AF324020

Study of Women and Legal Profession –A Feminist Approach

CONTENTS

DETAILED CONTENTS

CHAPTER VII

CHAPTER VIII

TABLE OF STATUTES

Australia

- Legal Practitioners Act 1981.
- Legal Profession Act 2004.
- Legal Profession Act 2006.

Canada

- The British North America Act, 1867.

India

- Hindu Widows Remarriage Act, 1836.
- High Courts Act, 1861.
- The Bengal Land-revenue Regulations, 1793.
- North Western Provinces and Oudh Act.1793
- Legal Practitioners' Act, 1879.
- United Provinces Act, 1890.
- Guardians and Wards Act, 1890.
- Legal Practitioners (Women) Act, 1923.
- The Child Marriage Restraint Act, 1929.
- Hindu Women's Rights to Property Act, 1937.
- The Constitution of India, 1950.
- Andhra State Act, 1953.
- The Suppression of Immoral Traffic in Women and children Act, 1954.
- Special Marriage Act, 1954.
- Hindu Marriage and Divorce Act, 1956.

- Hindu Adoption and Maintenance Act, 1956.
- Hindu Minority and Guardianship Act, 1956.
- Hindu Succession Act, 1956.
- Immoral Traffic Prevention Act, 1956.
- The Kerala High Court Act, 1958.
- Orphanages and other Charitable Homes (Supervision and Control) Act, 1960.
- Bombay Re-organisation Act, 1960.
- Orphanages and Other Charitable homes (supervision and Control) Act, 1960.
- The Dowry Prohibition Act, 1961.
- The Maternity Benefit Act, 1961.
- Equal Remuneration Act 1976.
- The Child Marriage Restraint Act, 1979.
- The Indecent Representation of Women (Prohibition) Act, 1986.
- The Commission of Sati (Prevention) Act, 1987.
- The Protection of Human Rights Act, 1993.
- The Family Courts 1984.
- Bihar Re-organisation Act, 2000.
- Madhya Pradesh Re-organisation Act, 2000.
- U.P. Re-organisation Act, 2000.
- The Juvenile Justice (Care and Protection of Children) Act 2000.
- Hindu Succession (Amendment) Act 2005.
- Domestic Violence Act, 2005.

Scotland

- Representation of the People (Scotland) Act, 1868.
- Universities Elections Amendment (Scotland) Act, 1881.

- Interpretation Act, 1910.
- Solicitors Act, 1843.
- Solicitors (Scotland) Act, 1980.

United Kingdom

- Custody of Infants Act, 1839.
- Matrimonial Causes Act 1857.
- Municipal Franchise Act 1869.
- Solicitors Act 1870.
- 1870 Education Act.
- Married Women's Property Act, 1874.
- Representation of the People Act 1918.
- Sex Disqualification (Removal) Act, 1928.
- Education Act 1944.
- Equal Pay Act 1970.
- Sex Discrimination Act 1975.
- Guardianship of Infants (Amendment) Act 1999.

United States of America

- Civil Rights Act 1964.
- Educational Amendments (1972).
- Sex Discrimination Act 1975.

LIST OF CASES

Canada

Edwards v.Attorney General for Canada (1930) A.C.124.

England

Charlton v. Lings (1868-9) LR. 4 CP 374,p. 392.

Beresford-Hope Vs Lady Sandhurst [1889], 23 QBD 79.

Ball Vs Incorp, Society of Law Agents (1901).

Nairn Vs University of Andrews, 1909 A.C. 147.

R v Harald [1872] LR VII QB 361.

Schle vs. Incorporated Law Society (1909) TS 363.

Incorporated Law Society vs. Wookey (1912) .

India

In re Regina Guha (1916) ILR 44, Cal 29.

Sudhangshu Bala Hazara (1922) AIR 1922 Patna 299.

Vishakha versus State Of Rajasthan (1997) 6 SCC 241.

Apparel Export Promotion Council versus A K Chopra (1999) 1 SCC 759 .

Gita Hariharan vs. Reserve Bank of India (1999) 2 SCC 228.

Upendra Baxi v. State of U.P., (1987) 2 SCC 402.

Mackinnon Mackenzie & Co. Ltd. v. Audrey D'Costa, (1987) 2 SCC 469.

Lena Khan v. Union of India (1987) 2 SCC 402.

Air India v. Nergesh Meerza (1987) 2 SCC 469.

Government of A.P. v. P.B. Vijay Kumar (1995) 4 SCC 520.

Madhu Kishwar vs State of Bihar AIR 1996 SC 1868.

Sarala Mudgal vs. Union of India, AIR1995 SC 1531.

Ahmedabad Women Action Group (AWAG) vs. Union of India, AIR 1997 SC 3614.

South Africa

Law Society Vs Wookey (1912) A.D. 623 .

United States of America

Bradwell v. State of Illinoi, (1873), US 83, 16 WALLS, 130.

In Re Bradwell, 55 Ill, 535(1870).

Re Mabel P. French 1 D.L.R. U.S., 1873.

Minor Vs Happier Sett, 11 88 US 162 (1875).

Reed v. Reed, 404 U.S. 71 (1971).

Wimberly v. Labor & Industrial Relations Commission, 107 S. Ct. 821 (1987).

Roe v. Wade, 410 U.S. 113 (1973).

Taylor v. Louisiana, 419 U.S. 522 (1974).

Kohn v. Royall, Koegel and Wells, 59 F.R.D. 515, 518-19 (S.D.N.Y.1973).

Hishon v. King & Spalding 467 U.S. 69. 104 S.Ct. 2229. 81 L.Ed.2d 59.

Hurley v Mustoe [1981] IRLR 208.

California Federal Savings v. Guerra, 107 S. Ct. 683 (1987).

EEOC v. Sears Roebuck & Co., 581 F.2d 941 (D.C.Cir. 1987).

Geduldig v. Aiello, 417 U.S. 484 (1974).

Hopkins v. Price Waterhouse, 618 F. Supp. 1109 (D.D.C. 1985).

Kahn v. Shevin, 416 U.S. 351 (1974).

LIST OF TABLES

CHAPTER-I

CHAPTER-III

LIST OF FIGURE

CHAPTER-I

CHAPTER- I

INTRODUCTION AND METHODOLOGY

"The soul has neither sex, nor caste nor imperfection,

The best thermometer to the progress of a nation is its treatment of its women,

There is no chance for the welfare of the world unless the condition of women is improved,

Woman has suffered for aeons, and that has given her infinite patience and infinite perseverance

The idea of perfect womanhood is perfect independence."

—Swami Vivekananda

Complete Works of Swami Vivekananda, (CW, V.4, P.176)

1.1. CONCEPTUAL FRAMEWORK

Women's entry and rising representation in the legal profession is one of the most remarkable changes, some claim 'revolutionary', in the legal profession over the past 50 years.[1] Historical and comparative research has documented women's arduous battles to gain entry to the profession through litigation, lobbying efforts, formal appeals to law societies, and at times their engagement in legal work on the boundaries of professional jurisdictions. Initially, it was the women in the United States who led the way first by entering the legal profession in the 1860s, several decades ahead of women in other countries. Yet, women continued to be excluded from several American law schools until the 1960s.[2]

Women's admission to law was confronted with the initial challenge to male exclusivity in the legal profession. Few women lawyers found a warm greeting in their chosen profession when they entered in their profession or sought their jobs in the years before the 1970s. Women who secured legal work were often offered opportunities in low-status specialties deemed suitable for women, such as probate law and family law. They received lower pay, were denied partnerships, and rarely

1 Kay Fiona, Gorman Elizabeth, *"Women and the Legal Profession,"* Annual Review of Law and Social Science, December 2008, Vol. 4: pp. 299-332.

2 Ibid.

served on the bench. Discrimination and exclusion in various forms persisted well into the twentieth century for women lawyers.[3]

While there have been very few studies in India, wider studies in Western countries have revealed the gender bias operating in many ways, including in the tacit or open assumption of the average textbook that the lawyer is a male and that the women involved are either plaintiff, defendants, witnesses, or secretarial staff at best. There is an assumption that women cannot be among the, leave alone, to become a best judge of the country. From the beginning, the society has looked on women lawyers with attitudinal bias. Even today the discrimination continues.

Women's entry to law remained a trickle through much of the first half of the twentieth century. The most dramatic increases in women's entry rates took place only since the 1970s. In 1970, women comprised 8 percent of the total law school enrollments in the United States.[4] By 2006, women had achieved near parity with men in law school. Similarly in Canada only 1 in 20 lawyers in 1970 was a woman. As of 2005, 1 of every 3 three lawyers was a woman, with the majority under 35 years old. The dramatic influx of women to the legal profession paralleled across many countries.[5]

In the present time we are constrained to admit that the legal profession in India is extremely patriarchal. Even after close to three decades of struggles by feminists and human right activists, it still remains a male domain in many ways. The present work is an attempt to study with special focus on legal profession in the feminist perspective. The study deals with women's legal education, their entry in legal profession, problems related to carving their identity and building a status of their own. The study mainly focuses on number of women advocates, women judges, and their professional hazards and difficulties.

---

3 Epstein, Cynthia Fuchs; *Women and Law,* Basic Books, Inc. Publishers, 1981, New York, pp.79-83.

4 Kay Fiona, Gorman Elizabeth; "Women and the Legal Profession," *Annual Review of Law and Social Science,* Vol.4, December, 2008, p.30.<http://arjournals.annualreviews.org/> on 9th March 2010.

5 Morrel Peter;"Women lawyers", <http://en.wikipedia.org/wiki/User:Peter_morrell/women_lawyers>last visited on 9/02/10

The discussion in this chapter has been divided under the following heads:

Conceptual Framework

Statistical Reality

Situation in India

- Women Judges in India
- Disproportionate Representation of Women
- Factors leading to Disproportionate Representation of Women

Literature Review

Prior Research on 'Women and Legal Profession' in India and findings that emerge

Objective

Research Questions

The Take off Stage

Methodology

Theoretical Framework

Focusing on the study

1. 2. STATISTICAL REALITY

In Unites States of America, women are now a permanent and integral part of the legal profession, comprising 24 percent of the nation's lawyers. The percentage of women lawyers has nearly doubled since 1985, when it was 13 percent, and is eight times the percentage of women who practiced law in 1971 (three percent). The percentage of female lawyers has climbed from 15 percent in 1983 to 26 percent in 1995. Women's place in the profession continues to grow. Forty-four percent of all law students are women, and it is expected that women will make up 40 percent of the legal profession by 2010. At the same time, current projections suggest that the legal profession will never be 50 percent women, even though women are more than 50 percent of the population.[6] But the starling finding of this study of women in the legal profession is that women are disproportionately located in different spheres of the profession in virtually every country. In1980, women as licensed lawyers comprised 8 percent. While in 1991, it increased to 20 percent. In 2000, the number further increased to 27 percent. [7] The data is shown in Table - 1.1. The Lawyer Statistical Report of American Bar Foundation estimated the total lawyers around 1,180,386 and women currently represent approximately 31 percent of the legal profession as shown in Figure -1.1.[8]Women comprised 19.2 percent as partners, 46.6 percent as Summer Associates, and 45.7 percent as Associates. The data is shown in Figure - 1.2.[9] In 2009, women as District Court judges comprised 24.7 percent, Circuit Court judges as 26.9 percent, International Trade judges as 33.3 percent, State Courts of last resort as 32.4 percent and Chief Justice as 34 percent. The data is shown in Table - 1.2.

---

6 Morrell, Peter; "Women lawyers," <http://en.wikipedia.org/wiki/User:Peter_morrell/ women_lawyers> on 9th March 2010.

7 "Lawyers Demographics," The Lawyer Statistical Report, *American Bar Foundation,* 1985, 1994, 2004 edition, p.1. < http://new.abanet.org/marketresearch/PublicDocuments/ Lawyer_Demographics.pdf>on 9/03/10.

8 Ibid.

9 Ibid.

TABLE 1.1

NUMBER OF LICENSED LAWYERS-2008

	1980	1991	2000
MALE	92%	80%	73%
FEMALE	8%	20%	27%

Sources: "The Lawyer Statistical Report," *American Bar Foundation,* 1985, 1994, 2000 edition

FIGURE 1.1

A CURRENT GLANCE OF WOMEN IN LAW, 2009

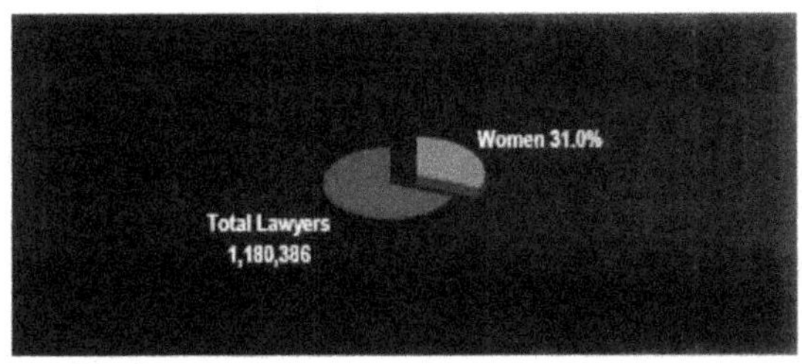

Source: "Lawyers Demographics." The Lawyer Statistical Report, *American Bar Foundation* 1985, 1994, 2004 edition, p.1. <http://new.abanet.org/marketresearch/PublicDocuments/Lawyer_Demographics.pdf>on 9/03/10.

FIGURE 1.2

WOMEN IN PRIVATE PRACTICE

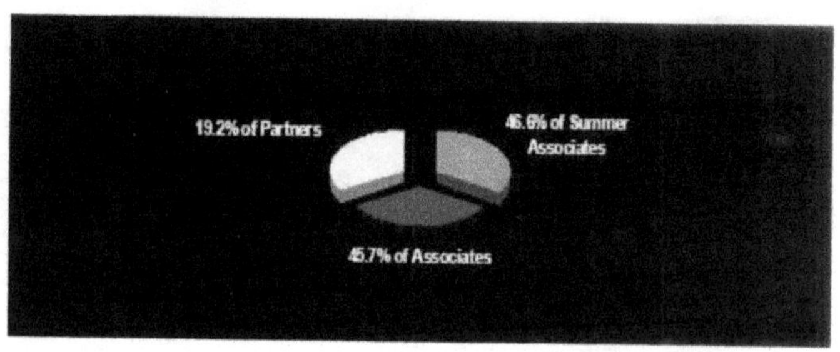

Law Firm Diversity Demographics Show Little Change, Despite Economic Downturn, National Association for Law Placement, October 2009.

Source: "Lawyers Demographics," The Lawyer Statistical Report, *American Bar Foundation*, 1985, 1994, 2004 edition, p.1. <http://new.abanet.org/marketresearch/PublicDocuments/Lawyer_Demographics.pdf>on 9/03/10.

TABLE 1.2

DEMOGRAPHIC VIEW OF WOMEN IN FEDERAL JUDICIARY AS ON 2009

TYPE OF COURT	TOTAL NO.OF SEAT	WOMEN	% OF WOMEN
District Court Judges	680 current seats – 25 vacancies	168	24.9%
Total Circuit Courts	167 current seats -11 vacancies	45	26.9%
International Trade	9 current seats	3	33.3%
United States Supreme Court	9	2	22.2%
State Court of last resort	349	113	32.4%
Female Chief Justice	53	18	34.0%

Source: Alliance of Justice, Judicial Selection Database and Statistics provided by National Center for State Courts, Knowledge & Information Services Division, and November, 2009.

- In Canada, women make up 36 percent in Canada, approximately one-third of Canadian lawyers. They are under-represented in private practice (26 percent) and over-represented in the public sector (40 percent) and 60 percent are more likely to leave law than men.[10]

- In UK, the position of women in the legal profession, in many ways, mirrors that of the USA. The Law Society of England and Wales confirmed that there has been a dramatic rise in the number of women in the profession. In 1987 women comprised less than one fifth of all solicitors. By 1999 women held 35 percent of practicing certificates, an increase of 14 percent since 1989. Although women have been in the majority since 1992-93, most are assistant solicitors, only one quarter of female solicitors becoming partners, compared with over half of male solicitors.[11]

- Women lawyers tend to remain clustered at the lower levels. The statistics for the Bar are no more encouraging. Women represent 26 percent of barristers in independent practice, with men representing 74 percent of these, only 8 percent of Queen's Counsels are female. Of the judiciary, there are no female lords of appeal in ordinary. Only 6 percent of appeal court judges and 7 percent of high court judges are female, whereas 19 percent of deputy district judges and 15 percent of district judges were female. Of pupils registered with the Bar Council in 200-01, 48 percent were female and 52 percent were male. Women account for 11 percent of all judges in England and Wales. In 1998, 1 in 10 judges in the courts were women.[12]

- In Scotland, the most striking feature of the current law student population is the proportion of women. In 1970 less than 20 percent were women. By 1980 the figure had risen to between 35-40 percent. Now, it is very close to parity.[13]

---

10 Morell, Peter; "Women lawyers," <http://en.wikipedia.org/wiki/User:Peter_morrell/women_lawyers> on 9th March 2010.

11 Ibid.

12 Ibid.

13 Abel, Richard L;"The Legal Profession in Scotland," *Lawyers in Society*, 1988, The Regents of University of California, California, p.87.

- In Australia, in 1947, out of the total of 4576 lawyers, women comprised only 2.4 per cent. While in 1961, out of the total of 6736 lawyers, women comprised 3.9 percent. In 1976 women comprised 7.5 percent. In 1981, women comprised 11.4 percent. In 1986 women as full time professionals comprised of 18.5 percent. In 1991 out of the total of 34075, the number of women lawyers increased to 8971 i.e. only 26.3 percent.[14] The data is shown in Table 1.3. As of June 2002, there were some 11,490 legal practices in Australia (7,566 solicitor practices, 3,670 barrister practices, 41 patent attorney businesses, 18 government solicitor/public prosecutor, 8 legal aid authorities and 191 community legal centers. There were 36,124 solicitors and barristers (with total employment by legal practices of 93,753 people, e.g. paralegal and secretarial staff), with 3,670 barristers (of whom over 83 percent were male).[15]

---

14 Anleu, Dr.Sharyn Roach; "Women in the Legal Profession: Theory, Research and Practice," *Journal of Sociology,* Vol. 28, No. 3, 391-410 (1992), < http://jos.sagepub.com/cgi/content/abstract/28/3/391>on 6th August 2009.

15 "Law: The Legal Profession," *Caslon Analytics law.* < http://www.caslon.com.au/lawnote9.htm> on 9th March 2010.

TABLE 1.3

LAW PROFESSIONALS,* AUSTRALIA

Year	No Women	% Women	Total
1947	109	2.4	4576
1961	258	3.9	6636
1976	970	7.5	12909
1981	1993	11.4	17516
1986	4396	18.5	23824
1991	8971	26.3	34075

Australia Bureau of Statistics (1947-1986) Census of the Commonwealth of Australia, ABS, Canberra.

*Law Professionals; judges, magistrates, barristers, solicitors and legal officers.

Source: Dr.Sharyn Roach Anleu; "Women in the Legal Profession: Theory, Research and Practice," *Journal of Sociology,* Vol. 28, No. 3, p.195.

- In Germany, women represented 36 percent of advocates in 1983.From 1993 to 2000 the number of advocates rose by 55 percent. The data is given in Table -1.4. Women as lawyers have played their part in this development. In recent years their share in admissions have ranges in between 36 percent (1996) and 42 percent (1999).At present, females account for, on average, a quarter of the nation's lawyers.[16]

---

16 Schultz, Ulrike and Shaw, Gisela; *Women in the world legal profession*, Hart Publishing, 2003, Oxford, p.285.

TABLE 1.4

WOMEN IN GERMAN ADVOCACY AND WOMEN NOTARIES

	Female advocates (Anwaltinmen) %	Total increase in advocates (m & F) % and absolute figures	Increase in advocates (f) % and absolute figures	Advocate notaries (f) (Annwaltsnotarinnen) %	Solo-notaries (f) (Nur-Notarinnen)
1985	12.04			4.42	
1991	16.08			4.87	14.44
1996	20.03			7.41	18.95
1997	21.21	96-97:7.97(6283)	14.32(2261)	7.85	18.65
1998	22.40	97-98:7.53(6411)	13.53(2442)	8.03	18.36
1999	23.66	98-99:6.86(6275)	12.89(2642)	8.24	18.40
2000	24.59	99-00:6.42(6276)	10.59(2450)		

Source: Ulrike Schultz and Gisela Shaw; "The Status of Women Lawyers in Germany," ***Women in the World Legal Profession***, Hart Publishing, 2003, Oxford, p.385.

- In Holland, women attorneys comprised 8 percent in 1960.From 1959, the percentage of female attorneys rose steadily and in 1970 it was 11 percent. In 1980, it increased to 18 percent .In 1990 it was 26 percent and in 1993, it was 30 percent.[17] The data is shown in Table -1.5.

[17] Ibid p.342.

TABLE 1.5

SHARE OF WOMEN AMONGST LAW STUDENTS, JUDICIALTRANEES, JUDGES, PUBLIC PROSECUTORS, ATTORNEYS, JUNIOR ATTORNEYS AND NOTARIES IN HOLLAND

Year	Students%	Judicial trainees%	Judes%	Public prosecutors%	Attorneys%	Junior notaries%	Noraties%
1959-52	30		>1	0	6	3	>1
1960	26				8	5	1
1970	20	41	3	>1	11	3	1
1975	24	30	8	7	16	4	2
1980	33	32		18	18	6	2
1986	44	51	16	12	21	9	3
1990	48	59	20	16	26	16	3
1991			60			27	
1992		60			27	27	
1993		65			30		
1994		68				42	3
1995	51	68	34	33			

Source: Leny E De Groot-Van Leeuwan; "Women in the Dutch Legal Profession," *Women in the World Legal Profession,* Hart Publishing, Oxford and Portland, Oregon, p.382.

- In Poland, from 1968 onwards women as lawyers have increased steadily. In 1974, they comprised 15.8 percent. While in 1980, they were 19 percent .In 1992, women comprised 27.4 percent, even when the numbers of men dropped. In 1998, women as lawyers comprised 29.5 percent.[18] The data is shown in Table in 1.6. In January 2000, there were 660 women and 1066 men on the Chambers roll, giving women share of 38 percent. Overall it remained very modest.

[18] . Ibid p.382.

TABLE 1.6

WOMEN ATTORNEYS IN POLLAND

YEAR	WOMEN	MEN	TOTAL	%
1968	732	4988	5722	12.8
1974	913	4853	5766	15.8
1980	1073	4567	5640	19.0
1992	1939	5146	7085	27.4
1998	2130	5086	7216	29.5

Source: Malgorzata Fuszara; "Women Layers in Poland under the Impact of Post 1989 Transformation," ***Women in the World Legal Profession***, Hart Publishing, Oxford and Portland, Oregon, p.382.

In the post war period the share of female judges broadly increased in tandem with women studying law, with the proportion of male and female judges equalizing around 1980.Yet within the judicial profession, the participation of women was not evenly spread across all levels of judicial hierarchy. Rather it was structured in the shape of a pyramid, with the highest numbers being found in the courts of lower instance. By 1990, women had come to form a majority in the higher instance courts as well. But here too there were internal imbalances. While in district courts women represented 69.5 percent of judges, in regional courts it was 55.3 percent. While the total percentage of women judges were 61.6 percent. This total profile has not changed significantly by the year 2000 as the total percentage of women judges were 63.6 percent.[19] The data is shown in Table - 1.7.

[19] Ibid p.375.

TABLE 1.7

WOMEN JUDGES IN POLLAND

YEAR	WOMEN	MEN	TOTAL	%
1968	890	1791	2681	33.2
1970	952	1655	2607	36.5
1975	1272	1636	2908	42.4
1980	1489	1529	3018	49.3
1985	1971	1751	3722	52.9
1990	2850	1778	4628	61.6
1995	3745	2265	6010	62.3
1996	4016	2399	6415	62.6
1997	4207	2480	6687	62.9
1998	4436	2542	6978	63.6
1999	4586	2636	7222	63.5
2000	4594	2629	7223	63.6

Calculation based on information provided by the Polish Ministry of Justice

Source: Malgorzata Fuszara; "Women Layers in Poland under the Impact of Post 1989 Transformation," *Women in the World Legal Profession*, Hart Publishing, Oxford and Portland, Oregon, p.371.

- In Finland, the share in the Finnish legal profession in 1928 was 0.7 percent. There was a mild increase to 1.7 percent in 1940 and 6.2 percent in 1960.In 1975 it was 13.6 percent which increased to 19.9 percent in 1982.In 1984 it was 24 percent, while in 1989 it was 28 percent. In 1999 it rose to 42 percent and was 43 percent in the year 2000.[20]The data is shown in Table - 1.8.

[20] Ibid p.390.

TABLE 1.8

THE SHARE OF WOMEN IN FINNISH LEGAL PROFESSION

YEAR	PERCENTAGE
1928	0.7
1940	1.7
1960	6.2
1975	13.6
1982	19.9
1985	24.0
1989	28.0
1999	42.0
2000	43.0

Data provided by the Association of Finnish Lawyers,

Source: Harriet Silius; "Women jurist in Finland at the turn of the century," *Women in the World Legal Profession*, Hart Publishing, Oxford and Portland, Oregon, p.390.

- In Denmark, women comprised 31 percent as judges .While in Norway, although 54 percent of law students are women but a smaller number enter the profession. In 1995, women as judges comprised 31 percent. In 1995, in Sweden, women as judges comprised 37 percent. [21] The data is shown in Table- 1.9.

21 Ibid.

TABLE 1.9

THE SHARE OF WOMEN IN THE NORDIC COUNTRIES IN THE MID 1990S

COUNTRY	YEAR	NUMBER OF JURIST	%
Denmark	1994	25,418	31
Finland	1994	12,030	29
Norway	1995	10,556	31
Sweden	1995	12,388	37

Source: Harriet Silius; "Women jurist in Finland at the turn of the century," ***Women in the World*** *Legal Profession*, Hart Publishing, Oxford and Portland, Oregon, p.390.

- In Belgium, there are comparatively fewer judges; women represent a disproportionally low number of judges.[22]

- In Brazil, women comprise 24.6 percent of law graduates, only 20.9 percent of law professionals are women.[23]

- There have been women lawyers since the 1920s in Egypt but ascending to the bench has been all but impossible for them.[24]

- In Malaysia, fewer lawyers are staying in the profession than their male counterparts for a shorter time.[25]

- In Pakistan, women are appointed as judges in the lower judiciary but the ratio of female judges is much less than male judges. Recently women judges were appointed in the High Courts. This is a major breakthrough for women in the legal profession.[26]

- In Nepal, only 800 of Nepal's 10,000 lawyers are women. Most female lawyers are advocates, many don't practice law, and only 36 of Nepal's 67 districts are home to even one female lawyer.[27]

1.3. SITUATION IN INDIA

Women started entering into the legal profession in a good number only during the decades of 1971-81. In 1981 the total number of, men were 22,128 and

---

22 Menkel-Meadow, Carrie; 'The Comparative Sociology of Women Lawyers: The Feminization of the Legal Profession," the Conference Papers, Volume III. 1986-87, Institute for Social Science Research, 1987, Los Angles, p.8.

23 Ibid p.6.

24 Ottaman, Sharon; "Egypt's changing career climate," *The Christian Science Monitor*, 21stMarch, 2006. <http://www.csmonitor.com/2006/0331/p18s02-hfes.html> on 9th March 2010.

25 Yusufzai, Rashida; "Number of lawyers in Malaysia grows," *ALB Legal News*, 8th February 2010. <http://asia.legalbusinessonline.com/news/breaking-news/number-of-lawyers> on 16thFeb.2010.

26 "Political Rights of Women," Article 7, ChapterVII, Constitutional ND Legislative Framework, P.39. <http://www.pakistan.gov.pk/divisions/women-development-division/media/08chp7.pdf> on 9th March 2010.

27 Jones, Chelsea; "Nepali women demand equality," *fall, 2009, Herizon*, Kathmandu.< http://findarticles.com/p/articles/> on 9th March 2010.

women were 5,778 i.e. 2.5 percent were women. In 1986, 3.86 percent women as lawyers were enrolled.[28] The modern Indian legal profession is the creation of the Advocates Act, 1961. It is conceptualized as a service oriented profession and not as a profit oriented trade. The Indian Bar consists of about 10 lakh and 20 thousand lawyers. In addition, there are about 740 law colleges and 11 national law universities under the control of the statutory body representing the profession, the Bar Council of India.[29] The structure of the Indian legal profession is essentially centered around a senior advocate and his/her junior advocates or colleagues with few law firms in existence in the major metros like Mumbai, Delhi, Kolkata and Chennai.

The profession is guided by a code of conduct and ethics framed as part of the rules of the Bar Council of India. The Bar Council of India and the State Bar Councils are created under the Advocates Act which is mainly entrusted with the induction of the new entrance into the profession, taking care of the conduct and discipline of advocates, safeguarding the privilege and welfare of advocates and finally maintaining and improving the standard of legal education in the country.

The available data from the Bar Council of India clearly indicates a gradual increase of women entering into the profession of law. As per the latest statistics made available by the Bar Council of India there are 8, 58,294 advocates enrolled in the country.[30] While sex wise distribution of different categories of professionals in India clearly indicate that decadal growth in women's enrollment. In 1950-51 women's enrollment was 10.9 percent which increased to 16.2 percent in the year 1960-61. In 1970-71 it was 22 percent, while it increased to 27.2 percent in 1980-81. In 1990-91 there was just a marginal increase of 2 percent, while in 2000-01 it increased to 39 percent which experienced an increase by 10 percent as shown in Table 1.10.[31] However, the data's beyond 2001 were not available.

---

28 Raju, M.P; "Women legal news and views," December, 1998, pp. 13-17.

29 Sinha, Suraj Narain Prasad; "Chairman's page," Bar Council of India,< http://www. barcouncilofindia. org/bar-council/chairman.php> on 7th March 2010

30 Lahoti, Justice R.C; "Speech on Law Day," 26th November r, 2004, (2005) 2 SCC (Jour)1.

31 "Report, Science Career for Indian Women; An examination of Indian women's access to and retention in sciencetific career," 2004. < http://www.ias.ac.in/womeninscience/INSA_1-17.pdf> on 3rd March 2008.

The data available from the Bar Council of Maharashtra and Goa reflects more women are attracted to enter in the legal profession. [32] The data is shown in Table-1.11. However, the data beyond 1999 were not available. The data collected from Bar Council of West Bengal shown in Table-1.12 indicate the gradual increase of women as lawyers in West Bengal.

[32] Maine, A.D; "Women's place at the Bar,"< http://mshrc.maharashtra.gov.in/Speech/> on 17th March 2010

TABLE 1.10

DECADAL GROWTH IN WOMEN'S ENROLLMENT: YEAR, TOTAL, PERCENT

Year	Total	%Women
1950 – 51	3, 96,745	10.9
1960 – 61	10, 49,864	16.2
1970 – 71	19, 53,700	22.0
1980 – 81	27, 52,437	27.2
1990 – 91	49, 24,868	29.2
2000 – 01	83, 99,443	39

Source: "Report, Science Career for Indian Women; An examination of Indian women's access to and retention in sciencetific career," 2004.

TABLE 1.11

WOMEN'S ENROLLEMENT IN THE BAR COUNCIL OF MAHARASTRA

Year	Total	Women	Men
1992	2371	587	1784
1993	2390	613	1777
1994	2292	660	1632
1995	3099	857	2242
1996	1259	348	911
1997	1013	285	728
1998 (till May)	0624	207	417

Source: Maine, A.D; "Women's place at the Bar," < http://mshrc.maharashtra.gov.in/Speech/>

TABLE 1.12

WOMEN'S ENROLLMENT IN BAR COUNCIL OF WEST BENGAL

Year	Total	Women	Men
2001	2040	405	1635
2002	2298	540	1758
2003	2070	494	1576
2004	1075	320	755
2005	935	223	712
2006	1032	262	770

Source: Bar Council of West Bengal, Kolkata.

1.3.1. WOMEN JUDGES IN INDIA

Even as women are breaking their way into the practice of law, the fight to attain judgeships is still slow though they form a permanent and integral part of the legal profession. The Supreme Court and various high courts have been lamenting that a particular section of society is inadequately represented in service or in education. Ironically, one field in which women are grossly underrepresented in India is the higher judiciary itself.

The Judges strength of the High Courts is being reviewed periodically. 163 posts of Judges have been created in various High Courts during the years 2006, 2007 and 2008.[33] The appointments of Judges of the High Courts are made under Article 124 1and 217 of the Constitution of India that does not provide for reservation for any caste or class of persons. However, from time to time the government has addressed letters to the Chief Justices of various High Courts requesting them to locate women from the Bar who are suitable for appointment as High Court Judges. But very few initiatives have been taken so far to increase the number in order to bring gender equality. Experts do say that with time, the situation may improve. Some 269 posts of high court judges are currently lying vacant and some of these are sure to be filled by competent women.

But the situation is believed to be much better in subordinate courts where the proportion of women judges is healthier than in the higher judiciary. Some of these judges will also be elevated to high courts in the coming years. More than three crore cases are pending in Indian courts, and while Supreme Court judges hear 80 cases a day, five days a week, more than 50,000 are pending there. Subordinate courts have worse data. Clearly, justice is not available at a reasonable price to most citizens, and that at a time when most of the states are becoming more ruthless in dealing with democratic struggles and people's movements.[34] Is Indian establishment's denial of justice is by design or by inefficiency?

---

33 Ministry of Law and Justice, *Press Information Bureau,* 15th December, 2008, New Delhi.

34 Singh, Sach Kanwal; "Courting Justice," *World Sikh News*, 10th March, 2010.

In May 2001, out of 21 High Courts, there were only 19 women judges. In the Supreme Court, out of the sanctioned strength of 26, only one was a woman. On 23rd October 2009, the Delhi High Court had eight women judges, the highest in number, followed by Bombay with seven. The High Court with the maximum judges in the country, Allahabad, has five women judges, out of a total number of 78 judges. In contrast, six of the country's 21 High Courts — Chhattisgarh, Himachal Pradesh, Jammu and Kashmir, Sikkim, Rajasthan, and Uttarakhand — have no women judges at all.[35] Karnataka, Kerala, Gujarat and Patna, Madras and Madhya Pradesh have four women judges each. The High Court at Calcutta has two women judges. While Andhra Pradesh, Gauhati, Orissa, Jharkand, and Punjab and Haryana have a total strength of 160 judges; has one women judge each as on 10th May 2007. The statistics may be surprising. A parliamentary committee report tabled in October 2008 said that women, among other weaker sections of society, were 'inadequately represented' in high courts and the Supreme Court. In spite of the tall talks regarding women empowerment, India has meager 5.8 percent women as judges in High Courts and none in Supreme Court for nearly four years.[36]

In 2003, there were 17 women judges out of a total of 514 judges in the Supreme Court and High Courts in India.[37] While in 2005-06, the total approved strength of judges in Supreme Court was 26, the actual strength was 25 with one vacancy.[38] On 17th May 2006, the total numbers of women judges in high courts were 38. On 16th August 2007, the high courts and Supreme Court taken together had a total of 597 judges, out of which only 39 women had made it to this slot. In 2008, there were only 42 woman justices in 21 high courts and none in the Supreme Court.[39] While in 2009, out of 617 high court judges in the country, only 45 are women.

---

35 Ibid.

36 Ibid.

37 "Women in Law,"24th December, 2007. < http: http://www.outlookindia.com/article. aspx?236336//> on 2nd April 2009.

38 Raghavan, B.S; "Ensuring Speedy Justice-reducing the backlog of cases," *Business Line,* 25th August, 2004. <http://www.thehindubusinessline.com/2004/0> on 2nd April 2009.

39 <http://southasia.oneworld.net/todaysheadlines/divided-views-on-womens-quota-in-higher-judiciary> on 6th Feb.,2009.

On 31stDecember, 2007, against a sanctioned strength of 15,917 trial court judges, there were only 12,524 judges available to man the trial courts which left a huge shortfall of 3,393 judges. The average disposal per judge comes to 2,538 cases in high courts and 1,182 cases in subordinate Courts, if calculated on the basis of disposal in the year 2007 and working strength of judges as on December 31, 2007.Applying this average, we require 1,475 high court judges and 21,432 subordinate court judges only to clear backlog in one year. The requirement would come down to 737 high court judges and 10,716 trial court judges if the arrears alone have to be cleared in the next two years.[40]

1.3.2. DISPROPOTIONATE REPRESENTATION OF WOMEN IN JUDICIARY

Although women are well-represented in entry to the legal profession, progression to the senior ranks of the profession remains a major issue: senior advocates in the case of the Bar, partnership in the case of solicitors, and progression to judicial office. Even after more than thirty years of feminism and dramatic changes in the number of women entering the legal profession, legal scholars and researchers continue to debate the impact of women's presence on the administration of justice.

Central to this debate is the question of whether gender affects legal outcome. From the available statistics it is also clear that women are greatly underrepresented in the more prestigious profession like Judiciary though the government is making effort to make 33 percent reservation to women in State Assemblies and Lok Sabha.Though the government has taken interest to appoint either men or women judges to clear the backlog of cases, yet it has failed to solve the problem. Apparently, there is no discrimination against women in the judicial service but there are not many women in the higher echelons of the judiciary in India. Whenever the government has filled in the vacancies, the appointments have usually been men. However, the government says that its hands are tied by the Constitution on the issue.

---

40 "Judiciary pitches for increased judges' strength,"17th, April,2008. <http://www.thaindian.com/newsportal/politics/judiciary-pitches-for-increased-judges-strength_10039031.html> on 2nd April 2009.

1.3.3. FACTORS LEADING TO DISPROPOTIONATE REPRESENTATION OF WOMEN

Admittedly there are many factors known or unknown that ultimately lead to the disproportionate representation of women in legal profession, higher judiciary, law firms, corporate bodies etc. Hawthorne's research and Crozier's work have argued that these earlier explanations in organizational theory and research that differences between women and men were due to biology, socialisation, attitudes and role commitments are not sufficient. They suggest that the difference could also be due to differential and selective recruitment of women, and differences in the mechanism to supervise women and men in the organization.[41] Dumelow and Griffiths' (1995) research similarly found that there were a number of barriers facing women which they classified as role conflict and organizational culture. The role conflict included career breaks, child-care and difficulties combining professional and family. Organizational culture included career structure, male prejudice, opportunities available and working practices. In their overview of career obstacle for women, Reed and Buddeberg – Fischer (2001) listed four obstacles: domestic responsibilities and circumstances, rigidity in career structures; discrimination; and psychological barriers.[42]

The following are some of the factors found to be exercising the influence in the causation of unrepresentation and gender inequalities of women in this field.

A) PARTITION AND ITS EFFECT

The first two decades after independence in India hardly experienced any organized resentment against the inequalities in the inherited legal system. The partition of British India into India ad Pakistan affected millions of women and men as they fled from both the countries. The division of British India into India and Pakistan in August 1947 was accompanied by the dislocation of between twelve and sixteen million people and the violent deaths of around a million. Punjab and Bengal,

---

41 Acker, Joan and Houten, Donald R. Van; "Differential Recruitment and Control; The sex structuring of an organization," *JSTOR*, *Administrative Science Quarterly*,Vol.19.No.2, June1994,p.152.

42 Miller, Karen and Clark Donna; "Knife before wife: An exploratory study of gender," Caledonian University, Glasow. < http://www.emeraldinsight.com/> on 4th March 2010.

the two provinces that were divided, were the most affected but so were other parts of the country. After all, mixed populations (Muslim, Hindu, Sikh, Christian, and so on) were more the norm than not in rural and urban India, making the very notion of two homelands, one with a Muslim majority and another with a Hindu majority, somewhat difficult to realize. Individuals, families, and communities that found themselves on the 'wrong' side of the border were dispossessed of land and home, faced with the threat of bodily harm, spent months on the road and in refugee camps, and began the long process of resettlement. The place where the shock and disbelief first register, as do attempts to negotiate an impossible history of violence is the literary text. It was a gendered narrative of displacement.[43] This affected Indian women in making entry into the legal education.

B) WESTERN CONCEPT OF LEGAL EDUCATION

The western concept of legal education is alien and was not readily acceptable to the traditional society of India. A more subtle difficulty was whether India would completely understand some of the very basic assumptions that underlie the rules in Western law and its applicability in the Indian society. Its understanding was not always well accepted. The traditions and requirements of Indian society required a legal order that was more acceptable, rather than drawing its nature from the common law which needed more adjustment. This was one of the obstacles in the development of legal profession in India and women's entry into it.

C) PATRIARCHY

Feminism focuses on the theory of patriarchy as a system of power that organizes society into a complex of relationships producing what feminists claim as a 'male supremacy' that oppresses women. The desire for supremacy, the psychological pleasure of power is identified as the motivating forces of patriarchy. The patriarchal theory maintains that the primary element of patriarchy is a relationship of dominance, where one party is dominant and exploits the other party for the benefit of the former. The feminist writers have chronicled the pervasiveness of the hierarchy of gender by showing how women have been left out in education.

---

43 Kamra, Sukeshi.; "A Messy History and its Many Messy Texts: An Essay on Partition (India, 1947) and its Narratives," *Literature Compass,* Volume 3, Issue 5, Blackwell Publishing,2009, Published Online: 25 July, 2006, pp.1160 – 1185.

D) DISCRIMINATION

A woman may experience discrimination on the basis of gender and religion, or gender and caste, at the same time... The underlying causes of gender inequality are related to social and economic structure, which is based on informal and formal norms, and practices. Women here may find legal task to be performed that would depend upon the work setting, types of client to interact and also to negotiate fees in terms of the professional work. Many a time's clients do not have confidence on the women lawyers especially when the lawyer has to perform mainly corporate work, drawing up contracts, defending the client against criminal charges etc.[44]

Client brings various issues, concerns and experiences to the solicitor that they express in various everyday discourses. Rather than inevitably subordinating or controlling the client and their desired outcomes, the lawyer translates and reconstitutes the issues in terms of a legal discourse that has trans-situational applicability. For example, a client's concern, that his or her children should inherit any real estate (a concern for family relation) will be translated into legal questions about the type of tenancy and the resulting ownership potentialities and capacities. The skill of the lawyer derives from the extent to which the statements that she or he formulates in legal discourse produce a legal outcome that is congruent with the outcome that the client articulates in everyday non legal language. It is at this point that the clients becomes choosy in selecting lawyers and often their choice falls on the basis of a lawyers' popularity, recognition and influence on the bench. Thus the client prefers to have a male lawyer in arguing his case.

E) CONCEPT OF INTERSECTIONALITY

The concept of intersectionality allows us to reflect on this multiple and intersecting oppression in law. There are multiple and diverse ways in which women are oppressed and gender discrimination may be based on intersectionality. A woman may also face intersectional discrimination that refers to the ways in which each of the multiple grounds for discrimination becomes intertwined and inseparable. It becomes impossible to single out one form of discrimination. To speak only of discrimination on the basis of sex or gender is to obscure the multiple and intersecting experiences of

---

44 Anleu, Sharyn L. Roach; *Law and Social Change,* Sage Publication, 2006, London, p.84.

discrimination for many women. It allows us to make more specific claims, which can more accurately represent the material specificity of women's oppression. As Kimberle Crenshaw, who first developed the concept, describes the fundamental enquiry of intersectionality is how simultaneous membership 'within at least two groups that are subjected to broad societal subordination bears upon problems traditionally viewed as 'monocasual', that is, 'as resulting from a single cause, commonly either gender or racial discrimination'. Intersectionality is intended to capture the ways in which individuals may be discriminated against on multiple and simultaneous grounds. In Crenshaw's words, the ways in which a woman may be 'situated within overlapping structures of subordination', and the ways in which any particular disadvantage or disability is sometimes compounded by yet another disadvantage emanating from or reflecting the dynamics of a separate system of subordination.[45] The idea of intersectionality seeks to capture both the structural and dynamic consequences of the interaction between two or more forms of discrimination or systems of subordination. It specifically addresses the manner in which racism; patriarchy, economic disadvantages and other discriminatory systems contribute to create layers of inequality that structures the relative positions of women and men, races and other groups. Moreover, it addresses the way that specific acts and policies create burdens that flow along these intersecting axes contributing actively to create a dynamic of disempowerment.

An analysis sensitive to structural intersection explores the lives of those at the bottom of multiple hierarchies to determine how the dynamics of each hierarchy exacerbates and compounds the consequences of another. A woman may experience discrimination on the basis of gender and religion, or gender and caste, at the same time. And the discrimination that she faces is more than simply adding two or more different kinds of discrimination together. Intersectional discrimination refers to the ways in which each of the multiple grounds for discrimination becomes intertwined and inseparable. It becomes impossible to single out one form of discrimination.

Thus, women may also experience discrimination on the basis of religion, ethnicity, caste, physical ability and/or sexual identity. To focus only on sex

---

[45] Ibid.

discrimination is to obscure the ways in which women particularly women in minority and disadvantaged communities experience multiple forms of subordination. These forms of subordination and discrimination are not discrete and separate but connected. The way in which the lower caste women experiences discrimination is intricately connected to her location in structure of both gender and caste subordination.

F) NATAL

This is another reason for slow pace of women access to education. Preference for boys over girls to have education, gender inequality can manifest in many forms.[46] Despite a general move towards greater equity, disparity remains strongly in favour of boys. Disparity is evident in access to education, in educational processes within schools, and in completion rates. Girls suffer in two ways: they have less access to education because of distance or unsafe conditions; and they are more likely to drop out, or be withdrawn due to economic or other extenuating circumstances, even when they do have access. They either do not get a chance to attend school or they are pulled out first when circumstances dictate, for example, to help in household duties at home, to care for younger siblings or older relatives. Long distances between home and school and the shortage of proper sanitation facilities for girls are contributing factors to lack of legal education. The result is there are less number of women law teachers in India.

G) SOCIAL

Associated with patriarchal power relations is a gender-linked allocation of social roles. The heterogeneity of Indian experience reveals that there are multiple patriarchies. We can see the act of unjust on women in our society in many ways due to our societal and cultural belief on account of inheritance, succession, laws relating to marriage and divorce, guardianship, custody, adoption etc. Discrimination based on caste is a major factor for women not achieving higher education like law. In India so far higher education is concerned, boys are preferred to girls. Women of higher caste get higher education than women of lower caste. In Crenshaw's words, the ways in which a woman may be 'situated within overlapping structures of subordination',

---

46 Sen, Amatya; "Many faces of Gender Inequality,"*The Frontline,* Volume 18 - Issue 22, Oct. - Nov, 2001.<http://www.hinduonnet.com/fline/fl1822/18220040.htm> on 5th March 2009.

and the ways in which any particular disadvantage or disability is sometimes compounded, reflects the dynamics of a separate system of subordination. An analysis from sensitive to structural intersection explores the lives of those at the bottom of multiple hierarchies to determine how the dynamics of each hierarchy exacerbates and compounds the consequences of another.[47]

For the purposes here it can be seen as a set of social relationships that provide for the collective domination of men over women. Patriarchy is just one of the hierarchies. Relational hierarchies between women within the same family are more adverse. Here women are pitted against one another. Not all women are powerless at all times. Caste-community identities intensify all other hierarchies.

H) POLITICAL

Power is exercised in everyday practices. Despite equity legislation, discrimination in some cases is found in governmental educational politics. In Sweden, for example, many of the educational programmes that attract women, for instance, vocational academic programmes such as nursing and those for elementary school teachers were formally designed in a way that prevented students from proceeding to post graduate or doctorate levels. These circumstances could partly explain the lack of women in higher levels.

I) PREFERENCES

Male select males, thereby reproducing male hierarchies. Men have increased their share of employment in all management tiers in women dominated agencies, while the proportion of women in agencies dominated by men continues to be under same low level. Men are being more preferred in higher education like law, while women are left behind.

Further, men are perceived by society to be superior and women to be subordinate. According to feminist theories (Hirdman 1990) men argues that women may have fewer but more substantial publications than men have. An emphasis on

---

[47] Patel, Pragna; "Notes on Gender and racial discrimination,"< http://www.eurowrc.org/13.institutions/5.un/un-en/12.un_en.htm> on 9th March 2010.

quality instead of quantity could, therefore, positively influence the evaluation of merit than women. In a study by Maume, (1999), having a college diploma was a significant predictor of wage promotion for women but had no significant impact for men who were promoted anyway. According to nine meta-analyses by Eagly and Karau (1991), gender differences in emergent leadership depend on the type of leadership measured. Women emerged more frequently in social leadership, while men emerged more frequently in general unspecified and task oriented leadership. As Alimo-Metcalf (1995) points out, if new managers are appointed to mirror the existing senior managers who are mostly men the criterion will be gender biased are seen by society as the 'standard', and consequently women's merit are not recognized. Based upon the findings women academic, biologist receives more citation per article than men, Sonnert (1995-96).[48] Radical feminists have therefore claimed 'that men use social systems and other methods of control to keep women suppressed.'

1.3.4. FEMINIST APPROACH IN INDIAN CONTEXT:

In India, women were not only engaged in an autonomous struggle for equality and better treatment but also continued to campaign even after the arrival of Mahatma Gandhi and the development of the supposedly all encompassing nationalism. Gandhi came up with the term 'stree shakti' for the concept of womanhood. Gandhi legitimized and expanded Indian women's public activities by initiating them into the non-violent civil disobedience movement against the British Raj. He exalted their feminine roles of caring, self-abnegation, sacrifice and tolerance; and carved a niche for those in public space. Mahatma Gandhi extended the logic of "feminine" modes of protest to the whole of the nationalist movement. It is argued, credibly, that Gandhi "feminized" nationalist politics by emphasizing *satyagraha* and passive resistance and creating a special space for women. He drew to the nationalist movement groups and numbers of women as never before. The Bengal women showed the way during the non-cooperation protests of 1921. Basanti Debi, Urmila Debi, and Suniti Debi (members of C.R. Das's family) joined picketing lines, courted arrest, and precipitated a broadening of the movement.

---

48 Åhmansson, Gabriella; "Male Hierarchies and Gender-balanced Boards," *Indian Journal of Gender Studies*, Vol. 15, No.3, 2008,pp. 485-505.

Women's Indian Association was launched in 1917, followed by the National Council of Indian Women (1925), the All-India Women's Conference (1927) and the National Federation of Indian Women (NFIW).Women were in the forefront of all the main items on the agenda of the social reform movement. For reformers, women's emancipation was a prerequisite to national regeneration and an index of national achievement in the connected discourse of civilization, progress, modernity, and nationalism.

One strand in the movement concentrated on legislative remedy. At this time natal inequality was much prevalent in the Indian society. In this type of inequality a preference is given for boys over girls that many male-dominated societies have. Therefore, gender inequality manifested itself in the form of the parents wanting the newborn to be a boy rather than a girl. There were spectacular barbarities in the everyday customs of India, including sati (burning widows alive on the funeral pyres of their dead husbands), female infanticide (especially common in northwest and western India), enforcement of celibate and ascetic widowhood, and pre-pubertal marriages (especially in northern India). Colonial officialdom and missionary rhetoric singled out such practices to characterize the status of Indian women as especially low and Indian men exceptionally violent. A series of campaigns resulted in the abolition of sati in 1829 and the enabling of widow remarriage in 1856. In the end the *Child Marriage Restraint Act* was passed .The minimum age of marriage for women was set at 14 and for men at 18. The age of consent was not mentioned. Another strand was concerned with creating the female counterpart of the new male elite, "New Women", who would share the sensibilities of the men in the family and be able to sustain their new class roles. The chief instrument was formal education but the issue became inextricably linked with the gender segregation and seclusion (purdah) practiced by the upper castes and classes and, by extension, with a reworking of public-private gender roles. Women were grappling with the issues relating to the scope of women's political participation, women's franchise, communal awards, and leadership roles in political parties.

During this period, however, social reform movements raised the issue of amelioration of the woman's position in society. There were legal reforms such as the Caste Disabilities Removal Act, 1850, the Hindu Widow Remarriage Act, 1856, the

Hindu Inheritance(Removal of Disabilities) Act, 1928, the Hindu law of Inheritance(Amendment) Act, 1929, the Hindu Gains of Learning Act, 1930, the Hindu Women's Right to Property Act, 1937, the Hindu Married Women's Right to separate Residence and Maintenance Act, 1946 were all enacted to give relief to those who are not content to abide by ancient shastras.

The women''s movement in India has played an important role in bringing gender issues to the forefront of development planning and defining feminist politics. The movement also addressed the issue of women's education. Women who struggled to gain an education and a place in India's public life, neither of which flowed automatically or easily from their class or caste status. Even when there is relatively little difference in basic facilities including schooling, the opportunities of higher education may be far fewer for young women than for young men. Indeed, gender bias was prevalent in higher education also. Women often earned "freedom" at the price of social ridicule, ostracism, and harassment. And while some women were aided by well-intentioned male relatives, others faced severe familial resistance. Still, the achievements were remarkable. Take the case of Rassundari Devi (born around 1809), who was entirely self-taught and wrote the first autobiography by an Indian woman: Other women became doctors, teachers, and educators. Women's education also proceeded apace in urban centers like Bombay, Poona, and Madras. Remarkable women like Pandita Ramabai, Anandibai Joshi, Tarabai Shinde, Haimavati Sen and Saraladevi, some privileged and some not, challenged patriarchal constraints, at least in their own lives, and some went on to participate in the emerging nationalist movement.

Women were "neither the subjects nor the objects" of this discourse, but merely the "site" on which the debates were conducted. This recast tradition came to occupy the core of modern Indian identity, gender as the exemplary site (or symbolic expression) became and remains central to political and cultural processes of identity formation.

Gender, thus, had been a central 'issue' in India. One prominent gender concern was status— that is, the rewards and benefits that accrued to women on India's journey to self-determination, statehood, democracy, progress, modernity, and development. The Hindu Law Committee was appointed in 1941 to look into a comprehensive legislation covering all Hindu laws. The committee under the chairmanship of Sir B.N. Rau and made recommendations of Rau committee as a result series of acts were passed in 1955 and 1956, to regulate marriage succession, guardianship and adoption. *The Hindu Marriage Act, 1955* deemed spouses as equals in a monogamous relationship and stated they had equal rights and responsibilities to each other. *The Hindu Succession Act,1956 gave equal rights in matters of succession* while *the Hindu Minority and Guardianship Act, 1956*,gave rights in matters of guardianship.Finally, the *Hindu Adoptions and Maintenance Act, 1956* gave the right to the Hindu wife to claim maintenance even while living separately.[49] Women's participation in the freedom struggle developed their critical consciousness about their role and rights in independent India resulted in the introduction of the franchise and civic rights of women in the Indian constitution.

In the 1960s, a more general movement for gender equality developed based on women's liberation and feminism. Gender and particularly the role of women was widely recognized as vitally important However, actual changes in attitudes continued to focus on specific issues. In 1961, the Parliament of India passed the *Advocates Act*, which amended and consolidated the law governing the Indian legal profession. The Act provided for the establishment of an All India statutory body called "The Bar Council of India". The Bar Council was made responsible for recognizing Universities whose degree in law would be qualification for a graduate's enrolment as an "advocate", a lawyer qualified to practice law in all courts and tribunals. However,a general acknowledgement of the importance of understanding how the situation of Indian women is embedded in these contexts was intrinsic to the new, self-consciously feminist women's movement that emerged in the late 1970 and early 1980s. This often means a focus on gender-equality, ensuring participation, but includes an understanding of the different roles and expectation of the genders within the community. The movement resulted in changes to laws, either relating to particular issues or general anti-sex discrimination laws. A change to attitudes to equality in education opportunities for boys and girls has also undergone a cultural shift. Some changes came about by adopting affirmative action policies.The *Equal*

---

[49] Flavia (1999) *Law and Gender Inequality: the Politics and Women's Rights in India*. Oxford University Press,New Delhi:

Remuneration Act in 1976 provides for equal remineration for men and women for equal work.[50] Hence the change also involved changes to social views, including "equal pay for equal work" as well as most occupations being equally available to men and women, in many countries. For example, many countries now permit women to serve in the armed forces, the police force and to be fire fighters. Also, an increasing number of women are active in politics and occupy high positions in business.

Conversely, men increasingly are working in occupations which in previous generations had been considered "female occupations", such as nursing. Also, in the home, while acknowledging the biological differences between men and women, most notably in relation to child bearing, the role of child rearing is not as widely considered to be an exclusively female role. Another manifestation of the change in social attitudes is the non-automatic taking by a woman of her husband's surname on marriage, as well as a wife being free to pursue her career after marriage.[51] Feminist analysis explains that the neat division between public and private spheres overlooks the fact that the public sphere acrivities undertaken by men are only possible because there is a particular kind od public sphere inhabited by women.This analysis conceptualizes law as operating in a specific social and economic context and it brings into the argument the effects of gender hierarchy.[52]

Formal legal equality was one of the earlier gains of the feminist movement.The *Hindu Marriage Act of 1955* amended in 1976 provides the right for the girl to repudiate a child marriage before attaining maturity whether the marriage has been consummated or not.The *Immoral Traffic(Prevention) Act* of 1956 as amended in 1986 makes sexual exploitation of male or female ,a cognizable offence.An amendment brought in 1984 to the *Dowry Prohibition Act of 1961* makes women's subjugation to cruelty a cognizable offence.The *Medical Termination of*

---

50 Patel, Dr Vibhuti; *Empowerment of Women and Legal provisions*.<http://www.scribd.com/doc/42646310/Vibhuti-Patel-on-Empowerment-of-Women-Legal-Provisions-in-India>on 21st March2011.

51 *Gender equality*, From Wikipedia, the free encyclopedia. < http://en.wikipedia.org/wiki/Gender_equality> on 21st March2011.

52 Parashar,Arachana and Dhanda Amita; Gender problem in India:*Feminine Jurisprudence in India*,Deep and Deep publication,2008p12.

Pregnancy Act of 1971 legalises abortion by qualified professionals on humanitarian and medical grounds.A new enactment of *Indecent Representation of Women (Prohibition) Act* ,and the *Commission of Sati Prevention Act 1987* have also been passed.However formal legal equality did not result in eradication of women's subordination.

While in some universities, gender or women found its way into courses and were readily added to the list. The focus was on ensuring girls' full and equal access to and achievement in good quality basic education. The study focused on our own history, the centrality of the women's question in nationalist discources,the history of women activism and organizations.There were conscious raising groups and women studies became the focal point of many NGOs in India.[53] Pertinent also is the National Policy for the Empowerment of Women, issued by the Government of India in 2001, which recognizes the need to create an environment through a set of policy prescriptions which cover a wide range of issues: changing laws, civil and property rights, equal access to health care, quality education, participation indecision making.

1.4. LITERATURE REVIEW

The study explores the several dimensions of the term 'feminization' of the legal profession. On the one hand, we can consider the profession feminized simply by the increased number of women in the profession. On the other hand, the question of whether the profession will be 'feminized'—that is, changed or influenced by women in the profession—is an issue of a different order. There is some level of complexity even in the definition of 'feminized'. For those who attribute 'feminine' qualities to women (or to men), the legal profession becomes feminized when those feminine qualities are recognized, appreciated and absorbed into the performance of legal tasks and functions (empathy, relatedness, nurturance, collectiveness) For others the profession becomes 'feminized' not by stereotypic attributions of gender qualities but by a 'feminist' influence on the profession which includes particular

---

53 Choudhary Maitryee; *Learning through teaching the sociology of Gender*,The Indian Journal for Gender studies2002,sage publicationp209. <http://www.jnu.ac.in/Faculty/maitrayee/Learning%20through%20Teaching.pdf.0n24th March2011.

substantive changes, not only in the practice of law (i.e., adaptation of work to family) but in the law itself (ranging from employment discrimination issues to family law and criminal law).

The issues here, which derive in part from important work being done in the field of feminist jurisprudence, are concerned with whether women who enter the profession will conform to a 'male' model of what it means to be a legal professional or whether the profession will innovate and adapt to new, previously excluded, entrants who may have new perspectives to offer on how the practice of law can be conducted.

Answers are based on both quantitative and qualitative analyses, using a variety of conceptual frameworks relevant to the present topic. Many books written by number of authors have been consulted in order to evaluate the situation of women in the legal profession in both common and civil law countries. Three countries are covered: the United States, United Kingdom, and India as comparative analysis in the study of legal education and legal profession. While an analysis of Australia, New Zealand, England, Germany, the Netherlands, Poland, Finland, France, Italy, Brazil, Korea, Japan, Afghanistan, United Arab Emirates, Nepal have been made. The focus ranges from women judges and public prosecutors, to law professors, lawyers (attorneys), notaries and company lawyers. National differences are clearly in evidence, but so are the common features.

With the review of the existing literature available on the subject in the United States, United Kingdom, Canada, Australia and India, the researcher surveys women's experiences in law schools, career entry and hiring, and enduring patterns of sex segregation in law practice. It also examines gendered experiences of legal work, specifically disparagement, sexual harassment, and work/family conflict. It evaluates contemporary patterns of gender difference in promotions and upward mobility, earnings, emotional lives of lawyers, and exit paths from law.

Most literature on the subject has focused on testing for and explaining the wage gap between, for example, equally productive male and female workers.

Some of the early discussions took place by Cynthia Fuchs Epstein (1981) in her book *Women in Law* who finds in her study that the proportions of women in the profession remain low, as the larger society does not believe in occupational success and progress of women in the society. Even where women have achieved professional successes, they are usually judged by a set of standards, which are different from those, applied to men. Hence male dominated system of society controls the motivation and participation of women in society. This is ambivalence on the role performance of women lawyers. Therefore, women have to pass through tough time in building their career due to structural differentiation and situational constraints.[54]

Jana Evertt (1984) discussed the experiences of women lawyers. In her paper she explores the prejudices faced by women in law and other difficulties such as securing work, long workdays, and late hours in dealing with clients. The analysis of the study reflects the understanding of prejudices regarding women, female lawyers' participation in media, and campaigns of legal awareness in the society. Thus not only women lawyers involve in law practice but also engage themselves in developing consciousness in society. However, Evertt herself admits that her study cannot be considered a representative of Indian women lawyers as the study is based on the views of urban cosmopolitan successful women lawyers who belong to upper class families than those of rural areas.[55]

Richard L Abel (1988) in *Comparative Sociology of Legal Profession: an Explanatory essays* has pointed out that women lawyers has pointed out that women lawyers were likely to anticipate new perspective on legal issues and the improvement of standards and ethics. The reason for women joining the profession was social service. Women wee also likely to see 'intellectual challenge' as an important reason for becoming a lawyer.[56]

Carrie Menkel-Meadow the author of 'The Comparative Sociology of Women Lawyers: the Feminization of the Legal Profession' has addressed the women's entry

---

54 Epstein, Cynthia Fuchs; *Women in Law*, Basic Books, 1981, New York, p.57.

55 Evertt Jana; "Social Politics," *International Studies in Gender, State & Society*, Volume 5, Number 3,Oxford University Press,1988, pp. 314-337.

56 Abel, Richard L; "Comparative Theories," *Lawyers in Society*, The Regents of University of California, 1988, California, p.80.

in the legal profession and the problematic themes and tensions related to it. It has been published in the book *Lawyers in Society*.[57]

Michael Burrage has tried to identify the common characteristics in the book titled *Revolution and the Collective Action of the French, American and English Legal Professions* and concludes that the common invariant basis demonstrates the motive and interest underlying lawyers. The French, American, and English legal professions are compared in terms of four common goals: to control admission and training, to protect their jurisdiction, to regulate the behavior of their members, and to enhance their cooperative status. [58]

Richard A. Posner in the book titled *Overcoming Law* covers wide ranging topics which includes the structure and behavior of the legal profession, constitutional theory, gender, sex and race theories, interdisciplinary approaches to law, the nature of legal reasoning, and legal pragmatism.[59]

Jean McKenzie Leiper makes contemporary assessment of modern women lawyers. She discussed the professional standards, dress codes that are embedded in the masculine culture and traditions of law practice. In her book titled *Bar Codes: Women in the Legal Profession* she makes a striking note of the struggles faced by the first women lawyers continue in various forms even today. The book fills a particular gap in the interdisciplinary scholarship on women lawyers.[60]

Bernard F. Lentz and David N. Laband in the book titled *Sex Discrimination in the Legal Profession* have shown the statistical data and interpretation which gives an idea of gender bias in American legal practice. The book gave an in-depth study

---

57 Menkel-Meadow, Carrie; "The Comparative Sociology of Women Lawyers: the Feminization of the Legal Profession," *Lawyers in Society*, The Regents of University of California, 1988, California, p.221.

58 Burrage, Michael; "Revolution and the Collective Action of the French, American and English Legal System," *JSTOR, Law and the Social Inquiry*, Vol.13, No.2, Blackbell pulishing, American Bar Foundation, 1988, pp.225-277.

59 Posner, Richard A; *Overcoming Law*, Harvard University Press, 1995, U.S.A.pp.17-51.

60 McKenzie Leiper, Jean; *Bar Codes: Women in the Legal Profession*, UBC Press, 2006, Vancouver.

and helped in this study.[61] Gender in Practice demonstrates and explains how the structure of legal practice has changed in recent decades, often to the disadvantage of women. The issues addressed here such as conflicts between careers and family, departures from practice, and barriers to women's promotions and earnings are of great importance to members of the profession.

Looking at the careers of both men and women and using the book *Gender in Practice: Study of Lawyers Lives,* it traces and reveals occupational and personal experiences and analyzes these patterns in terms of work and gender.[62]

Catharine A. MacKinnon, a noted feminist in the book titled *Feminism Unmodified,* explores and develops her original theories and practical proposals She argues that viewing gender as a matter of sameness and difference--as virtually all existing theory and law have done--covers up the reality of gender, which is a system of social hierarchy, an imposed inequality of power. She reveals a political system of male dominance and female subordination that sexualizes power for men and powerlessness for women. She analyzes the failure of organized feminism, particularly legal feminism, to alter this condition, exposing the way male supremacy gives women a survival stake in the system that destroys them.

While in the book titled *Lloyds Introduction to Jurisprudence,* M.D.A., Freeman gives a critical understanding of jurisprudence and the question that it deals impinges the consciousness of the lawyers.[63]

Anleu Sharyn L. Roach in the book titled *Contemporary theories of law and Social Change* provides an introduction to the sociology of law and its role as a social institution and social process. This book provides coverage of major classic and contemporary social theories of law. Discussing current theory and key empirical research from a diverse range of perspectives, *Contemporary theories of Law* and

---

61 Lentz, Bernard F. and Laband, David N; *Sex Discrimination in the Legal Profession,* Greenwood Publishing Group, 1995, U.S.A.

62 Hagan, John and Kay, Fiona; *Gender in Practice: Study of Lawyers' Lives,* Oxford University Press, 1995, London, pp.21-115.

63 Freeman, M.D.A; *Lloyds Introduction to Jurisprudence,* Sweet & Maxwell Limited, 1994, London.

Social Change gives relevant examples, from various cultures and societies, to provide a sociological view which goes beyond more jurisprudential approaches to law and society.[64]

Carol Gilligan in the book titled *In a Different voice: Psychological theory and Women's Development* has studied women's psychology and girl's development which was useful in the development of this research. This book challenges the traditional way of looking at women's psychological development, focusing on the importance of relationships in women's lives.[65]

There are hardly any books or memoirs that provide detailed information of women in the legal profession during the British rule. There is hardly any proper study of women lawyers' in India except for few based on non-empirical literature.Much of it is contributed by foreigners particularly American scholars.The existing literature, understandly, leaves much to be desired on all fronts - substantive and theoritical.

To begin with, the substantive part of the study of legal practioners have received attention but less than the multiple complexes of organizational aspects.There are more gaps than trends on this dimension.Secondly, there is hardly any systematic study on Women and legal profession from the feminist viewpoint.That is to say,what kind of men and women dominate the bar,how do women and men lawyers get their clients,what professional hazards do women lawyers face,how decision are made in the Bar Council of India and State Bar Council.

Preliminary study of legal profession began in India in 1958 with the publication of the report of the Law Commission of Indiaon reform of judicial administration.[66] This was followed by another study of the growth of Indian middle

---

64 Sharyn L Roach Anleu; *Law and Social Change*, Sage Publications Ltd, 2010, London.

65 Gilligan, Carol; *In a Different voice: Psychological theory And Women's Development*, Harvard University Press, 1983, U.S.A., pp.8-66.

66 Reform of Judicial Administration (14th Report,1958).

classs in modern times by B.B.Mishra in 1962.[67] A systematic study of the legal profession in India appeared in the later half of the 1960s w.Just after three years, *Comparative studies in Society and History* carried a few perceptive articles dealing with the same theme.It was only in 1980 that a full length book on legal profession authored by J.S.Gandhi.[68] But no work was done on women's contribution to the legal progession nor was any descriptive study made on them.

One of the important article titled *Advent of women in the Legal Profession* written by Ramo Devi Gupta discussed how on 29th August, 1916, a Special Bench of Calcutta High Court, *In re*, Regina Guha, reported in (I. L. R. 44 Cal. 290), consisting of the Chief Justice and four other Judges, refused the enrolment of Miss Regina Guha as a Pleader, relying on the case of Bobb versus The Law Society.[69]

A sketch on the Development of Legal profession in India written by Samuel Schmitthener is also one of the first books written on the legal profession of India. Thereafter there has been no such book on the legal profession, in particular, and the impacts of women entering into it.Some few books were also consulted.

Women have been considered as weak, vulnerable and in a position to be exploited. In the year 2003, the book on *Women and Crime* edited by A. Kumar has discussed crime and violence against women. Gender injustice, taking the shape of crimes against women is escalating the world over but in India it has ancient cultural roots. He has made an attempt to ascertain the views of the women lawyers, on some vital questions and also the motive behind for joining the profession, difficulties experiences by them and contribution and impact on the legal profession.[70]

Mary Jane Mossman in the book titled *The First Women Lawyers: A Comparative Study of Gender, Law and the Legal Profession published* in February 2007 is among the current books.She has made a comparative study which explores

---

67 Mishra,B.B;*The Indian Middle Classes:Their Growth in Mordern Times*(1961)

68 Gandhi, J.S. ; *Saints and Sinners- On Gandhi's lawyers and Touts A study in the Sociology of Legal Profession*,Hindusthan Publishing,New Delhi 1982,p.889

69 Gupta,Ramo Devi; "Advent of women in the Legal Profession,"<http://www.allahabadhighcourt.in/event/AdventofWomenInTheProfessionMrsRDGupta.html>

70 Kumar, A; *Women and Crime*, Anmol Publications (Pvt.) Ltd., 2003, New Delhi, p.38

the lives of some of the women who first initiated challenges to male exclusivity in the legal professions in the late-nineteenth and early-twentieth centuries. The book has been of immense help in understanding the lives of some of the first women lawyers in six jurisdictions: the United States, Canada, Britain, New Zealand and Australia, India, and Western Europe. As a comparative study of the first women lawyers in several different jurisdictions, the book reveals how a number of quite different women were engaged with ideas of gender and legal professionalism at the turn of the twentieth century.[71] The writer explores how legal professions responded to women entering a male profession, how women characterized their right and interest in admission to the legal professions, and why some women were successful in their challenges while others were not. She shows how women challenged notions of gender in the legal professions and how these challenges were received by both legal institutions and the public. The book's focus on the late nineteenth and early twentieth centuries when efforts for women's suffrage were taking place, also lead to a number of interesting conclusions. Mossman begins by asking what impact the introduction of women lawyers had on the law and the legal professions and explores whether women assimilated the norms of men or developed their own.By citing examples of the first women lawyers, the writer shows the choices the first women lawyers made in the larger context of their personal lives, the legal profession and historical evolution of women's rights.

While previous research has been published on both the subject of the women's entry into the legal profession as well as the evolution of notions of legal professionalism, Mossman's work offers a new perspective on these matters by analyzing their intersection.

The article titled "Gender justice in India" written by Vijay Pal Singh, a research scholar, deals with the harsh reality that women have been ill-treated in every society for ages and India is no exception. In the article the author says that women are discriminated at two levels, firstly they suffer because of their gender and secondly due to grinding poverty. He discusses the various legislations that were enacted in the colonial rule like the abolition of Sati in 1829, widow remarriage made

---

71 Mossman, Mary Jane; *The First Women Lawyers: A Comparative Study of Gender, Law and the Legal Professions,* Hart Publishing, 2006, Oxford, pp.16-98.

legal in 1856 etc.[72]Though the *Sex Disqualification and Removal Act* of 1919 put an end to such disability in England and women were allowed to enter all professions, including law. A British woman called to the Bar was allowed to practice in India as well, but an Indian woman or a woman who qualified in India was not allowed to practice even in her own country. Prejudices existed followed by the enactment of the *Sex Removal Disability Act* yet Cornelia Sorabji could gain entry in the Legal Profession in India. This has been dealt by A. D. Mane in the article titled "Women's Place in the Bar".[73]

Suparna Guptu in the book titled *India's Pioneer Women Lawyer* on *Cornelia Sorabji* says that Cornelia Sorabji from1866-1954 occupies a significant place in Indian history, as she played a crucial role in trying to open up the legal profession to women much before they were formally allowed to plead before the courts of law.[74] This detailed biography uses rich and hitherto unused data to illustrate a remarkable individual who has remained neglected in studies on India's transition to modernity and also in the historiography of women and gender.This book has been recently published and was only made available in 2010

Women lawyers feel that they can make significant contribution towards the legal profession. It was found that women lawyers joined in the profession mainly due to their interest in the field, desire for social work, to stand in the profession on their own merit and also due to hereditary reasons. In the beginning of their practice women lawyers experience difficulties to deal with clients. However mostly were of the view that it cannot be the monopoly of male lawyers. They also win the confidence of their clients and respect of their colleagues through hard work, sincerity and commitment.

Justice Leila Seth's autobiography *On Balance,* launched in 2003 in New Delhi talks about her early years of homelessness and struggle, her straying into law

---

72 Singh, Vijay Pal; "Gender Justice in India,"< http://www.legalserviceindia.com/articles/gen_j.htm>.

73 Mane, A. D; "Women's Place in the Bar,"<mshrc.maharashtra.gov.in/Speech/upload/file%2051.pdf> on 4th August 2008.

74 Guptu, Suparna; *India's Pioneer Women Lawyer on Cornelia Sorabji,* Oxford University Press, 2006, India, pp 5-78.

while in England with her husband Premo, and later practicing in Patna, Calcutta and Delhi.It includes the experience of bringing up three remarkable children. This book has helped in this proposed study to peep in the life of women judges.[75]

Sexual harassment is a serious and real problem for working women in a large number of occupations, and employments, and may have disastrous consequences both for the victims and the employers. Notwithstanding the absence, so far, of any statute in India that specifically deals with the problem of sexual harassment at work, victims of sexual harassment have remedies under different types of law such as the Indian Constitution, Labour Laws, Criminal Laws, the *National Commission for Women Act*, 1990, *Protection of Human Rights Act, 1993*, as also Torts Law. The author Alok Bhasin of the book Law *Relating to Sexual Harassment at Work has* explained the circumstances under which are employers may be held vicariously liable for the sexual torts of its employees.[76] While Mamata Rao's book on *Law relating to Women & Children* have dealt with women issues which was helpful in this study.

Recent developments in women in India indicate growing concern with in adequate representation in the decision making bodies. Women's participation has not only seen as the central to the functioning of the democracy but also to the ability in the struggling for their rights and challenging the ideologies and hierarchies that keep women in subordinate positions. Kumud Sharma in the article titled "Power and Representation: Reservation of women in India" has discussed the reasons and problems of women underrepresentation in decision making bodies. [77]

The issue of gender and law reform with reference to the politics and history on India has been explored in the book on *Law and Gender Inequality: the Politics and Women's Rights in India written by Flavia Agnes.* It also explores the strategies,

---

75 Seth, Leila; *On Balance*, Penguin Books Pvt. Ltd., 2008, India, pp.8-68.

76 Bhasin Alok; *Law Relating to Sexual Harassment at Work*, Eastern Book Company, Lucknow,2007

77 Sharma, Kumud; "Power and Representation: Reservation of women in India," *AJWS*, Vol.6, No.1, Centre for Women Studies, New Delhi, pp.47-87.

which could safeguard the women's rights in a country like India, which has a typical social, cultural and political background.[78]

The priority of man against woman and dominance of masculine against feminism is a progressive factor. Women are deprived of economic resources and are dependent on men for their living. Women works are often confined to domestic sphere, she had to do all house hold works, which are not recognized and unpaid. In modern times many women are coming out to work but has to shoulder the double responsibility; one she has to work where she is employed and secondly she also has to do all the house hold works, moreover, she is last to be considered and first to be fired as she is considered to be less productive than her counterpart. Her general status in the family and in the society has been low and unrecognized.

We cannot put assistance to woman,when we are coming across to their problems and worries.They may put their plight and problem through published paper,writing,media or otherwise.Gokulesh Sharma in *Feminist Jurisprudence in India ; Womens right* have compiled works of writers in this regrd.[79] The book has helped in the study and understanding of the feminist jurisprudence in India.

Women have been victims of exploitations by male dominated society. They need to be empowered and men need to be oriented about their obligations towards women. Women empowerment may enhance their self-confidence and their ability and willingness to challenge oppression. "Legislative and Judicial Initiatives towards Empowerment of Women" discusses the legislative and judicial initiative towards empowerment of women written by R.Seyon.[80]

The Universal Declaration of Human Rights (1948) reaffirmed faith in fundamental human rights in the dignity and worth of human person and in equal rights of men and women. Justice R.C. Lahoti has discussed the need for women's

---

78 Agnes, Flavia; *Law and Gender Inequality: The Politics and Women's Rights in India.* Delhi: Oxford University Press, 1999.

79 Sharma, Gokulesh; *Feminist Jurisprudence in India ; Womens right,*Deep and Deep publication,New Delhi,2008.

80 Seyon,R; "Legislative and Judicial Initiatives towards Empowerment of Women," <http://www.airinfotech.in/legislative.htm> on 4th August 2008.

empowerment by law and legal means in the article titled "Women's Empowerment – Role of Judiciary and Legislature."[81] While the title "A review of gender justice since independence" written by Dr. V.S. Elizabeth has discussed the objective of the constitution of India.[82]

Scholars of legal history, sociology, economics, organizational behavior, and law have examined various dimensions of the feminization of the legal profession. They document and assess the theoretical explanations of gender inequalities that persist across legal education, hiring, remuneration, promotions, and other professional opportunities in law. The article "Women in Legal Profession" by Fiona Kay and Elizabeth Gorman has dealt that in recent years, the legal profession has undergone significant changes with rapidly rising numbers of women among its membership. The authors also examine women's responses to their experiences and women's impact on the law and the profession.[83]

Apart from these, international instruments and conventions like Universal Declaration of Human Rights, 1948,[84] Declaration on the Elimination of Violence against Women, 1993,[85] Convention on the Elimination of All Forms of Discrimination against Women,[86] an International Covenant on Economic, Social and Cultural Rights,[87] The Mexico Plan of Action (1975),[88] the Nairobi Forward Looking Strategies (1985),[89] the Beijing Declaration, the Platform for Action (1995)[90] and the Outcome Document adopted by the UNGA Session on Gender Equality and Development & Peace for the 21st century, titled "Further actions and initiatives to

---

81 Lahoti, R.C; "Women's Empowerment – Role of Judiciary and Legislature," (2005) 2 SCC (Jour) 49

82 Elizabeth, V.S; "A review of gender justice since independence,"<http://www.nls.ac.in/gender/vselizabeth.html> on 4th August 2008.

83 Kay, Fiona and Gorman Elizabeth; "Women in the Legal Profession," Annual Review of Law and Social Science, Vol. 4: 299-332.

84 <http://www.un.org/en/documents/udhr/> on 4th August 2008.

85 <http:// www.un.org/documents/ga/res/48/a48r104.htm>

86 , <http://www.un.org/womenwatch/daw/cedaw/ >on 2nd June 2008.

87 <http://www2.ohchr.org/english/law/pdf/cescr.pdf> on 2nd June 2008.

88 <http://www.un.org/womenwatch/daw/followup/session/.../hist.htm >on 2nd June 2008.

89 <http://www.un.org/womenwatch/confer/nfls/ >on 2nd June 2008.

90 <http://www.un.org/womenwatch/daw/beijing/platform/declar.htm> on 2nd June 2008.

implement the Beijing Declaration and the Platform for Action" have been of great relevance in the study.

The National Commission for Women was set up by an Act of Parliament in 1990 to safeguard the rights and legal entitlements of women. The reports of the National commission for women, The West Bengal State Commission for women,[91] National Human Rights Commission, National Policy for the empowerment for women, 2001 and The National Knowledge Commission on Legal education have been referred.[92] Within the framework of a democratic polity, our laws, development policies, Plans and programmes have aimed at women's advancement in different spheres. From the Fifth Five Year Plan (1974-78) onwards has been a marked shift in the approach to women's issues from welfare to development. In recent years, the empowerment of women has been recognized as the central issue in determining the status of women. The philosophy of empowerment – Vision of the Eleventh plan-Integrated policy and strategy for economic and social empowerment of women has been looked into.[93] The 73rd and 74th Amendments (1993) to the Constitution of India have provided for reservation of seats in the local bodies of panchayats and municipalities for women, laying a strong foundation for their participation in decision making at the local levels. For the research various Law Commissions Reports have been looked into. The Fifty Nine Report,[94] Sixty Fourth Report,[95] Sixty Six Report,[96] Law Eighty First Report,[97] One Eighty Fourth Report, [98]of the Law Commission of India has been referred in the study.

---

91 < http://www.wbcw.org/> on 3rdMarch2008.

92 <http://www.un.int/india/india_and_the_un_hr.html> on 3rdMarch2008.

93 Eleventh Plan Vision and Strategy (2007-2012), 19th December2007. <http://www.karunadu.gov.in/SPB/Reports/> on 5th May 2008.

94 "The Fifty Nine Report, Law Commission of India," March1974, India.

95 "The Sixty Fourth Report, Law Commission of India," March,1975,India.

96 "The Sixty Six Report, Law Commission of India," May 1976, India.

97 "Eighty First Report, Law Commission of India," December, 1979, India.

98 "One Eighty Fourth Reports, Law Commission of India," December2002, India.

1.5. PRIOR RESEARCH ON 'WOMEN AND LEGAL PROFESSION' IN INDIA AND FINDINGS THAT EMERGE:

Not many studies have been undertaken on the issue of "Women and Legal Profession" from the feminist perspective. Some discussions have been undertaken on the struggle of early women lawyers in India and earlier decisions of the court regarding entry of women, which concluded that women were not entitled to practice law, and rejected women's claim to gain admission to the bar until legislations were enacted after World War I.

Some of the findings that emerge from these studies are:

- In the North- East Province (later known as United Province and now Uttar Pradesh) a regulation was made in 1802 for appointment of Vakils and Pleaders in Civil Courts. *Legal Practitioners Act, 1879* consolidated laws and regulations governing the lawyers. The Advocates, Vakils or Attorney of a High Court, Pleader, Mukhtar or Revenue agents were all brought under the jurisdiction and on the rolls of the High Court. The High Court was empowered to make rules regarding their qualifications, fees, suspension and dismissal.[99]

- The claims initiated by early aspiring women lawyers were unsuccessful in the courts, and were vigorously opposed on the ground that the earlier legislations such as the provisions of the *Legal Practitioners' Act, 1879*, did not contemplate the extension of the privilege to women in India.[100]

- Many judges clearly deferred on the question of women's eligibility to practice law. Individual women adopted different legal arguments in litigating cases, or devised particular strategies to overcome barriers to professional

---

99 Ambwani, Justice Sunil; "Ethics and the Legal Profession," < http://www.ijtr.nic.in/webjournal/2.htm>.

100 Gupta, Ramo Devi; "Advent of Women in the Profession of Law,"<http://www.allahabadhighcourt.in/event/AdventOfWomenInTheProfessionMrsRDGupta.html>.on 2nd June 2008.

work, but most of the decisions reflected that women were considered weaker sections of the society and therefore had no right to appear in public sphere.

- The enactment of the *Sex Disqualification Removal Act, 1919* removed the disability in England, but Indian women did not have this right for many years.

- *In Regina Guha (1916) 21 CWN 74* the Calcutta High Court,[101] and in *Sudhangshu Bala Hazara (1922) ILR 1 Patna 104,*[102] the Patna High Court held that women otherwise qualified were not entitled to be enrolled as Vakil or Pleader. To remove the doubts *Legal Practitioners (Women) Act,* 1923 declared that notwithstanding the Letters Patent of any High Court no woman shall be disqualified to be enrolled as legal practitioners.[103]

- The Allahabad High Court took the lead and changed the history by enrolling Miss Cornelia Sorabji, as the first Indian Lady, Vakil of Allahabad High Court, on 24th August 1921. In the face of stupendous opposition, Miss Cornelia Sorabji decided to enter the profession. Here she was up not only against the racial biases of the rulers, but also against those of her own kind.

- A Parsi Christian from western India, Sorabji was the first woman to complete the examinations for the B.C.L. degree at Oxford in 1892, and her appearance for the defense in the 1896 murder case was reported all over the common law world.[104]In this way, women who aspired to become lawyers were necessarily pushing the women's equality agenda to its fullest potential.

- In addition, these new idea of women's equality were occurring along side changing ideas about the nature of professions, including law, and many jurisdictions in the late nineteenth century.

---

101 Ambwani, Justice Sunil; "Ethics and the Legal Profession,"< http://www.ijtr.nic.in/webjournal/2.htm> on 2nd June 2008.

102 Ibid.

103 Ibid.

104 Mossman, Mary Jane; "Reflections on the First Women Lawyer," *Osgoode Hall Law Journal,* Vol.45, No.2, 2007, p.395.

- The first women lawyers grew up in families that enjoyed middle class status or aspired middle class values. Arguably, their entry to the profession provided opportunities for independence and adventure, circumstances that were not available to other workingwomen.

- Thus in confronting competing ideas about 'women's equality' and about 'legal professionalism' at the end of the nineteenth century, they relied on the rhetoric of equality and opened up opportunities to women to become lawyers, even though this rhetoric substantially failed to challenge the most fundamental aspects of professional culture in the practice of law.

- At the same time, it is clear that at least some of the time, some of these first women lawyers challenged, or at least destabilized, traditional ideas about women's roles and about the gentleman's profession of law. In this way, the history of the first women lawyers is an essential part of both the history of women's equality and the history of the legal professions.[105]

- Women successes or failures were reasoned with prejudices, which they had to overcome It painted a picture reflecting that women are but male subjectivity glorified, objectified, elevated to the status of reality. It recognizes patriarchal myths that are projection of the male psyche.

- Women face barriers in getting recognition in the legal profession.

- Women struggling there way to create an identity of their own faced gender bias, harassment and other social issues.

- After some years of practice, woman lawyers working in the courts leave the profession. Hence the numbers keep receding from time to time.

---

105 Ibid.

1.6. OBJECTIVES

In recent years, the legal profession has undergone significant change, with rapidly rising numbers of women among its membership. The study assesses how shifting and contested ideas about gender and about legal professionalism shaped women's opportunities and choices, as well as both support for and opposition to their claims. Although research has been carried out on the career patterns of women who have been working in the legal profession for several years in western countries very little is known about Indian women lawyers during their course of their practice in India.

The study is an attempt to explore:

1. How some women initiated gender challenges to the legal profession in a number of different jurisdictions including their entry to law i.e. from gaining admission to the profession, entry in all legal specialties, practice settings, and higher echelons of status and influence?

2. What barriers to gender equality persist within the profession? How have women lawyers responded to the organizations in which they work, particularly when these organizations have been reticent to change or resisted to change altogether?

3. To explores gender-related psychosocial aspects, such as the differences between the career patterns of men and women and to evaluate critically the differences between the career patterns of men and women in the legal profession. The applicability of several career development theories to women and to understand the career psychology that is particularly relevant to female law students in pursuing the study of law--traditionally dominated by men.

4. To assesses the theoretical explanations of gender inequalities that persist across legal education, hiring, remuneration, promotions, and other professional opportunities in law. To analyze how gender influences affect the career decisions of women. To explore and identify some of the key

issues related to the career development of women in legal profession and judiciary, in general.To examine several career development theories that are applicable to women, followed by implications and specific suggestions for career counseling that address the unique experiences and needs of women studying in law.

5. To assess the parameters of integration and inequality in the careers of women and men in the contemporary legal profession.

6. To evaluate the impact of women's presence and rising numbers in the legal profession that stimulated change.

1.7. RESEARCH QUESTIONS

There are a number of questions that are coming in the present socio-legal context, such as; how did legal profession respond to women challenges to the male exclusivity of a 'gentleman's profession'? How did women characterize their right to gain admission to legal profession? What impact have they had on the profession that has for so long been a preserve of male domination? What are the major determinants of career satisfaction for women attorneys? What are the specific factors-formal and informal that inhibits career satisfaction? What are the gender dynamics that influence career trajectory of women lawyers? Whether the increased presence of women in the last ten years so far India is concerned might lead to alternative ways of seeing what lawyers do and how they do it. More profoundly, has women's presence and rising status in the legal profession stimulated change in either the substance of law or the organization and activities of lawyers? Will the women who practice law transform the legal profession?

- *The Research Question of this study, therefore, is what are the factors that lead to discrimination and barriers or restrictions of Indian women entering a legal profession and practicing in a field or her elevation into the bench.*

1.8. THE TAKE –OFF STAGE

There are over sixty lakhs practicing lawyers in India.[106] The general conception is that it is a noble profession. But globalization has changed the perception of legal profession yet the status of women lawyers in India has remained unchanged. It is no secret that the very thought of facing the courts in India leaves the common man with a sense of dread and despair; cases drag on interminably, and justice sometimes seems like an afterthought. The picture is not a flattering one.

From the available statistical data, the researcher traces that not significant numbers of women have entered in the Bench/Judicial Service as compared to men. The Bar has been set long time ago. Members of legal profession, day in and day out argue matters of justice and equality. Why then, women have no fair percentage in the High Court/Supreme Court? What is the cause of this poor representation of women in judiciary?

How are lawyers and the judicial system in India perceived today? Who or what is responsible for this situation? Where have we lost our way? Can we presume that the increased influx of women, who are born builders in the legal profession, might help mitigate?

This prompted the researcher to undertake this topic as her research study.

1.9. METHODOLOGY

The methodology of this study is broadly characterized as analytical method involving analysis of case laws, statutes by applying logic and reasoning and identifying the legal issues, barriers encountered by women in legal profession. By using the available data relating to position and role played by women lawyers in the world in general, and in India in particular, the study analyzes the various changes and its impact both in legal profession and in legal education.

---

106 Joshi, Swapnil; "Changing Face of Legal Profession in India in the era of globalization," Legal Service India .com, < http: //www.legalserviceindia.com/articles/lprof.htm.> on 6th May2008.

The data on women's participation in legal profession in India in particular, has been principally taken from secondary sources. Statistical data furnished by Bar Council of India, Bar Council of West Bengal, and National Commission for women, Law colleges in Kolkata, law firms, quasi-judicial bodies etc has been used. This analyzed stratification, socialization, professionalization, networks of lawyers both men and women and clients. It was of important relevance. Data has also been taken from journal, newspapers, articles, books and electronic sources. Hence, at times the research has been empirical based.

By citing cases and the effects of the decisions, these cases reflect how some women initiated gender challenges to gain access in the legal profession. In this context my research questions about women lawyers focuses on the history of claims presented by the first women who challenged male exclusively in the legal profession: to what extent the women become lawyers without challenging gender and discrimination in legislation and the legal profession.

By utilizing a multi-method approach grounded in feminist theory, this research expects to provide insight in the challenges of women lawyers and their career experiences. Policy implications for creating equal opportunities for women in legal profession have been discussed by taking help from the views of feminist scholars who have offered some insights and have shed light on these questions. The proposed study assesses women's impact on the legal profession and styles of legal practice.

Therefore, the exploratory study is from the feminist perspective.

Despite the fact that women made up half of the students graduating from law school in the past 15 years, the legal profession remains a male-dominated world. The inescapable conclusion is that it is the product of the discriminatory, systemic and structural practices in the legal profession that have been well documented in recent years and which prevent female advocates from getting the same opportunities as male advocates. It can't also be due to lack of ability or numbers. The results of this study reveal that women attorneys are also victimized by less obvious forms of discrimination. The proposed study determine that although earnings of female lawyers differ appreciably from those of male lawyers, the incidence of promotion from associate to partner is greater for men than for otherwise comparable women. There are also evidence of sexual harassment and other less-tangible aspects of sex discrimination in the legal workplace though very few cases have been reported in newspapers. Such harassment has serious implications for lawyers and legal employers, resulting in emotional, physical, and social consequences; lost productivity; increased turnover; impaired reputations; and greater risk of liability and litigation expenses.

Experts do say that with time, the situation may improve. Some 269 posts of high court judges are currently lying vacant and some of these are sure to be filled by competent women. Moreover, the situation is believed to be much better in subordinate courts where the proportion of women judges is healthier than in the higher judiciary. Some of these judges will also be elevated to high courts in the coming years.

1.10. THEORETICAL FRAMEWORK

Feminist theories demonstrate the ways in which this gentleman's profession and practices discriminate women and reinforce gender inequality. Despite some change the legal profession remains a male dominated profession. Feminist theory is based on the belief that the law has been instrumental in women's historical subordination. There are different feminist jurisprudence. Cain offers a useful categorization into four schools Liberal, Radical, Cultural and Postmodern.[107]

Liberal approach emphasizes to equality that amounts to equal opportunity. Liberal feminist identify the law as sexiest and biased and advocate reform as a remedy. Some recent liberal approaches rely on Carol Gilligan's work to argue that women have a different morality or voice than men. Women's identities are defined in

107 Cain, Patricia A; "Feminism and the Limits of Equality," 24 Ga. L. Rev. 803 (1989-1990)

a context of relationship and that female values are characterized by responsibility, intimacy, and connection.[108]

Other feminist legal theorist disagrees that the maleness of law can be changed by increasing women's participation or by placing more value on so called female qualities. Law is seen as maintaining 'male domination'. Radical feminists, such as Littleton and MacKinnon, focus on differences between women and men and support affirmative measures to challenge inequalities. Cultural feminists also emphasize difference, but view it more positively. Radical feminist like MacKinnon and Littleton are critical of the traditional approach to equality. Littleton's critic of equality is based on 'gender complements'. By matching a female gender difference to its male complement and then treating them equally in terms of compensation, status and opportunity for promotion into decision making process. Catherine MacKinnon is probably the most influential of feminist legal scholars. In the extract from the book titled *Feminism Unmodified*, she argues that feminists should concentrate on identifying dominance. This treats gender equality issues as questions about the distribution of power, about male supremacy and female subordination.[109] Thinkers such as Carol Gilligan and Robin West use the rhetoric of equality to advocate change that supports the values caring, relational connectedness of this difference. They argue that the category 'women' has been not so much misdefined by men as undervalued.[110] The fourth school of thought, postmodern feminism admits that gender qualities as well as equality doctrines are social construct that are products of patriarchy and are in need of feminist reconstruction. But post modern feminist rejects the search of one new truth to replace the old. It denies that there is a single theory of equality that will benefit all women.[111]

To Ann Scales, 'Feminism proceeds from the principle that 'objective reality is a myth, with patriarchal myths as projections of the male psyche'.[112] Ann Scales'

---

108 Sharyn, L Roach Anleu; *Law and Social Change*, Sage Publications Ltd, 2010, London, p.65.

109 Mackinnon, Catherine; *Feminism Unmodified: Discourses on Life and Law*, Harvard University Press, 1987p.56.

110 Anleu, Sharyn L Roach; Law and Social Change, Sage Publication Ltd, 2009,London,p.65.

111 Weisberg, D. Kelly; *Feminist Legal Theory: foundations* Temple University Press, 1993, Philadelphia, p.217.

112 Ibid p.6.

look to a feminist jurisprudence is a one that examines on domination, disadvantage and disempowerment of women. Gilligan, a developmental psychologist, has argued that women's moral development reflects a focus on responsibility and contextually, whilst men's relies more on heavily on rights and abstract justice.

Postmodernist theorists question the homogeneity and stability of social and legal categories, including those used by other feminist. They shift attention to the ways in which law constitutes gender, especially gender differences, and the converse. Rather than looking on the women as a category, post modernist examines the ways in which these laws affect different kinds of women.[113]

The researcher has taken the radical approach of feminist jurisprudence in this study.

1.11. FOCUSING ON STUDY

The focus of study is on Women and Legal Profession from the feminist perspective. The study examines several contemporary dynamics of gender in the legal profession. The study divided the discussion into the following areas:

1. ***An introduction and methodology.***
2. ***The Legal profession — a historical perspective.***
3. ***Women in legal education and legal profession.***
4. ***Professional hazards of women lawyers.***
5. ***Women lawyers around the world.***
6. ***Women in judiciary.***
7. ***Feminization of Legal Profession — its impact.***
8. ***A critical Appraisal***

---

113 Ibid p.68.

CHAPTER- II

THE LEGAL PROFESSION - A HISTORICAL PERSPECTIVE

"Modern readers ... ... know that women's lives are complex and that region, period, personality, and circumstance crucially influence what a subject is able to make of herself. ... And modern women lawyers know that the biographies of women who chose to locate their professional lives in the law are likely to be stories of piecemeal progress and circumscribed success."

-Carol Sanger; "Biography and Early Women Lawyers," *(1994)*
Stan.L.Rev., Vol. 46, p.1257

2.1 AN OVERVIEW

In the previous chapter, the representation of women in the legal profession has been manifested through analysis of statistics offered by official and non-official agencies all over the world. The review of the literature on the subject highlights multi-dimensional scourge of problems. The magnitude of the problem prompted the researcher to take up the study.

In this chapter, the researcher flips through the pages of history to trace the history of discriminatory practices in the legal profession. The study explores the struggle of women seeking entry to a gentleman's profession. They were confronted with contested ideas about women's roles and about legal professionalism. These women were unique as they first challenged the male exclusively in legal profession, tried to persuade the male judges and legislatures to reinterpret the law that made entry into the legal profession unthinkable.

The study critically examines as to what difference it made when Cornelia Sorabji, Clara Brett Martin, Myra Bradwell took admission in the course of Law (a profession in which their presence was not only unthinkable but also illegal) and succeeded in becoming lawyers in 1897.In the years of waiting, some women with legal qualifications assumed subordinate legal roles akin to those of paralegals, such as Elizabeth Orme in England, or they gave up on the law altogether. These women were those who were prepared to beat a path, through the jungles of convention, so as to pave the way for future generations.

The story of the women in the profession began very recently Entry to the so called learned profession – law, medicine and ministry---- was prohibited by law in many countries until well into the twentieth century. Even where entry was lawful social and ideological barrier were substantial. Women generally participated in activities that had not been professionalized. The history of discriminatory practices in the legal profession can be traced from the very first decision in *Bradwell v. State of Illinois, (1873), US 83, 16 WALL, 130.*[114] The main point that was argued was whether the 'persons' admitted to the bar could be women where the Supreme Court ruled that the word 'person' meant only 'male'. In the cases that follow, the central legal issue was whether women could be considered to be "legal persons" or to be included within definitions of 'person' or 'man' in legislation governing various professional and civic rights and duties, for example, the right to practice law, to vote, or to hold public office.[115]

Some of the other cases worth mentioning are *Re Mabel P. French 1 D.L.R. 80,*[116] *Charlton v. Lings (1868-9) LR. 4 CP,*[117] *Beresford-Hope Vs Lady Sandhurst [1889],23 QBD 79, Beresford-Hope Vs Lady Sandhurst [1889],23 QBD 79,*[118] *Ball Vs Incorp., Society of Law Agents (1901),*[119] *Nairn Vs University of Andrews,* 1909 A.C. 147, p.161.[120]

114 *Bradwell v. State of Illinoi,(* 1873), US 83,16 WALL, 130.

115 Ibid.

116 *Re Mabel P. French,*37 N.B.R.359(S.C).

117 *Charlton v. Lings (*1868-9) LR. 4 CP 374,p 392.

118 *Beresford-Hope Vs Lady Sandhurst* [1889], 23 QBD 79,p. 91.

119 *Ball Vs Incorp. Society of Law Agents* (1901).

120 *Nairn Vs University of Andrews,* 1909 A.C.147, p.161.

The discussions in this chapter has been divided into the following headings-

Early Women Lawyers: Historical Background

- USA
- Canada
- Britain
- South Africa
- Indian Scenario

Feminist theories

A Sum Up

2. 2. EARLY WOMEN LAWYERS: HISTORICAL BACKGROUND

2.2.1. UNITED STATES OF AMERICA

Entry of women in to the legal profession relates back to 18th Century. In 1860, in the United States of America, women first began to attend university law schools and to gain formal education in the University State bars. For a century women lawyers had been struggling which began in 1869 when Arabella Babb Mansfield achieved formal admission to the Iowa bar of the United States of America. The Iowa court approved her application in 1869; Mansfield became the first women in the United States to achieve formal education to the bar of any state. This gradual transformation is important to the history of the women's entry to the legal profession. The aspiration of women who wanted to become lawyers was quite consistent with the goals of the women's movement, including the opening up of educational opportunities and access to the profession.[121]

Feminist social theorists argued about whether women's 'marginal' status endowed them with altruistic attitudes that would 'purify' humankind if women were granted the vote, allowed to practice their separate professions of social work and teaching, and able to accomplish their social reform agendas of protective labor

---

121 Mossman, Mary Jane. *'The First Women Lawyers - a Comparative study of Gender, Law and the Legal Profession'*, Hart Publishing, 2006, Oxford, p. 49.

legislation. They were opposed by those who stressed the 'homogeneity of the human mind'. Throughout the nineteenth century in both England and the United States most of the activists, but not all, stressed the 'special qualities of women.' Nevertheless, the history of women in the professions is peppered with strong individual achievers who do not fit easily into either camp.

The history of the first women lawyers is relevant to an understanding of contemporary issues of gender and professionalism. In describing how 19th century women lawyers struggle to balance their gender and professionalism, for example, Virginia G. Drachman explained how they adopted clothing styles for legal work which "mirrored the suits of male lawyers and revealed women lawyers" professional identification with their male colleagues.[122] It was a great concern for a woman lawyers who entered into the courtroom to argue cases. As a proper lady of her day, social etiquette required that she wear a hat in public. But as a lawyer, professional etiquette demanded that she removed her hat when she entered the courtroom. As a result the question of the hat once again confronted women lawyers with the enduring challenges of reconciling their traditional role as women with their new professional identity as lawyers. The burden of the 19th century women lawyers and their conflicts between their identities as women and as lawyers were not so easily reconciled when they appeared in court. Some other scholars have examined the ideal of 19th century legal culture as 'gentleman's profession'. Maleness was a defining feature of the idea of profession: an occupation could not be called a profession 'if it was filled with women'.[123]

Women entering into the profession in the nineteenth century generally assimilated to prevailing western ideologies such as the 'cult of domesticity' and 'women's separate spheres' by arguing that women had special contribution to make.[124] With their zeal and effort, they initiated gender challenges to the legal

---

122 Drachman, Virginia D; "Women Lawyers and the Quest for Professional Identity in Late Nineteenth Century America," *JSTOR, Michigan Law Review*, Vol.88, No.8.1990, pp.2414-1443.

123 Gidney, RD. and Millar, WPJ: *Professional Gentlemen: The Profession in Nineteenth-Century Ontario*, Toronto, University of Toronto Press, 1994, p. 239.

124 Abel,Richard; "Feminization of the Legal Profession," *Lawyers in Society*, University of California Press, 1988,California, p.199.

profession and tried to establish their identities as professional women by facing insurmountable hurdles. This was at a time when the ideology of women's natural place was ideally at home as a mother and a wife. Thus, the fact that the first women lawyers in the United States, Canada, Britain and India who had made access to the legal profession is useful for understanding the efforts the first pioneers had taken in challenging male hegemony in the legal profession.

The history of discriminatory practices can be traced from the very first decision about whether the 'persons' admitted to the bar could be women where the Supreme Court ruled that the word 'person' meant only 'male'. This was in the year 1894, and the decision denied the women the right to practice law on the grounds that the word 'person' meant men only. The history of legal profession shows that in the United States, Myra Bradwell fought her case right up to Supreme Court and lost in 1872 in *Bradwell v. State of Illinois, 1875, 83 U.S. 130; 21 L. Ed. 442; 1872 U.S.*[125] Some of the other cases are *Re Mabel. French [1.Barrister (Section I A — 6) — Right to Practice — Admitting Women as Barristers and Solicitors.], Beresford-Hope Vs Lady Sandhurst (1889)23 QBD 79, Hall Vs Incorporated Society of Law Agents (1901), w 3 F, 1059, and Nairn V University of Andrews, 1909 A.C. 147, p. 161* in which the House of Lords expressly held that women did not fall within the meaning of the term person.[126]

In Bradwell v. State of Illinois, 1875, 83 U.S. 130; 21 L. Ed. 442; 1872 U.S, the Supreme Court of Illinois having refused to grant to a woman a license to practice law in the courts of that State, on the ground that females are not eligible under the laws of that State. It also held that such a decision violates no provision of the Federal Constitution. The Supreme Court disagreeing with Bradwell upheld the decision of the Illinois court ruling that the Privileges or Immunities Clause of the *Fourteenth Amendment* did not include the right to practice a profession.

The judgment of Justice Barker is notable. To quote him ".......the civil law, as well as nature herself, has always recognized a wide difference in the respective spheres and destinies of man and woman.....The natural and proper timidity and

---

[125] *Myra Bardwell v. State of Illinois* 83 U.S. 130; 21 L. Ed. 442; 1872 U.S. LEXIS 1140.

[126] Ibid.

delicacy which belongs to the female sex evidently unfits it for many of the occupations of civil life. The constitution of the family organization, which is founded in the divine ordinance as well in the nature of things, indicates the domestic sphere as that which properly belongs to the domain and functions of womanhood. The paramount destiny and mission of women are to fulfill the noble and benign offices of wife and mother. This is the law of the Creator." Further, the US Supreme Court in Bradwell Vs Illinois (1875) also held that 'a State could preclude a married woman from practicing law'. The doctrine of coverture, which barred married women from owing property in their own names and making contracts, prevented them in entering into the profession as well as others. Even when it was removed by the by the *Married Women's Property Act* in many eastern and mid western states, the courts drew on the 'divine ordinance' to confine women to the home, ruling that the 'proper delicacy' and 'timidity' suited them to care for husbands and children but not to enter the rough and tumble of public life.[127]

Myra Bradwell was unsuccessful in her efforts to gain admission to the bar of Illinois, not only before the Illinois Supreme Court (*In re Bradwell, 1869*) but also in her subsequent appeal to the Supreme Court of the United States. Notwithstanding her lack of success, however, her case remains important because the case illustrates the variety of legal arguments used to decide the issue of whether women were eligible to become lawyers in the United States in the 19th century, arguments that were later adopted in jurisdictions, particularly Canada.

In stark contrast to the reasoning in Mansfield's case in Iowa, however, the Illinois court concluded that the judges had no jurisdiction to admit persons 'not intended by the Legislature to be admitted, even though their exclusion [was] not expressly required by statute'. As Nancy Gilliam suggested, the judicial role in this case was one of deference to the legislature, particularly on a novel question such as women's roles in the professions. Thus, while Mansfield had successfully gained

127 Abel, Richard; "Feminization of the Legal Profession," *Lawyers in Society*, University of California Press, 1988, California, p. 201.

admission to the bar in Iowa in 1869, Myra Bardwell's application was denied in Illinois just a few months later.[128]

The language of the Bradwell decision expressed very clearly an unqualified acceptance of the idea of difference between men and women. It was, thus, evident that the ideas he expressed were those that were prevailing in the cultural and professional milieu in which he lived. Accepting these ideas, and applying them in the decision, the judgment was a significant reinforcement of the idea of gender-based difference. In 1894 a U.S. Supreme Court decision denying women the right to practice law on the grounds that the word person meant men only. Though the problem in the US was partially solved by ratification of the *19th Amendment* to the US Constitution (1920) permitting women over 21 to vote.[129]

More importantly, the Bradwell decision included a concurring opinion by Justice Bradley that confirmed that women were barred from the practice of law because women and men occupied 'separate spheres'. According to this view, 'it was the law of nature that women both lived in separate spheres from men and that the practice of law was closed to women.' Thus the Bradwell case not only provided a precedent from the highest court in the United States, one which clearly denied women's right to practice law, but it also confirmed that 'separate spheres' existed, as a matter of law, for men and women. As a result it was firmly entrenched a 'jurisprudence of separate spheres,' not only for the women in the United States, but also in other jurisdiction where judges used Bradwell to deny claims submitting by aspiring women lawyers.

Mary Jane Mossman explains that this idea of "women as delicate, unstable by nature and as suited to a function within the domestic sphere whilst unsuitable to the demands of the public realm had a great effect on middle-class women who became

---

128 Mossman, Mary Jane.: *The First Women Lawyers - a Comparative study of Gender, Law and the Legal Professions,*Hart Publishing, 2006, Oxford, p. 43.

129 Pretty Ones, 21st April, 2006. < http://kvtrust.blogspot.com/2006/04/pretty-ones.html> on 5/07/07.

confined to the home, than upon working class women who were employed in factories."[130] The difference was social as well as biological.

Two years later in the case of *Minor Vs Happier Sett,*[131] it was conceded that women were citizens as well as persons but held them to be a special category of non-voting citizens. Bradwell name lives in legal history because of the Supreme Court's 1873 Bardwell decision, upholding the lower court ruling that denied her a license to practice law on the grounds that she was a married woman.[132]

The second case was a 1905 decision of the New Brunswick Court of Appeal, *In Re Mabel. French* reported in 1 D.L.R. 80, (British Columbia Court of Appeal). The issue was whether Mabel French was entitled to be admitted as an attorney. The governing legislation referred to 'persons' having the requisite qualifications as being entitled to become lawyers. To quote C.J.A Macdonald, "I think we can take judicial notice of the fact that no woman has been admitted in England as an attorney or solicitor. To my mind, having regard to the common law disability above referred to, this fact that no woman has ever been admitted in England is conclusive that the word 'person' in our own Act was not intended to include a woman. The context of our Act refers to a profession for men, and men alone."[133] Again the judges held that women were not within the meaning of the term 'person'. The trend of authority at common law is that women are not eligible. No case can be found in English or Canadian jurisprudence in support of the appellant's application. The only direct authority is the other way, and there are many inferentially against it. In the United States the cases are conflicting, but the one, which was decided by the highest authority there -- the Supreme Court -- and which is based upon the common law of England, is against the appellant.

That there are cogent reasons for a change, based upon changes in the legal status of women, and the enlarged activities of modern life, may be admitted, but if

130 Mossman, Mary Jane.: *The First Women Lawyers -a Comparative study of Gender, Law and the Legal Professions,* Hart Publishing, 2006, Oxford, p. 47.

131 *Minor v. Happersett,* 88 U.S.162 (1874).

132 Epstein, Cynthia Fuchs; *Women in law,* Basic Books, Inc, 1981, New York, p.33.

133 *Re Mabel French,* 1, D.L.R.80, British Columbia Court of Appeal, January 9th, 1912.

we were to give effect to these considerations, we should be usurping the functions of the legislature rather than discharging the duty of the Court, which is to decide what the law is, not what it ought to be." While to quote Justice Irving, "The expression used in all those Acts is 'person', "I think we can take judicial notice of the fact that no woman has been admitted in England as an attorney or solicitor. To my mind, having regard to the common law disability above referred to, this fact that no woman has ever been admitted in England is conclusive that the word 'person' in our own Act was not intended to include a woman. The context of our Act refers to a profession for men, and men alone. It is not necessary to go through all the earlier B.C. statutes. They are very interesting, but it is sufficient to say that by the Order in Council of 4th April, 1856, establishing the Supreme Court of Civil Justice of the colony of Vancouver Island, the Court was authorised to admit certain 'persons'; and the same expression is used in the Order of Court made by Justice Matthew Baillie Begbie, in the Court of British Columbia in 1858, for the admission of attorneys to practice in the colony on the mainland; and in all the Acts since passed, the word 'person' has been used."[134]

The court reviewed two kinds of arguments about women's eligibility to become lawyers: first, that there was a right at common law for women to be admitted to the bar; and second, that the language of the statute, which authorised the Barristers' Society to make rules for the admission of 'persons', included women as well as men.[135]

The judges considered the meaning of the word 'person' taking into account the provincial Interpretation Act, which provided that the word 'person' included anyone to whom 'the context is capable of applying'. However, since the context included the fact that women had never been lawyers in the past, the court decided that the legislature had never intended that women be included as 'persons' in the bar statute. Thus, rejecting all of the arguments, the five judges who heard French's case concluded that there were no legal principles which supported French's claim to

---

134 Ibid.

135 Ibid.

become a lawyer. Rather concluded that French's application was a matter for the legislature.

In examining the context of the bar statute as a whole, however, the judge surveyed the history of the legal profession and concluded that 'no women either in literary France, or in practical England' had ever made any attempt to become a member of the legal profession prior to the enactment of the statute governing the bar in Quebec in 1849. He also examined English authorities and a number of American cases in which married women had been denied the right to practice law.

Thus of the fifteen judges who decided these cases in New Brunswick, British Columbia and Quebec in the decade between 1905 and 1915, all but one concluded that women were not eligible to become lawyers. The courts unanimously concluded that there was no common law right which entitled women to become lawyers, and that the use of the word 'person' in their relevant statutes, as interpreted in the context of each statute as a whole, was not intended to include women as well as men.[136]

2.2.2. CANADA

This conception of the female role was employed on the basis of the judicial conception of the nature of the women originated in the dominant social thinking of that time.[137] The concept of 'woman' has changed a number of times over the past several decades. Although women won the right to vote in several Canadian provinces, that status of women remains to be defined. The legal recognition of women as persons with rights was not obtained at the same time as the suffragette movement. Up until 1929, the legal term for person did not apply to women according to the Canadian Constitution.

While women were granted the right to vote in most Canadian provinces, lobby groups seeking to improve the status of women on a social, economic, legal and even political level, continued to argue their case. Indeed, women were not legally

---

[136] Mossman, Mary Jane.: *The First Women Lawyers: A Comparative Study of Gender, Law and the Legal Profession,* Hart Publishing, 2006, Oxford, pp. 89 – 95.

[137] Bridgeman, Jo and Millns, Susan; *Feminist perspective on Law,* Sweet and Maxwell, 1998, London, p.19.

recognized as 'persons'. Furthermore, when women married, they lost all of their rights. This was as the result of a real struggle on the part of the group of women now known as the Famous Five. The state did not simply hand over this victory to women; it had to be fought for. It was the 'Famous 5' (Emily Murphy, Henrietta Muir Edwards, Irene Parlby, Louise McKinney and Nellie McClung) who contested the legal interpretation of the word 'person' before the Supreme Court of Canada in 1927.

The third case was the famous Canadian *'Persons'* case – *Edwards v.Attorney General for Canada(1930) A.C.124* which was decided in October 18,1929.It is also known as the 'Persons Case' – is a famous Canadian and British constitutional case where it was first decided that women were eligible to sit in the Canadian Senate. In this case, five prominent Canadian women brought a reference to the Supreme Court of Canada for interpretation of the sections in the *British North America Act, 1867* which set out eligibility to be called as Senators. The sections referred to 'qualified persons' as being eligible; thus, the issue was again whether women were 'persons' recognized in law. The Supreme Court of Canada held in 1928 that women were not 'persons'. Their Lordships were of opinion that the word 'persons' does include women. The matter was taken on appeal to the Privy Council in London, England. This body was at that time the highest court of appeal for legal disputes throughout the Commonwealth. The Privy Council decisively held that women were indeed legal persons in 1930 even if not so defined at earlier times. Conventional legal wisdom was that women were not legal persons and that legislatures had not intended to include women within the terms 'person' or 'man' used in various statutes.[138]

The Persons Case was one of the most important milestones in the history of women's struggle for full citizenship. It has been described as the event that marked women's formal sexual emancipation. British newspapers hailed the judgment as 'the Canadian women's triumph'.

The 'Canadian women's triumph' was important for women in Britain in 1929 because they believed that the ruling would at last mean that British women could be admitted to the House of Lords, for which they had been campaigning since women

---

[138] Brittle, T. Dawson; "*Law and the Legal Person,*" <http://www.lawsite.ca/WLSC/LegalPerson_w.htm> on 10th May,2007.

had won the right to vote and stand for election to the House of Commons in 1918. Historically, however, of even greater importance was the fact that the judgment overturned arguments that had been used by lawyers and legislators for centuries to keep women out of public life. The judgment became the new landmark interpretation of women as persons in English common law throughout the Empire. The Persons Case was the vindication of a 60-year battle which had begun in 1867, and during which women in Britain and in Canada had sought - in vain - for a determination by the courts that they were entitled to hold public office and to enter universities and the professions.

The history of women's admission to the bar in Canada spans four decades from the end of the nineteenth century to World War II, women in provinces other than Quebec became eligible to enter the legal profession between the last decade of the nineteenth century and the end of the World War I. According to Linda Kealey, "the appearance of the new woman' in the 1890s was reflected in the experiments in dress reform, spiritualism and women's right, issues which were eventually transformed into a variety of reforms initiatives and new ideas about women's citizenship and voting rights." In this context, women's entry to the legal profession occurred as part of the 'progressive reform'. Nonetheless these new roles for women were still contested in the decades when women were first becoming lawyers in Canada. These views about women's roles were reflected in archival records that reveal how some male lawyers responded to the challenge of women's entry to the legal profession. In addition, legal journals in Canada published editorials with disparaging comments about women lawyers as early as 1869, in response to news of Arabella Mansfield's admission to the legal profession in the state of Iowa.[139]

Clearly, these cases reflected ideas about separate spheres for men and women, views which were frequently invoked in Canada and elsewhere to explain, and also to justify, limitations on women's role in the later part of the 19th century. Yet, there are certain differences between the ideas in the quotation adopted from Bradwell in French's case, and in the views expressed in Langstaff's case a decade later. In the Bradwell quotation, women may confined to their own sphere by being

---

139 Mossman, Mary Jane; *The First Women Lawyers: A Comparative Study of Gender, Law and the Legal Professions,* Hart Publishing, 2006, Oxford, pp. 66 – 67.

'elevated to a superior position,' a typical argument used to justify the idea of separate spheres in the United States and also in England.

All these comments make clear and reflected different views about the continuing validity of separate spheres for men and women. During World War I ideas and expectations about proper role for women were changing, even though for Justice Saint-Pierre, women's new role were regarded as highly exceptional, acceptable only in the context of war. Yet, if the views of Justice Saint-Pierre were inconsistent with new ideas about women, it was nonetheless reflected a view of law including the legal profession as a 'gentleman's profession. Gidney and Millar examined the doctrine of separate spheres as well as the economic interests of male professionals. They suggested that while any 'new' entrants to the professions (including women) created additional competition for male lawyers, the entry of women to the legal profession was doubly challenging.[140]

2.2.3. BRITAIN

Conventional legal wisdom was that women were not 'legal persons' and that legislatures had not intended to include women within the terms 'person' or 'man' used in various statutes. Judicial pronouncements had the effect that women were not included in the term 'persons' which meant in practice that women were barred or prevented from equal participation with men in public life. What they meant in law was 'non-persons' did not exist as active agents in the legal process. For example, Blackstone, in his "Commentaries on the Laws of England," had found it to be a self-evident principle of law that "by marriage the husband and wife are one person in law; that is, the very being or legal existence of the woman is suspended during marriage, or at least is incorporated into that of the husband, under whose wing, protection and cover she performs everything..."[141]

But, women successfully fought their way out and compelled the Government to amend the laws and permit the entry of woman in the profession of law in terms of equality with their male counterparts. In the case of Charlton Vs Lings, (1868-9) LR.

---

140 Ibid pp. 96 – 99.

141 Brettel, T. Dawson; T; "*Law and the Legal Person,*" <,http://www.lawsite.ca/WLSC/LegalPerson_w.htm> on 10th May2007.

4 CP, the word 'man' was used. Despite an Act, similar to our General Clauses Act, in England, masculine includes feminine the court held that women were not included in the term 'man' and were not entitled to vote.[142] The situation in Britain as late as 1912, the Court of Appeal ruled that women were not eligible to practice as solicitors of the Supreme Court because only 'persons' could do so and that referred exclusively to men. Then started the series of cases where the court held that women were not included in the term 'person'. These cases are as follows: Beresford-Hope Vs Lady Sandhurst, (1889) 23 QBD 79, lnn Vs Incorp Society of Law Agents (1901),w 3 F,1059, and Nairn v University of St. Andrews, 1909 A.C. 147, p 78 L.J.P.C. 54.[143]

Gray's Inn refused to enroll Berthe Cave in 1903. The House of Lords in Nairn Vs Scottish University (1906) expressly held that women did not fall within the meaning of the term 'person'.[144] In 1913, three other women with outstanding university qualifications applied to the law society to take the preliminary examination to become solicitors but the society refused their application. They initiated legal challenges. The Law Society refused to allow four women to sit in the Law Society examinations. The women took the case to the Court of Appeal. The Court of Appeal upheld the Law Society's decision. Justice Joyce ruled that women were not 'persons' within the meaning of the *Solicitors Act of 1843.*[145] Yet, in spite of being represented both on trial and on appeal, both courts concluded that the language of the statutes should be interpreted in accordance with 'long usage' in the common law.

In 1914, a young lady called Bebb brought an application against the Law Society which is reported in *Bebb v Law Society* 1914 (1) Chancery 286,[146] for a declarator that she was a person within the meaning of the Solicitors' Act and that she was entitled to write a preliminary examination which would give her entry to apprenticeship. The court also concluded that it was clear that the women were under

---

142 "Pretty Ones," 21st April, 2006.

143 Ibid.

144 *Nairn -v- University of St Andrews* [1909] AC 147.

145 Morel,Peter; "women lawyers," < http://en.wikipedia.org/wiki/User:Peter_morrell/women_ lawyers> on 2nd December 2008.

146 *Bebb v. Law Society* (1913), 29 T.L.R. 634.

a common law disability, which had not been removed by the used of the word 'persons' in the *Solicitors Act*, 1843.This case was first of its kind allowing women to practice law.[147]

Infact, the history of the women and legal profession reveals that women in Britain had been demonstrating an interest in widening the sphere of women's activities to encompass careers in law even before Margaret Hall, Bertha Cave and Gwyneth Bebb initiated their legal claims at the beginning of the twentieth century. Clearly, the only solution was legislative action. Yet although numerous bills were presented to Parliament to permit women to become barristers and solicitors in Britain in the years immediately after the Bebb decision, they were not successful. Finally the *Sex Disqualification (Removal) Act, 1919* was enacted, permitting women to become solicitors and barristers in Britain.[148]

These cases reveal that the general notion in common law was that women were incapable of serving in public offices. These cases reveal the existence of the myth of male protectiveness. Women were variously described as refined, delicate and pure, quite as worthy as noble as men, but different. One judge shared the widely held view that women were intellectually inferior to men, and was particularly incapable of severe and incessant work. While another judge expressly left open the question of whether the women were fickle in judgment and liable to influence. But the general view spoke of the unfitness of women for public life based on inferiority.[149] If there is one calling in the world for which women are conspicuously unfitted it is the law. There was no doubt that on the merits of the question there was a feeling among the majority of the members of both branches of the profession, in England a well as in this country, that an exception to the qualification of women to enter the profession is well founded. Though there were views that women should have a Parliamentary vote, and even · Parliamentary representation, the instinctive objection to their entering the public profession of the law was a wholesome one.

---

147 "75 Years of women solicitor," *BBC News*, 19th December, 1997.

148 Mossman, Mary Jane; *The First Women Lawyers: A Comparative Study of Gender, Law and the Legal Professions*, Hart Publishing, 2006, Oxford, pp. 115 – 118.

149 Sachs.A, and Wilson, J.H; *Feminist Perspective on Law: The myth of male protectiveness*, Sweet and Maxwell, 1998, London, p.21.

Most of the men in the legal profession felt that in the present state of competition, it does not seem right that an already overcrowded profession should be inundated by a deluge of women, many of whom might find it difficult to obtain a lucrative practice for abilities, which might be more profitably employed in other directions.

Whilst much has been achieved in recent decades to secure greater equality for women, gender inequality-remains a significant feature of both public and private life for women and men. Such gender inequality is reflected in traditional ideas about the role of women and men and, though they have shifted over time, the assumptions and stereotypes that underpin those ideas are often very deeply rooted. Indeed, they so permeate our view of the world that they often appear to reflect no more than 'common sense'. Thus, it seems innocuous to assume that a woman will have children, look after them and accordingly take a break from paid work (if indeed she ever takes it up) to accommodate the family. However, such assumptions and stereotypes can and often do have the effect of seriously disadvantaging women. It is perhaps not surprising that gender inequality persists. Women were legally subordinate to men in a number of ways until well into the twentieth century. For example, marriage under the common law, known as 'covertures', caused and amounted to a legal expiry of a woman's being: The very being or legal existence of the wife is suspended during the marriage or at least incorporated and consolidated into that of the husband under whose wing, protection and cover she performs.

When legislation granted women the municipal franchise in 1869 (*Municipal Franchise Act 1869*) it was interpreted promptly by the judges to exclude married women on the grounds that upon marriage a woman's 'existence was merged with that of her husband' and she could not therefore vote (*R v Harald [1872] LR VII QB 361,* as cited in Discrimination Law). Women were not entitled to vote until 1911.[150]

Thus, there is a long and recent history of inequality between men and women, sanctioned by law and apparently supported by the judiciary whose intransigence on occasions did much to impede the promotion of equality. Whilst many of the formal

---

150 "Women and Equality: Equal Treatment Bench Book," *Judicial Studies Board*, Chap.6.2, September2005.< http:// www.jsboard.co.uk/downloads/etbb/etbb_6_gender_08.pdf> on 12th Sep, 2008.

barriers to equality have of course been removed, assumptions about the proper role of men and women continue to obstruct true equality and often do not reflect reality. For example, assumptions about the primary role of women as bearers and careers of children and of men as breadwinners do not necessarily reflect the true life experience of many people. Women remain significantly underrepresented in the judiciary, particularly at senior level. Thus women are underrepresented in all areas of law making.

As late as 1909, the courts refused to accept that the gender-neutral word 'person' could include women. In *Nairn v University of St. Andrews, 1909 A.C. 147, p 78 L.J.P.C. 54*, a case about whether women could vote for the old university seats in Parliament. Women graduates of St Andrews and Edinburgh, who, as graduates, were members of the general council of their university, sought a declarator that they were entitled to vote under section 27 of the 1868 Act. The section provided that 'every person' whose name was on the register of the general council, if of full age 'and not subject to any legal incapacity' was to be entitled to vote for the member of Parliament for the university. Lord Loreburn LC commented and held that the section did not confer a right to vote on women graduates. Lord Ashbourne said: "If it was intended to make a vast constitutional change in favour of women graduates, one would expect to find plain language and express statement." "It is incomprehensible to me that any one acquainted with our laws or the methods by which they are ascertained can think, if, indeed, any one does think, there is room for argument on such a point. It is notorious that this right of voting has, in fact, been confined to men." (***Representation of the People (Scotland) Act 1868 27 - Universities Elections Amendment (Scotland) Act 1881***).[151]

No one seeks to deny the existence of differences between the sexes, differences subtle, deep seated, and ineradicable. But these, being admitted, afford no justification for the usurpation by man of the right to say what duties and responsibilities woman may be allowed to undertake, and what must be withheld from her because of her sex. Such a theory can only be upheld on the old tradition of the East that woman is one of the lower animals over whom lordly man was given

151 Ibid.

dominion. The harem is the logical outcome of this belief. It is only by removing the disabilities and restraints imposed upon woman; and permitting her to enter freely into competition with man in every sphere of human activity, that her true position and function in the economy of life will ultimately be settled. We can at present form no conception of what woman is capable of being, or doing. We have no data upon which to base any real conclusions. Nowhere is woman treated as the free and equal companion of man. Thus in Scotland, a woman speaks of her husband as her 'man', whilst in Staffordshire he is always spoken of as 'the master'. The universality of this subjection of woman is assumed by many as an-infallible testimony to the truth of the theory that woman must in some way be inferior to man.[152]

With emancipation of women in the 1920s in many nations, things slowly began to change. It was a Canadian case on appeal to the UK in 1930 that ended the fraternity of solicitors and barristers and opened the door to women. In 1919, when the *Sex Disqualification Act* was passed; women were allowed to practice law. The basic purpose of the Act was to amend the Law with respect to disqualification on account of sex. Its broad aim was achieved by Section 1, which stated that: "A person shall not be disqualified by sex or marriage from the exercise of any public function, or from being appointed to or holding any civil or judicial office or post, or from entering or assuming or carrying on any civil profession or vocation, or for admission to any incorporated society (whether incorporated by Royal Charter or otherwise), [and a person shall not be exempted by sex or marriage from the liability to serve as a juror."[153]

The first women to pass the examination were Maud Crofts, Carrie Morrison, Mary Pickup and Mary Sykes in 1922. Carrie Morrison was the first woman to be admitted to the role of solicitor. She and Maud Crofts graduated from Girton College, Cambridge with First Class Honors, the university authorities refused to award them their degrees because they were women. Although they were allowed to study, attend lectures and sit exams, women could not hold degrees. Maud Crofts, who was

---

152 Hardie, Keir; "The Citizenship of Women: A Plea for Woman's Suffrage," a speech given in 1905, <http://en.wikisource.org/wiki/The_Citizenship_of_Women:_A_Plea_for_Woman's_Suffrage>, on 14th Sep. 2008.

153 *Wikipedia*; "Sex Disqualification (Removal) Act 1910,"<http://en.wikipedia.org/wiki/Sex_Disqualification_(Removal)_Act_1919> on 17th Sep 2008.

involved in the 1913 Court of Appeal case, was a prominent suffragette. When she went into practice with her father and brother, her clientele included wealthy and influential members of the women's suffrage movement. Although these women were breaking new ground in Britain and it continued to be an uphill struggle for women even after 1922. If women did not have fathers or husbands who were lawyers, it was often financially impossible for them to get articles, for which there was a yearly premium of something between 300-500 guineas (£15-25). Although wealthy parents may have been willing to invest in their sons, paying this amount for daughters was rare. In 1931, nine years after Carrie Morrison had been admitted; only about 100 women had qualified as solicitors. The numbers continued to rise relatively slowly until the last decade or so. In 1967, only 2.7percent of solicitors holding certificates were women. Judges were even slower in catching up. Of 96 High Court Judges, only seven are women, and there is only one Lord Justice of Appeal from a total of 35. All 12 law lords are men.

2.2.4. SOUTH AFRICA

South Africa deserves special mention. It is further of interest to note that a similar application had served before Justice Bristowe of the Transvaal Supreme Court *Schle vs. Incorporated Law Society (1909) TS 363,* where the learned Judge held that "in view of the long practice which has prevailed not only in this country, but in Holland and in England too, not to admit women to be solicitors, I feel that the proper course to be adopted, if an innovation is to be made, is to approach the Legislature and not the Court."[154] Miss Schlesin's application was accordingly refused. Thus it was decided that women were not 'persons' for the purposes of the relevant legislation governing the admission of attorneys in South Africa, notwithstanding the clear provision contained in s. 7 of *the Union Interpretation Act 1910*, that in every law, unless the contrary intention the words importing the masculine gender shall include females. This Act was not referred to at all in argument or in the judgment, although presumably the decision could still have been justified by the qualifying words 'unless the contrary intention appears'. Women in South Africa were not alone in being relegated to this non status, since a similar

---

154 Chanock, Martin; *The Making of South African Legal Culture, 1902-1936: Fear, Favour, and Prejudice*, Cambridge University Press, 2001, p.21.

position prevailed in Scotland as can be seen from *Hall's* case, and also in England, where even after the passing of the *Solicitors' Act 1843*, women were not permitted to qualify and practice as solicitors.

Though, later on, in a subsequent case in 1912 the Cape Supreme Court held that the term person included women and were entitled to become attorneys. It is said to be the first decision of its kind. But it did not last long. In an appeal against it, the appellate courts in the *Incorporated Law Society vs. Wookey (1912)* overruled the decision.[155] It decided that women were not included in the term 'person'. It was thus apparent, that women were not considered to be equal with men but were also valued less than men.

Women, who were aspiring to become lawyers at that point of time, took challenges in the contexts of new ideas about equality rights and emerging concept of legal professionalism. It was clear that in seeking access to the 'gentleman's profession' of law women were challenging 'gendered' exclusively in the legal profession.

2.2.5. INDIAN SCENARIO

It is not known when pleaders first had appeared in a Court of Law in our country. The earliest record is an account of the procession, which was taken out on 8th August 1672, when a Court of Judicature was established in Mumbai. There were no regular legal practitioners in India till 1793 when the first attempt was made to create an independent legal profession. In that year, the Governor-General in Council enacted *Regulation VII of 1793* in order to induce men of education and character to take up the practice of law as a distinct profession. The East India Company had established the Supreme Court in Calcutta. But there were no clear provision regarding lawyers, judges or the legal profession itself. The first step in this direction of organizing a legal profession in India was taken in 1774 with the

155 Blum, Karen; 'Portia Today: No need for drag', Johannesburg Bar, < http://www.sabar.co.za/law-journals/1990/april/1990-april-vol003-no1-pp12-18.pdf> on 20th Sep.2008.

establishment of the Supreme Court at Calcutta.[156] *The Bengal Regulation VII of 1793* for the first time created a regular Legal profession for the companies' courts.[157] Other, similar regulations were also passed to regulate the Legal profession in the Companies courts in Bengal, Bihar, Orissa, Madras, and Bombay.

It was *clause 11 of the Charter of 1774* that empowered the Supreme Court "to approve, admit and enroll such and so many advocates and attorneys-at-law," as it thought proper.[158] It also authorized the Supreme Court to remove them on a reasonable cause. So stringent was the provision that no other person could appear, plead or act for or on behalf of any party. Also no Indian had the right to appear before the court because according to the terminology of *clause 11* of the *Charter of 1774*. Only the British and Irish barristers and members of the Faculty of Advocates in Scotland or British attorneys were authorized to appear. A similar provision was made later in the charters that established Supreme Courts at Bombay and Madras. The provision effectively kept Indians out of the legal profession.

The *Legal Practitioners Act of 1846* enabled all persons certified by Sadar Adalats as persons of good character and duly qualified to be pleaders. Attorneys and barristers were authorized to appear in the Sadar Adalat and pleaders were permitted to enter into agreement with the clients for their fee. Subsequently, the Legal Practitioners Act, 1855 allowed the barristers and attorneys to appear before any of the Company Courts. In 1861 when the High Courts Act provided for replacement of the Supreme Court and Sadar Adalats by the High Court, clause 9 of the Letter Patent of 1865 establishing the High Court at Calcutta authorized that Court "to approve, and enroll such and so many Advocates, Vakils and Attorneys as the said High Court shall deem fit". They were entitled to appear and plead before the Court subject to its rules and directions. Similar

---

156 "Role of Legal Profession in Administration of Justice," *131st Report, of the Law Commission of India*, 1988, New Delhi.

157 Sinha, Suraj Narain Prasad; Bar Council of India. <http://www.barcouncilofindia.org/bar-council/history.php> on 6th March 2010.

158 Ibid.

provisions were made in the letters patents establishing the High Courts at Bombay and Madras.

The foregoing provisions of law did not apply to other Courts that came up later and, therefore, a comprehensive legislation to consolidate and amend the law relating to practitioners was passed in the *Legal Practitioners Act, 1879* which gave wide powers to the High Courts to enroll lawyers for different courts and also to take disciplinary proceedings against them. It authorized all High Courts other than the chartered High Courts to make rules, with prior sanction from respective provincial governments with respect to the qualifications and admissions of proper persons to be the Advocates and Vakils of the courts. Power to dismiss the advocates, after giving them an opportunity to defend was given to these High Courts. The High Courts were also authorized to make rules respect to qualifications and admission of pleaders and mukthars for the subordinate courts and revenue offices. Though different High Courts lay down different qualifications for the pleaders and mukthars generally the former were law graduates while the latter were not. While pleaders could practice in all subordinate courts, mukthars were allowed to appear only before the criminal courts, and at some places even before revenue officers.

The three-chartered High Courts added to the category of advocates and attorneys, the category of Vakils. The former two categories were of persons qualified in England, while the latter were Indian law graduates. However, under amended rules the Bombay and Madras High Courts had permitted even Indian law graduates to be advocates after passing a prescribed test. While an advocate could appear on original as well as appellate side of these High Courts, the vakil could not appear on the original side or even in appeals from original side. The Act of 1879 also empowered an advocate or vakil on the roll of any High Court to plead before any subordinate court in British India and also before any High Court with the permission of that Court.

Since Indians were not allowed to appear in the courts, the question of women having access to Legal profession was out of question. But, this sensitive controversy was resolved by the *United Provinces Act, 192,* which ordained that women could be enrolled as legal practitioners and could not be debarred from practice of law merely because of their gender.[159] Though, the enactment of the *Sex Disqualification Removal Act, 1919* removed the disability in England, but Indian women did not have this right for many years, A British woman called to the Bar in England, was allowed to practice in India as well, but an Indian woman or a woman who qualified in India was not allowed to practice even in her own country. In India, since long back, women were considered as an oppressed section of the society and they were neglected for centuries.

The link between feminist movement and the law goes back at least to the early suffragette demands that disparities between the formal rights of men and women should be eradicated.The initial focus of feminist writings on the law was to identify how legal rules either stopped short of treating men and women as equals or when formal equality was granted how much rules were manipulated to prevent women from exercising their rights.Very soon it became obvious that mere formal right to equality did not result reality between men and women and what was needed was reconceptualization of the categories af analysis.[160]

On 29th August, 1916, a Special Bench of Calcutta High Court, *In re, Regina Guha*, reported in *(I. L. R. 44 Cal. 290)*, consisting of the Chief Justice and four other Judges refused the enrollment of Miss Regina Guha as a Pleader, relying on the case of *Bobb versus The Law Society*, reported in (1914) 1 Ch. 286 relied on the positive prohibition of Common Law of England, founded on inveterate usage which imposed an absolute and positive prohibition against women practicing the profession of law and held that women could not be allowed to be solicitors.

Late Sri Madhusudan Dass, Vakil, a great patriot and social reformer, encouraged one Miss Sudhanshubala Hazra to enter the profession of Law, but her application for enrollment as pleader was refused on 28th November, 1921 by a Full Bench of the Patna High Court, *In re, Sudhanshubala Hazra, (I. L. R. 1 Pat. 104)*,

---

159 Mane, A D; "Women Place at the Bar,"<http://mshrc.maharashtra.gov.in/Speech/upload/file%2051.pdf.> on1st Nov.2008.

160 Parashar,Archana; *Feminism in Indian Legal Education*, Feminine Jurisprudence In India, Deep and Deep publication, New Delhi, 2008, p127.

consisting of Dawson Miller, Chief Justice, Mullick and Jwala Prasad, JJ., on the ground that the provisions of the *Legal Practitioners' Act, 1879*, did not contemplate the extension of the privilege to females. The use of the word 'Men' in Regulation VII of 1793 although subsequently in all enactments it was replaced by the word 'persons', led to the two decisions aforesaid. Relying on the case of *Bobb versus The Law Society*, supra. it was held in both the aforesaid cases that provisions of the General Clauses Acts of 1868 and of 1897 did not apply. The words importing the masculine gender shall not include the feminine, inasmuch as women were never there in the legal profession, either in the Mughal or British days. The Legislature never intended to bring about a change of such magnitude, so momentous and far-reaching by so furtive a process. It was further held that the words 'he', 'him', and 'his', in the subsequent enactments and the *Legal Practitioners' Act, 1879*, show that they invariably excluded women not by any direct prohibition but inferentially by words appropriate only to the male sex. Following Miss Regina Guha's case, it was held in Miss Hazra's case, "it was not the intention of the Legislature in the *Legal Practitioners' Act* to reverse the established policy or to introduce a fundamental change in long established principles of law and that to read the sections as including females was repugnant to the subject".

Justice Mullick thus observed in Miss Hazra's case, "If it were permissible to speculate upon the reasons of the legislators, all that can be hazarded is that having regard to the previous history of the relations of the sexes and the general position of women in the country, the Legislature was of opinion that it would be repugnant to ideas of decorum to permit women to join in what I may call the rough and tumble of the forensic arena." Thus, the Calcutta and Patna High Courts while dealing with the enrollment of women held that women were not included in the word persons and thus rejected the applications.

The Allahabad High Court, in spite of the above two decisions, took the lead and changed the history by enrolling Miss Cornelia Sorabji, as the first Indian Lady, Vakil of Allahabad High Court, on 24th August, 1921. This was done by a decision of the English Committee of the Court, consisting of the Chief Justice, Sir Grimwood Mears and other member Judges present. In his judgment Mr. Justice Jwala Prasad had remarked in the case of Miss Hazra, "No doubt the recent admission of Miss

Sorabji in the Allahabad High Court might create some anomaly inasmuch as ladies enrolled as Vakils in the Allahabad High Court may claim to practice in occasional cases in the courts subordinate to this Court. ..... This again is a ground for changing the present law". In 1929, Miss Shiam Kumari Nehru, and on 22nd February, 1933 Mrs. Meenakshi Amina Faruki Begum, got themselves enrolled in Allahabad High Court and actually practiced for some years.[161]

At that point of time, women all over the world were claiming equal rights with men at about the same time when the High Court at Allahabad was established. The majority of the statutes at that time used the phrase 'any person who has... is entitled to vote or to take admission or to practice'. And soon a question was raised. Does the word 'person' include women? The *Legal Practitioners Act* also used the word 'person'. It could be argued that the reasoning delivered in the case was gendered. It was patriarchal because the decisions reflected the men's eye rather than through the women's experiences and differences. Decisions on such cases had not embraced a version of equality rather than differences on sexes.

The High Court at Allahabad took the lead to enroll the first woman in India. Cornelia Sorabji (1866-1954) `was enrolled on August 9, 1921. Cornelia was not only the first woman to be enrolled in India but also the first to be enrolled anywhere in the world under the 'person' clause. The question did not arise subsequently because of the enactment of the *Legal Practitioners Women Act* in 1923.The *Legal Practitioners Act, 1923,* prohibited discrimination on the basis of sex in a matter of enrollment. *The Act of 1926* also provided that a specific rule be made by every Bar Council that a woman will not be disqualified to be an advocate on ground of sex alone.

It is not known whether Cornelia argued any case or not. At least none is reported. But, it is said that the court that enrolled the first woman denied the grace and charm of the fairer sex. Cornelia Sorabji was the first woman lawyer of India whose formative years coincided with the high noon of the British Empire. She was

---

161 Gupta, Ramo Devi; "Advent of Women in the Profession of Law," <http://www.allahabadhighcourt.in/event/AdventOfWomenInTheProfessionMrsRDGupta.html> on 6th Dec.2009.

the first women to have enrolled as an advocate in India and occupies a significant place in Indian history, as she played a pioneering role in trying to open up the legal profession to women much before they were formally allowed to plead before the courts of law. Having completed the BCL examination at Oxford and six months of practical work at Lee and Pemberton in London, Sorabji was ready to return in India in the spring of 1893. Sorabji began by professing herself to be ludicrously incapable of making speeches, but her modest beginning was then followed by a well organised and succinct outline of the property rights of Muslim and Hindu women in India. According to Sorabji, social customs that require Indian women to live in seclusion often made a difficult for them to enforce their substantive rights to property in practice. For Sorabji, the circumstances of Indian women living in purdah created a special task for women with knowledge of the law and a love for Indian women and their needs. Yet in defining this new role with legal training, Sorabji diplomatically suggested that they would pose no challenge to the work of male lawyers saying: 'We need not supplant men. There is enough to do if we will supplement them'.

In the 19th century India witnessed reforms and proposals for legislation to alter a number of indigenous religious practices, including child marriage, the prohibition of widow remarriage (the *Hindu Widows Remarriage Act),* the custom of sati, and unsatisfactory rules concerning Hindu women's married property. Among both British and Indian social reformers, education was viewed as a way of promoting 'civilization' in India. In this context, girls' schools were established, education for middle class girls spread rapidly; in Bengal, for example, where there were ninety-five girls' schools in 1863, the number increased to 2,238 schools by 1890.

Women also began to pursue university education; two women graduated for the first time from Calcutta University in 1883, and both Madras and Bombay Medical Colleges had opened their doors to women by that year. While Cornelia Sorabji was the first Indian women to graduate in law at Oxford and completed the requirements for the degree in 1892.

It is important to account of gender, as Sorabji's gender posed few difficulties for her. As the first women student at Deccan College, she described the challenge of attending the college while living at home and commuting a distance of five miles each day to attend lectures with hundreds of Hindus and Muslims. In the final degree examination, Sorabji obtained the highest marks in Bombay Presidency, and was therefore automatically entitled to the Government of India's scholarship to attend an English university, including traveling and other expenses. However, because she was female, Sorabji was excluded from this prize. 'It was in fact impertinent of any women to produce circumstances which were not in the mind of the authorities as a possibility when they dangled a gilded prize before eyes that should have been male eyes alone.'[162]

Cornelia Sorabji was identifying legal work for which she was then the only qualifying applicant. It was thus clear that her aspirations for a career as a women lawyer were completely entwined with the needs for legal service of more traditional, 'less civilized' Indian women. Cornelia Sorabji's opposition to Indian nationalism in the Gandhi an era led to a disapproval of her role and personality. Yet this Parsee and the daughter of a convert to Christianity was the first woman to study law at Oxford, the first Indian woman to be allowed to practice in the Calcutta High Court, became the first woman to be appointed to a senior bureaucratic office under the colonial government, and the first person to champion the cause of Indian women in purdah who owned property.[163]

The other woman who became a lawyer in High Court of Madras was Ms. B.Ananda Bai in the early 1920s. But it took fourty years when their numbers grew to quite a handful and they formed themselves as an Association in 1963. The founder President and Secretary were Ms. Lakshmi Panikar and Ms. Lakshmi Swami Nathan respectively. From amongst them have been three lady judges, Justices M/s Prabha Sridevan, Chitra Venkatraman and K. Suguna and two designated senior counsels.[164]

This was at a time; both the legal profession and the judiciary reflected the complex hierarchies of imperial administration in India. The processes for selecting

---

162 Mossman, Mary Jane; *The First Women Lawyers: A Comparative Study of Gender, Law and the Legal Professions,* Hart Publishing, 2006, Oxford, pp. 201 – 202.

163 Gooptu, Suparna; *Cornelia Sorabji:India's Pioneer Woman Lawyer,* Oxford University Press, New Delhi, 2006, pp.15-19

164 "High Court, Madras," a Report published by High Court, Madras, 2007, p.23. <http://www.hcmadras.tn.nic.in/lawday.pdf.> on 12th November, 2008.

judges for the Courts in India created tension especially between advocates and members of the Indian Civil Service. All the legislations enacted in 1861 had identified categories of appointees to the High Courts, but by the end of the 19th century, most candidates for Chief Justices were still being recruited from the practicing bar in Britain, and three quarters of them had spent their judicial career in Britain.

Common law education in India began in 1857, when three universities with Law Departments were established in Calcutta, Madras and Bombay. Initially, students were free to study other disciplines - History, Geography, Science etc. - along with Law, which was a part-time course. This arrangement continued for about a century, during which period institutions such as the Government Law College in Bombay, the Law College in Poona, the Symbiosis College of Law also in Poona, the University College of Law in Calcutta and the Law College in Madras, all affiliated to their respective Universities, created their own Law-teaching traditions. In 1961, the Parliament of India passed the Advocates Act, which amended and consolidated the law governing the Indian legal profession.

The feminist activism in India picked up momentum during later 1970s. One of the first national level issues that brought the women's groups together was the Mathura rape case. The acquittal of policemen accused of raping a young girl Mathura in a police station, led to a wide-scale protests in 1979–1980. The protests were widely covered in the national media, and forced the Government to amend the Evidence Act, the Criminal Procedure Code and the Indian Penal Code and introduce the category of custodial rape.Female activists united over issues such as female infanticide, gender bias, women health, and female literacy.[165]

Previously viewed as fundametaly patriarchal, now the state is analysed in its relations of power, class, social and economic groups in feminist perspective. Also state's instruments for subordination of women, structuration and influence of gender roles and relations, and in more positive vision - positive economic policies for lessening of the financial dependency of women on men, analyses of the promotion of

---

165 From Wikipedia, the free encyclopedia
Women in India, < http://en.wikipedia.org/wiki/Women_in_India>on 22nd March2011.

women's interests within the state, either through the action of 'femocrats' (feminist bureaucrats) working from within the state system to empower women, or when the state itself acts in a way to further women's status.An article on Status of Women in India –A depressing scenario which appeared in the Tribune of Chandigarh edition on 15th April ,1999 points out that rape takes place in every 54 minutes:eve-teaching in every 51 minutes :molestation once in every 26 minutes and dowry deaths in every 1000 minutes.

As regards education of women, according to the census of 1991, the general illiteracy rate was 52.11 per cent. The female literacy rate was 39.42 per cent. as compared to male literacy of 63.86 percent.These figures indicate that 60 per cent. Of our female population i.e., six out of every ten females – still remain illiterate.[166]

With the view to convert equality of women from de jure to de facto, educating the female would play an important role. The Law Commission of India realized that the legal education and the legal profession should undergo reforms to serve the country better. After years of deliberations and discussions, the first National Law School (NLS) was established in 1987 in Bangalore. Later, other NLSs were established in cities like Hyderabad, Bhopal, Kolkata and others. The concept of law schools was founded in America where law schools are not controlled by the government and thus are autonomous. National Law Schools in India are established under State Legislations, thus giving them the status of statutory institutions. Although India produces the most number of lawyers, second only to the United States, it has failed miserably in improving the legal system and the reasons are quite conspicuous.

Therefore India currently faces the major challenges in the field of providing legal education to respond to the global challenges. At present, professional legal education is being imparted by 913 colleges recognized by the Bar Council of India and 14 National Law Universities/ schools established under the State Acts. The Bar Council of India under the *Advocates Act,* 1961 has made rules to regulate the legal education but the standard of legal education does not meet the present day

[166] Anand, Justice A.S; *Justice for Women*, Universal Law Publishing Co.Pvt.Ltd.New Delhi, 2008, pp 46-47.

requirements of the legal profession. The matter relating to the legal education has been examined by the Law Commission of India in its 184th Report on Legal Education and Professional Training and Proposals for Amendments to the Advocates Act, 1961 and the University Grants Commission (UGC) Act, 1956 (2002).Within the academic discipline of law ,it is still an unresolved issue whether the study of law belongs in the universities or it is a professional training best imparted by its practitioners.Even though law is not taught everywhere ,the dichotomy between doctrinal study of law and a wider understanding of law as one among many institutions of society which continues to persisit.

In the recent past, the National Knowledge Commission (NKC) has made certain recommendations in its report particularly in the area of research in legal education. The National Knowledge Commission, while deliberating on issues related to knowledge concepts, recognizes legal education as an important constituent of professional education.It emphasized at revamping legal education to meet the needs and challenges of all sections of society and the development of contemporary curriculum to be integrated with other disciplines and devise a 'model' syllabus for all core and optional courses.. Legal education must also be socially engaged and sensitize students to issues of social justice.[167]

2.3. FEMINIST THEORIES

It was apparent that women who wanted access to legal profession were aspiring for economic independence. But sexual differences affected women's aspirations. These women were unique as they first challenged the male exclusively in legal profession, tried to persuade the male judges and legislatures to reinterpret the law that made entry into the legal profession unthinkable. Their decisions confirmed that women were not eligible as a matter of law for admission to the bar.

The challenge was made through law for attaining social positions of women. It was directed against the denial that women were also capable of becoming legal

---

[167] *Government mulls major reforms in legal education, 21st April2010.* <http://www.indiaedunews.net/Law/Government_mulls_major_reforms_in_legal_education>visited on 22nd March 2011.

persons entitled for legal rights. It was necessary to challenge the view of womanhood upon which the denial rested - a view which was set up as that women by nature were only suited to the task of tending for husband, children and home. The divisions of society into two spheres, public and private were considered as an appropriate division. The qualities associated with women were those that have traditionally been used to justify their subordination and relegation to the so-called private sphere.[168] The laws gave an appearance of neutrality but were in fact deeply biased.

Some Feminist scholars base this inequality on the notion of dominance and subordination. The statues reflected male concern and priorities. The idea that legal profession is 'male dominated' arises from the observation that most lawmakers and lawyers are indeed male. This transcends the starting point. The realization that legal profession is male dominated reflects how we think and perceive about it.

The argument of male domination further demonstrates the ways in which legal practice discriminated women and reinforced gender inequality. This approach is based on the 'dominance analyses' of Catharine MacKinnon, an American feminist scholar that is distinct from 'difference analyses'. She argued that men and women are different but the difference is that male dominate and women are subordinate. Legal Profession was seen as 'maintaining male domination' - a powerful conduct for reproduction and transmission of the dominant theory, a paradigm of maleness.[169]

Some cases cited in the above paragraphs shows that courts in the early part of the twentieth century interpreted the word 'person' to mean 'men' and adopted the notion of separate spheres to justify women's exclusion from the practice of law and other profession. This shows sex-discrimination that can be identified from their judgments. Once it is recognized that women suffer from a history of discrimination, it becomes easier to recognize discrimination. A rule or practice is discriminatory, in the inequality approach, if it participates in the systemic social deprivation of one sex because of sex. The only question for litigation is whether the policy or practice in

---

168 Bridgeman, Jo and Millns, Susan; *Feminist perspective on Law,* Sweet and Maxwell, 1998, London, p. 23.

169 Anleu, Sharyn.LRoach; *Law and Social Change*, Sage publications, 2010, London, p. 68.

question integrally contributes to the maintenance of an underclass or a deprived position because of gender status.

A court would no longer be justified in asking whether a particular discrimination is 'rational'. This culturally biased standard would be replaced by a scientific determination of whether the practice in question hurt women. If so, it would be illegal. As a result, sexual harassment could be outlawed as a practice that undermined sexual equality in the workplace. MacKinnon's 'inequality approach' was intended to be a powerful weapon of affirmative action on behalf of women. Where current law forced women to prove they had been the victims of discrimination, the inequality approach required only that they demonstrate that there was discrimination. MacKinnon was frank in declaring that the purpose of her approach was to give women the power to destroy any obstacle the stood in the way of equality. Women see the world, as men want them to see it. It follows that while they may believe themselves to be free, women cannot exercise free will.[170]

If one is not a legal person, one is not recognized as having, indeed, conceptually cannot have, rights and obligations as a subject in the law. One is literally, outside of the law, either as having n5o status (a non-entity) or as being an object (of property). The many cases brought by women who challenged the view that women did not have their own legal existence, constituted important threshold claims for women's inclusion as active agents in the legal process. In considering this idea of "legal personhood" it is important to note that it is an artificial or abstract concept of legal reasoning -- or gate keeping as to which entities may be legal actors.

The ways in which legal practice discriminated women and reinforced gender inequality demonstrates the argument of male domination. The view emerges and is based on the theory of 'dominance analyses' of Catharine MacKinnon, an American feminist scholar. She argues that men and women are different but the difference is that male dominate and women are subordinate. Legal Profession was seen as 'maintaining male domination' - a powerful conduct for reproduction and transmission of the dominant theory, a paradigm of maleness. The few cases that have

---

170 Finan, Christopher; "Catherine A. MacKinnon: The Rise of a Feminist Censor," 1983-1993, <http://www.mediacoalition.org/reports/mackinnon.html>, on 12th Sep., 2008.

been cited shows that courts in the early part of the twentieth century interpreted the word 'person' to mean 'men' and adopted the notion of separate spheres to justify women's exclusion from the practice of law and other profession.[171]

Catharine MacKinnon views such discrimination as hierarchy and not just a difference and argues that efforts to treat gender as a question of difference are misguided and that gender should be understood to be a matter of domination and subordination. Reflecting on women's exclusion from and subordination by law, Catharine A. MacKinnon traces the place of the legal guarantee of sex equality "from anathema to afterthought." In early attempts to change this, and continuing into the present, existing doctrine has been largely accepted as given. That is, demands have principally been to include women on the same terms as men. The Aristotelian notion of equality imposed by the courts, first on race then on sex, requires subordinate groups to be 'similarly situated' to dominant groups before they can receive equal treatment. Relying on litigation or legislation to alter women's status it reproduces patriarchal power relations. She argued that the most central inequality was gender, and thus followed the differences. She maintained that the liberal state coercively and authoritatively had constituted the social order in the interest of men as a gender. It embodied and ensures male control over women's sexuality at every level.[172]

As 'male' is the implicit reference for human, 'maleness' would be the yardstick of equality in sex-discrimination laws. The adoption of these values reproduced gender inequalities in the guise of neutrality and justice. The barriers and discrimination that the women pioneers encountered were overt and at times calculated to exclude women from the profession and hindered in the development of society. Legal Profession was seen as 'maintaining male domination 'based on dominant ideology'. Radical feminists locate the root cause of women's oppression in patriarchal gender relations.

---

171 Anleu, Sharyn L.Roach; *Law and Social Change,* Sage Publication, 2010, London, pp 68-69.

172 MacKinnon ,Catharine A ; "Reflections on Sex Equality under Law," *The Yale Law Journal*, Vol. 100, No. 5, Centennial Issue ,March, 1991, pp. 1281-1328< http://www.jstor.org/stable/796693> on 8th May2008.

Catharine MacKinnon views such discrimination as hierarchy and not just a difference and argues that efforts to treat gender as a question of difference are misguided and that gender should be understood to be a matter of domination and subordination.[173] Relying on litigation or legislation to alter women's status reproduces patriarchal power relations.

Based on the views of Catharine MacKinnon, it was apparent that the legal profession demonstrated social inequalities from the standpoint of subordination of women to men. Rejecting the notion of different voices, Mackinnon suggested and identified male dominance. She argued that the most central inequality was gender, and thus followed the differences. Focusing on differences served as ideology that neutralizes and rationalizes power inequalities. She maintained that the state coercively and authoritatively had constituted the social order in the interest of men as a gender. It embodied and ensures male control over women at every level. As male' is the implicit references for human, 'maleness' would be the yardstick of equality in sex-discrimination laws. The adoption of these values reproduced gender inequalities in the guise of neutrality and justice.[174]

The judgments in various cases in United States of America, Canada, Britain and India reflected a society were men ruled women. These legislations were a reflection of patriarchal society often rendering women passive victims. The barriers and discrimination that the women pioneers encountered were overt and at times calculated to exclude women from the profession and hindered in the development of society. The increase of women lawyers may help to wash the tear of women folk who are illiterate, poor, and downtrodden and victim of tortures in various kinds. Therefore, women occupy a place at the Bar, has a distinct role in the society. Women are equally competent to serve the nation, while practicing the law.

Legal Profession was seen as 'maintaining male domination 'based on dominant ideology. This shows sex-discrimination, which can be identified in their

---

173 Catherine A. Mackinnon.; *Feminism Unmodified: Discourses on Life and Law,* Harvard University Press, 1987, supra n.1, p.1087.

174 Anleu, Sharyn L.Roach; *Law and Social Change,* Sage Publication, 2010,London, p.68

judgments.[175] Moreover these legislations revealed the mindset of men. Many prejudices existed against women entering into different professions and fields of occupations. Two forms of discrimination could be identified. First, direct discrimination where a practice treats one person less favorably than others and second indirect discrimination where she is treated less favorably than men, for e.g. women could not gain entry in legal profession on the plea that the home is women's sphere and therefore they are unable to discharge public duties. The loss because of sex, of the chance of getting something that is thought to be of value is enough to constitute sex discrimination.[176] Denying the women the same opportunity as men, depriving them of the choice valued by them, the legislation did not promote equality. It was on the plea that the responsibility to run the home and take care of the children is that of women. It is the women who will do the household chores apart from attending to children and taking care of visitors.

The social reformers showed the path of redemption to them, and the exploited had to strive for it by their relentless efforts. The major success of the social reformer of the Renaissance was that they created an awakening among Indian women as a result of which they themselves came to assume the responsibilities of their own cause and began to raise the demand for their proper place in society. This consciousness awakened in them a sense of urgency in experiencing equality and social justice. The notion of equality has various dimensions and perceptions. Social justice provides strength to a woman. 'Women's place' is linked to the unequal distribution of resources, rewards, rights and authority between men and women, which in turn influence patterns of family and work life. In a society there are various hurdles in ensuring the participation of women who are highly stratified and are culturally and economically divided into small groups. The challenge of development of women, in the society, is not the problem of finance but was also of motivation and mobilizing them.

The campaigns of women's organizations to achieve greater equality and social justice within the societies led to law reforms. In the United States extensive

---

175 Ibid p.69.

176 Connolly, Michael; *Discrimination Law; Text, Cases and Material: Direct Discrimination,* Hart Publishing, 2005, Oxford, p. 171.

lobbying by women and sympathetic men gradually changes state laws, beginning with Iowa in 1870.In Great Britain the Sex Removal Discrimination Act achieved the same result.[177] While in India, a number of enlightened women established women's organization in different parts of the country in pre and post war years. Its activities brought social legislation with reference to women like *Hindu Women right to Property Act* in 1937 and in the early 50's, such as, *Women's Legal Rights,*1952, the *Suppression of Immoral Traffic in Women and children Act* in 1954, the *Special Marriage Act,* 1954, the *Hindu Marriage and Divorce Act,* 1956, *the Hindu Adoption and Maintenance Act,* 1956, the Hindu Minority and Guardianship Act, 1956, *Succession Act,* 1956, the *Orphanages and Widow Home Act* [The *Orphanages and Other Charitable homes (supervision and Control) Act,* 1960] and the *Dowry Prohibition Act,* 1961 to cite a few.[178] Many women's organizations use the processes associated with the Convention on the Elimination of All Forms of Discrimination against Women to put pressure on their governments. However, formal legal equality did not result in eradication of women's subordination.

2.4. A SUM UP

This chapter reveals the following findings:

(i) The Supreme Court decisions confirmed that women were not eligible as a matter of law for admission to the Bar.

(ii) The judicial decisions based on past legislations reveals pronounced gender bias and restricted women's entry into the public sphere including their access to high paying professional occupations and other profession.

(iii) The enforcers discriminated between men and women and unconsciously tend to reflect traditional and rigid attitudes towards women.

(iv) Women's natural differences were deployed for differential treatment in law. As 'male' is the implicit reference for human, 'maleness' was the yardstick of equality in sex-discrimination laws.

---

177 Abel, Richard; "Feminization of the Legal Profession," *Lawyers in Society*, 1988, University of California Press.

178 Kant, Ajani; *Women and the Law*, A.P.H.Publishing Corporation, 2008, New Delhi, p.15.

(v) The adoption of these values reproduced gender inequalities in the guise of neutrality and justice.

(vi) Gender was a question of power on male supremacy and female subordination.

(vii) The judgments in various cases in United States of America, Britain and India reflected a society where men ruled women.

(viii) These legislations were a reflection of patriarchal society often rendering women passive victims. This approach is firmly located within the patriarchal discourses.

(ix) The assumption was that women are weak, naturally different and that they are simply taken for granted and therefore cannot be in public sphere.

(x) Thus in both United States of America , Great Britain, and India, the professions were deemed unsuitable for women because of their assumed biological and psychological differences from men.

(xi) These differences were class based.

(xii) Women's challenges to enter into the legal profession were of continuous struggle, which were tied to professional structures and competition for control. Sometimes defeat revealed how male power and privilege were sustained within the orbit of professional control.

(xiii) The barriers and discrimination that the women pioneers encountered were overt and at times calculated to exclude women from the profession and hindered in the development of society.

(xiv) Important problems relating to the status and rights of woman had been dealt with by legislation in India.

(xv) There are yet loopholes in the existing legislations which need to be scrutinized more intensively, especially with a view to finding out to what extent it serves the present social and economic objectives of the nation and to ascertain how far it can deal adequately with current social problems.

CHAPTER – III

WOMEN IN LEGAL EDUCATION AND LEGAL PROFESSION

"Woman is the companion of man gifted with equal mental capacities. She has the right to participate in the minutes details in the activities of man, and she has an equal right and freedom with him."

- Mahatma Gandhi.
Wit and Wisdom.

3.1. AN OVERVIEW

In the previous chapter, we have noted the historical background of the study by describing the development of feminist jurisprudence in general and the struggle of early women in legal profession in particular. In this chapter, we are discussing the status and representation of women in legal education and legal profession. This discussion is subject to the limitations of available data in the area as separate data for women is only a recent development. The chapter begins with the apprenticeship system that was allowed only to men. In some cases women had to bring lawsuits, while in others, they mobilized the influence of fathers and husbands.

In this chapter, the researcher studies the experiences at the workplace, which contribute to the gender divide, such as work-family conflict, gender discrimination, major challenges etc in the entry of legal profession and other details, which are discussed as below.

American Legal education.

- Opening Legal Practice to Women,
- Growing Number Of Women Lawyers,
- Women lawyers using new laws,
- Challenging discriminatory practices,
- Law School Teaching,
- Legal Occupational Culture and Barriers,

British Legal Education

- Academic and Corporate Bodies.

Legal Education in India

- Participation of women in the Legal profession

A Sum Up

3.2. AMERICAN LEGAL EDUCATION

There were no law schools in colonial America. In 1779 Jefferson helped found the first professorship of law, at William and Mary College, installing his apprenticeship mentor, George Wythe. Yale, Columbia, the University of Maryland, and Harvard followed suit. Men could embark on a self-directed course of study; they could serve as an assistant in a clerk of court's office; or they could travel to England to study at the Inns of Court. The most common method of obtaining a legal education was through the apprenticeship system. The apprenticeship system only allowed men to acquire education and experience simultaneously by working under an experienced practitioner. Ideally, an apprentice would spend several years learning both the law and the practical aspects of a law practice. It was generally unavailable to women.

In 1784, however, proprietary law schools arrived and spurred the transformation of legal education. Proprietary law schools were essentially specialized. The first and most famous was Connecticut's Litchfield School. Its fourteen-month course provided instruction in subjects such as property, contracts, procedure, master-and-servant, and commercial law — similar to the subjects of some of today's first-year law school classes. The advent of law proprietary schools notwithstanding, apprenticeships remained the most common way to obtain a legal education until well into the nineteenth century.

Harvard, the first academic law school, was founded in 1817 by the outright adoption of a proprietary law school. In 1850 there were fifteen university law schools. By 1870 the number had barely doubled, but the modern era of legal education was about to begin. Part-time evening schools appeared, providing people with a lower income and less general education a way to obtain a legal education.

Women were notably absent from American legal education for its first 100 years in the United States of America. Margaret Brent was the first woman lawyer to practice in the mid-1600s, and tried over 130 matters. It was over 250 years before the United States had its second woman lawyer. The first women lawyer groundbreakers was Arabella Babb Mansfield who was the first woman to admitted to the bar in any state in the US (1869); others were early Clara Brett Martin of Canada's in 1897, Helena Normanton in 1919 was the first woman to became a pupil at the bar although Eliza Orme managed to practice as a lawyer from 1873 without being called to the bar or admitted to the solicitors' profession. While Carrie Morison was the first woman to qualify as a solicitor in 1923.

What difference does it make that Clara Brett Martin succeeded in becoming a lawyer in 1897 and what difference should it make that the legal profession increasingly includes large numbers of women as well as men?

Women were either excluded or obtained only limited access to the practice of law by formal or informal law school quotas or even by the absolute refusal to admit women (as was the case at Harvard University until 1951). They were barred from many law schools until well into the twentieth century. In fact the early pioneer women of the law are revered in all nations: in the United Kingdom and in its former colonies. As apprenticeship routes disappeared, even these limited opportunities for women to enter law were reduced by women's exclusion from the academic route. Although Washington University in St. Louis was the first law school to admit women in 1869, access to legal education remained very limited. Many law schools, particularly the most elite, denied admittance to women altogether. Columbia only opened its doors to women in 1928, and Harvard did so in 1950.

Even as women began to break their way into the practice of law, the fight to attain judgeships was still gearing up. The first women to ascend to these positions were often appointed to part-time positions as 'token' representatives of their gender, rewarded for their enterprising fortitude. For example, in 1884, the Diistrict of Columbia (now known as Washington D.C) trial court appointed Marilla Ricker to the position of United States Commissioner. In 1886, the first woman to graduate from Pennsylvania Law School was appointed master in chancery for the city of

Philadelphia. By 1907, Evanston, Illinois elected a woman, Catherine Waugh McCulloch to serve as a justice of the peace.

At this point of time, another pioneering woman to take the role of a judge was Georgia Bullock in 1914. The court, over which she presided, however, did not resemble those of her 'fellow' judges. Judge Bullock was the 'woman judge' of Los Angeles, in charge of a court which was segregated because of gender where 'she would serve as a model of Victorian ideals of womanhood for female misdemeanants.' Her appointment was considered as women began to break their way into the practice of law; the fight to attain judgeships was still gearing up. Her appointment was considered important, not because of concerns of equality, but because a women would be better served by a woman judge and could help them reform their ways.

The first women to ascend to these positions were often appointed to part-time positions as 'token representatives' of their gender, rewarded for their enterprising fortitude. For example, in 1884, the District of Columbia trial court appointed Marilla Ricker to the position of United States Commissioner. In 1886, the first woman to graduate from Pennsylvania Law School was appointed master in chancery for the city of Philadelphia. By 1907, Evanston, Illinois elected a woman, Catherine Waugh McCulloch to serve as a justice of the peace.

In 1920, the *Nineteenth Amendment* was ratified, granting women the right to vote and ushering a new era of women's rights. During this time, women began assuming judgeships, through both appointment and election. However, many of these women were the same handful who had broken ground in the end of the 19th Century. For example, in 1925, the first female lawyer in California, Clara Shortridge Foltz, was considered for a federal judgeship at the age of 76. Florence Allen became both the first woman to be elected to the positions of general jurisdiction court in 1920 and the first female state appellate judge through her election to the Ohio Supreme Court in 1922. She would later become the first female federal appellate judge, appointed to the 6th Circuit in 1933. The Los Angeles Women's Judge Georgia Bullock was finally appointed to an 'official' judgeship in 1931. The first female judge to serve on a federal district court, Burnita Shelton Matthews, was not appointed in 1949 to the United States District Court for the District of Columbia.

Beyond the courts of general jurisdiction, the specialized state courts also saw a rise in female judgeships. Many considered specialized courts more appropriate to the tasks of female judges; in these positions their positive womanly characteristics could be used to resolve issues such as juvenile crimes and domestic relations. Also, the 'token' aspect of female judges was seen in the temporary appointment of women to positions of prominence, such as the three female judges temporarily elevated to the Texas Supreme Court in 1925 after three male judges rescued themselves in a matter involving a fraternal society to which they belonged.

The struggle in which the women engaged in order to gain admission left an important legacy; they consistently have been over represented in legal reform efforts. By 1960s, women represented about 3 percent of American law students. By 1963-64 there began a yearly increase in the number of law school enrollments that fueled the profession's remarkable expansion. Despite increasing numbers of women applicants, women constituted only 3 percent between 1951 and 1965.Cecilia Morgan noted "the admission of the first woman law student did not result in a real 'revolution' for women in this particular profession, but neither did it result in a complete maintenance of the status quo."[179] While it was of great significance to remove some barriers for some women, the removal of barriers did not of itself lead to the next stage of dismantling attitudes and inequalities.

Title IX of the Education Amendments of 1972 (renamed in 2002 as *Equal Opportunity in Education Act*) was enacted on June 23, 1972 in United States. The law states: "No person in the United States shall, on the basis of sex, be excluded from participation in, be denied the benefits of, or be subjected to discrimination under any education program or activity receiving Federal financial assistance...."[180] By the 1970's, amid the tidal wave of feminist advocacy, the passage of Title IX, and

---

179 Morgan, Cecilia; "An Embarrassingly and Severely Masculine Atmosphere: Women, Gender and the Legal Profession 1920s-1960s,"(1996), 11 *Canadian Journal of Law and Society*, p. 21.

180 "Title IX of the Education Amendments of 1972,"< http://en.wikipedia.org/wiki/Title_IX. > on 3rd Feb.2010.

the empowering ruling of *Roe v. Wade, 410 U.S. 113 (1973)*, women finally began realizing the vision of equal opportunity in judgeships. This remained an ongoing struggle and negotiation. Mossman has pointed out; the underlying paradox is that "legal Profession remains both a facilitator and barrier to change." Despite the lifting of many of the formal restrictions during the early part of the twentieth century, the number of women lawyers remained negligible until the 1970s.[181]

Women started entering into the legal education in large numbers only in the late 1960s and early 1970s.The reason differed from country to country. From 1972 onwards, dramatic and significant changes were noticed due to international women's movement. Postwar prosperity and increased state subsidization of higher education was the cause of entry. Women gained entry easily in state universities in the West and Midwest. But encountered difficulty in the elite Ivy League schools of the Eastern establishment. Thus, in some cases they had to bring lawsuits, while in others they mobilized the influence of fathers and husbands.[182]

Until the 1970s, women remained less than 5 percent of the enrollment at ABA-approved law schools (Abel, 1989). Both faculty and men students made the educational environment inhospitable to women. While all students were subject to ridicule, particularly if they did not provide the right response when called on in class, women were rarely called on, and on such occasions, they were subjected to questions designed to embarrass them (e.g., being asked to explain the details of rape cases) or were humiliated by such comments as "better go back to the kitchen" if they stumbled in recitation

Civil rights laws contributed to change in the legal profession by opening the doors to law schools and legal work for women. *Title VII of the Civil Rights Act of 1964,*[183] *the 1972 Amendments to Title VII,* and *the Title IX of Educational*

181 Anleu, Sharyn L.Roach; *The legal Profession, Law and Social Change,* Sage publication, 2000, New Delhi, p. 94.

182 Abel, Richard; "Feminization of the Legal Profession," *Lawyers in Society*, 1988, University of California Press, Columbia, p 206.

183 "The Civil Rights Act of 1964," (Pub.L. 88-352, 78 Stat. 241, July 2, 1964).

Amendments Act, 1972 were of particular importance to aspiring women lawyers.[184] The *1972 Educational Amendments Act* prohibited sex discrimination in all public institutions of higher learning receiving federal monies, including major university law schools. In 1972, passage of *Title IX of the Higher Education Act* prohibited discrimination based on sex in the enrollment of students and hiring of faculty. Facing denial of federal financial assistance if they continued to discriminate, law schools finally began to admit more women and allow them to compete equally with men. This not only opened enrollment to women students, but also affected the distribution of scholarships and the hiring and promotion of women faculty members. It also made it illegal for law firms to openly refuse to interview or hire women.

Since that time, women's enrollments have grown dramatically.[185] But the 1965 study and in 1972 reviewed the existing admission pattern of major law schools in the country, and found a small proportion of female law students. Even when women were admitted, quotas and other restrictive barriers kept their numbers small. With a sufficient supply of qualified men applicants and in the absence of anti discrimination laws, the academic gatekeepers excluded or limited the numbers of men and women. For many decades, law classes typically had a maximum of three women. Although academics protested that the low numbers were due to women's disinterest, statistics that appeared in the Harvard Law Record in 1965 suggest a pattern of discrimination. Predictably, admission officers denied in interviews that qualified women were barred and stressed with family commitments and socialization to a more feminine' field. Just as early research found that women were disadvantaged by discriminatory views among professors; studies in the past two decades suggest that women continue to face a 'chilly climate' in law schools, and that such a chilly climate can strengthen gender differences in career aspirations and outcomes. What constitutes the chilly climate?

A contributing factor is the dearth of women in law academia. The percentage of female law faculty did not increase as quickly as the percentage of female law

---

184 "Title IX of Educational Amendments Act, 1972, *Title 20 U.S.C,* Sections 1681-1688,United States,Dept. Of Labor, < http://www.dol.gov/oasam/regs/statutes/titleIX.htm> on 3rd Feb.2010.

185 "Women Entering the Legal Profession: Change and Resistance. <http:// www.uk.sagepub.com/upm-data/12634_Chapter5.pdf - United Kingdom> on12th Dec. 2009.

students. By 2001, only 23 percent were full professors and 13 percent of law school deans are women. It was also found that women professors occupy non-tenure track positions in soft areas of law, such as legal writing and courses outside the core curriculum. As such, female students often have difficulty finding mentors, a process that may already be exacerbated by subtle bias in the classroom. The legal curriculum may have casebooks or class discussions, which may contain language or omit women's issues. Some also argue that the Socratic method in legal education produces a competitive and hostile environment that can further alienate and disadvantage female students, who generally prefer a more holistic style of learning and who already feel silenced in the classroom.

Numbers of women in the legal academy have increased, but some facts reveal tremendous feelings of marginalization by many women, exclusion from positions of power within their institutions. Many women are in the new of legal writing and clinical teaching; and so they are in lower status positions and do more labour intensive work. Many women do institutional 'care taking' work: advising and mentoring students, developing student-focused programs, participating as members of the committees within the institution. Their work is, like care taking work in the home, frequently invisible. Fewer women have chairs or are directors of centers or institutes. Many cannot negotiate higher salaries or positions if they are forced to 'leverage' these matters with outside offers, since they are more frequently locked in geographically by family or care taking needs.[186]

This modus operandi shows women's subjugation and identifies gender bias in legal education.

3.2.1. LEGAL PRACTICE BEING OPEN TO WOMEN

In the past four decades, there have been a number of major changes in the legal profession. These include an enormous increase in the number of law schools and lawyers; an opening of the profession to white women and people of colour; a shift in the type and organization of legal employment, including increases in firm

---

[186] Mossman, Mary.J; *The First Women Lawyers: A Comparative Study of Gender, Law and the Legal Professions*, Hart Publishing, 2006, Oxford, pp. 201 – 202.

size and bureaucratization; increases in the number of hours worked and the salaries paid to lawyers (particularly those in private practice); and a diminution of the legal profession's control over lawyers' behavior. Each of these changes has affected and been affected by the expanded role of women in law.

The hurdle for women lawyers after graduating from a law school was finding a job. Even women with training from elite schools faced employment discrimination that was openly practiced well into the 1970s.Women who were able to obtain legal work often were offered opportunities in low status specialties deemed appropriate for women, such as domestic relations and probate law. They received lower pay and were denied partnerships and opportunities for leadership in bar associations. For example, when former Supreme Court Justice Sandra Day O'Connor graduated third in her class at Stanford Law School in 1953, the only job that she was offered was as a legal secretary. [187]

Questions about women's competence lingered, and few women sought legal careers for the next several decades after they were permitted to do so. Across these diverse nations, many of the arguments used to exclude or limit women were similar: the law was and continues to be 'constructed as male' (i.e., presumed to be rational, logical, dispassionate, objective, professional, intimidating and demanding), while women are presumed to lack these qualities.

From 1960 to the present, there has been a phenomenal growth in the number of lawyers and in the ratio of lawyers to the general population. The number of lawyers in the United States grew from about 222,000 in 1950 to 35,000 in 1971,542,000 in 1980, 806,000 in 1991, and 909,019 in 2000.

As racial and sexual barriers to entry into law fell, the number of aspiring lawyers more than doubled, while the number of law schools rose by 25 percent. In 1960, women comprised only 3.5 percent of the enrollees at ABA-approved law schools; in 1970, they comprised 8.5 percent; in 1980, they comprised 33.6 percent; and in 1986, they comprised 40.2 percent. In 2004, they constituted about half (48

---

187 W. Huber, Peter; "Sandra Day O'Connor 1930,Supreme court justice - American Decades," *The Gale Group, Inc.,Encyclopedia.com,*2001.<http://www.encyclopedia.com> on12th Dec. 2009.

percent) of the students enrolled in law school and 51 percent of those awarded JDs (ABA, 2006). As of 2005-07, women represented virtually half (48 percent) of all law students in the United States (ABA, 2006).[188]

Using firm reported data very similar to that used by 'Building a Better Legal Profession'; the release of 'The American Lawyer's study of Women in Law Firms' shows nearly identical results. While the findings across the 210 firms that responded to 'The American Lawyer survey' were heartening to an extent, it was found that women make up 34 percent of lawyers and 45 percent non-partners and 19 percent partners. Still, little improvement has been made compared to previous studies cited in The American Lawyer.[189] With this rising tide of women being admitted, the percentage of lawyers who are women has risen sharply in the past two decades.

3.2.2. GROWING NUMBER OF WOMEN LAWYERS

But in what segments of the profession did this growing number of women lawyers found employment?

The percentage has doubled since 1985 when it was 13 percent. In the year 1971 there were only 3 percentwomen who practiced law. In 1980, 92 percent of attorneys were men and 8 percentwere women, compared to 73 percentmen and 27 percentwomen in 2000. The ratio of population to lawyers has decreased from 695:1 in 1951 to 303:1 in 1995.

The total JD enrollment: 129,397 in 1995-96, 125,184 in 1999-2000, and 137,676 in 2003-2004.In those years, male enrollment dropped from 56 percent to 51 percent, while the percentage of female enrollment rose from 44 percent to 49 percent According to the American Bar Association, there were 1,116, 967 licensed attorneys in June of 2006. The number rose to 1,128,729 by the end of 2006, and grew to 1,143,358 by the end of 2007. The American legal profession is the largest in the world. It is reported that there are over 6, 50,000 lawyers practicing in the United

---

188 <http:// www.uk.sagepub.com/upm-data/>, on 10th Dec.2008.

189 Schwieger, Matthew; "Building a Better Legal Profession: on Data and Women in the Legal Profession,", *Lexis Nexis*, <law.lexisnexis.com/webcenters/...–/Data-and-Women-in-the-Legal-Profession> on 12th Sep. 2008.

States. It is, therefore, an integral, important and significant segment of the Administration of justice.[190]

Though the above statistics show optimism for gender parity in the profession, research continues to find that women are over-represented in government and in public interest, but under-represented in private firms. Although women comprised 27 percent of the legal profession as of 2000, their numerical gains have not yielded equivalent increases in power, status, and income. Though the number of women in the legal profession has increased dramatically in the United States, research continues to document gender differences in career paths among lawyers. Specifically, a number of studies find that women are less likely than men to work in private firms, but more likely to work in the public and non-profit sectors and over represented in government, corporate/private industry, and legal aid and public defender (PD) work. Additionally, within each of these organizational hierarchies, women are concentrated in the bottom rungs of prestige and income; they are underrepresented in the ranks of partner, general counsel, and supervisors. While 75 percent of male attorneys work in private-practice settings, females were represented disproportionately in government practice locations (and were over represented by about 41 percent in that sector, based on their total numbers in the profession). Both women and minorities are disproportionately located in the "associate," not partnership, rank in the large law firms. For example, women still constitute less than 15 percent of all partners in law firms, and the figure for minorities is even lower. Occupational sociologists continue to study the "push-pull" effects of these phenomena. Are women and minorities "pushed" into government and legal aid positions because they are systematically excluded from or discriminated against by the private sector, or are they "pulled" by choice into work with greater social justice potential because of their own commitment to such work?[191]

According to McKinnon's model, the partnership selection process within these organizations produces a hierarchy of inequality because it tends to credit male

---

190 < http://wiki.answers.com/Q/What_is_the_total_number_of_lawyers_in_the_US> on 4 Feb.2008.

191 "Lawyers: Demographics and Social Structure: Issues Facing the Profession: Democracy in America," < http://law.jrank.org/pages/18750/Lawyers.html> on 4/02.08.

knowledge as normative, while treating the female experience as inconsequential. Thus, any attempt to reform the current power structure within law firms requires a better understanding of the lives of women lawyers and their continual struggle with gender inequality. For these women, dominance feminism serves as a call to action; it seeks to empower them as women, and not as women in relation to men.

Women remain severely underrepresented in positions of the greatest power, influence, and financial remuneration throughout most for-profit organizations in America. However, nowhere is this disparity more prevalent than in large U.S. law firms, where women account for only five percent of all managing partners, and male associates are nearly two to three times more likely than their female counterparts to attain partnership. The inner workings of these complex institutions offer critical insight into a variety of issues of particular importance to women, such as work-family conflict, the gender division of labor, and sex-based bias in the workplace. In evaluating the significant challenges faced by female attorneys seeking advancement in major law firms, feminism not only serves as a diagnostic tool, but also as a mechanism for generating possible solutions.

While it is important to recognize that no panacea exists for eliminating the barriers faced by women attorneys, MacKinnon's dominance perspective encompasses the greatest potential for explaining the under representation of women at the managerial level, and contemplating pragmatic strategies to confront the inherent structural and social biases found in many large firms.

The persistence of such gender segregation has implications on gender inequality in the profession. Consequently, as has been shown, the legal profession remains gendered despite dramatic changes in the past three decades. To understand why, it is necessary to examine other factors that also have affected both changes in the profession and women's place in it in the past fourty years.

3.2.3. WOMEN IN LEGAL PROFESSION - INITIAL ISSUES

Opening employment opportunities in law to women required lawsuits against the legal establishment. These suits gradually brought about changes in the legal professional treatment in practice, hiring, and the job market. At first, women students at New York University and Columbia Law Schools, with the participation of Columbia Law School's Employment Rights Project, set out to end exclusionary practices in elite Wall Street firms. Pooling information about job interview experiences, they concluded that these firms were not taking their applications seriously. They complained to their school's placement office, and with help from the Employment Rights Project (and funding from the Equal Employment Opportunity Commission), several women filed complaints with the New York City Human Rights Commission against 10 firms on behalf of all women law students in New York. In 1976, seven years after initiation of their suit, all of the firms agreed to settlements similar to those reached following findings of employment discrimination in two test cases.

In the first case decided in *Kohn v. Royall, Koegel and Wells*, the court determined that the firm had systematically discriminated against women in hiring. The next legal barrier was posed by the partnership decision. In *Hishon v. King & Spalding* (1984),[192] the U.S. Supreme Court legally recognized that promotion to partnership is an area covered under *Title VII*. Earlier, the courts had treated partnerships as voluntary associations that must be congenial for all concerned, because partners are liable for the negligent acts of any copartner. In the case of *Hishon v. King & Spalding* 467 U.S. 69. 104 S.Ct. 2229. 81 L.Ed.2d 59, the Court rejected the argument that the choice of partners was protected under the First Amendment right to freedom of association. It ruled that *Title VII* does not force partnerships to accept less qualified individuals. Nevertheless, consideration for partnership is a " term, condition, or privilege" of the original employment contract covered under *Title VII*, and, as such, a partnership decision must be made on a fair and equal basis without regard to the applicant's gender.

3. 2.4. CHALLENGING DISCRIMINATORY PRACTICES

The next hurdle for women was addressing discrimination in the actual decision making process. Women lawyers soon encountered discriminatory practices and gendered interactions in the courthouse that threatened their livelihoods. Such bias was defined as existing when people are denied rights or burdened with

192 *Hishon v. King & Spalding*, 59 F.R.D. 515, 518-19 (S.D.N.Y.1973).

responsibilities solely on the basis of gender. People are subjected to stereotypes about the proper behavior of men and women which ignore their situations. People are treated differently on the basis of gender in situations where gender should make no difference;[and] men or women as a group can be subjected to a legal rule, policy or practice which produces worse results for them than for the other group.

This is apparent from the statistics which shows that in United States of America, 16.5 percent of men lawyers worked for federal, state, or local governments, and 1.7 percent of women and 0.7 percent of men worked for 1993. Additionally, 25 percent of President.

Clinton's appointees were persons of colour, compared with 15 percent of President Reagan's and 12.4 percent of G. H. W. Bush's appointees.[193]

In 2000, female lawyers comprised24.7 percent in private practice,29.7 percent in Federal judiciary, 35.1 percent in local government,29.9 percent in local judiciary,36 percent in State government,36 percent in private industry,27.6 percent in private association,42.7 percent as public defenders and 44.1 percent in legal education.[194] The data is shown in Table-3.1.

---

193 www.bbr.unl.edu/archives/September1994.

194 Ryan, Justice C.J; "Women entering the Legal Profession: Change and Resistance,"p.119.<http:// www.uk.sagepub.com/upm-data/12634_Chapter5.pdf - United Kingdom>.

TABLE 3.1

EMPLOYEE DISTRIBUTION OF MEN AND WOMEN LAWYERS IN 2000

Employee Setting	*Male Lawyers*		*Female Lawyers*		*Females as Percentage of Category*
	Number	*Percent*	*Number*	*Percent*	
Private practice	506,829	75.0	1, 66,072	71.2	24.7
Federal judiciary	2,221	0.3	939	0.4	29.7
Federal government	18,572	2.7	10,049	4.3	35.1
State/local judiciary	16,231	2.4	4,548	1.9	21.9
State government	25,698	3.8	14,476	6.2	36.0
Private industry	54,972	8.1	14,476	6.2	36.0
Private association	3,285	0.5	20,973	9.0	27.6
Legal aid/public Defender	5,060	0.7	2,443	1.0	42.7
Legal education	5,060	0.9	3,997	1.7	44.1
Retired or inactive	5,908	5.5	3,135	1.3	15.3
Total	**675,729**	**100**	**233,290**	**100**	

Source: Justice C.J.Ryan; "Women entering the Legal Profession: Change and Resistance,"p.119.<http:// www.uk.sagepub.com/upm-data/12634_Chapter5.pdf - United Kingdom>.

3.2.5. LAW SCHOOL TEACHING

Only 1 percent of lawyers go into full-time law school teaching, as shown in Table 5, yet they have a disproportionate effect on the law as role models, gate-keepers, and shapers of the next generation of practitioners. In addition, their legal writing affects lawyers' arguments and judicial decisions.

Initially, the barriers to women achieving faculty positions in law schools were even higher than those facing legal practitioners. In 1950, there were only 5 women law faculty members; they accounted for less than 0.5 percent of tenure-track faculty in law schools. By 1977, the number of women had grown to 391 professors, who made up 8.6 percent of the tenure-track faculty, mostly at a few new and generally low-status law schools. A decade later, Richard Chused's survey of law school faculty composition during the 1986–1987 academic year indicated that women comprised 20 percent of full-time faculty, including 45 percent of the professional skills teachers of legal writing and clinical law (who often are not considered regular faculty). His study also provided evidence that women were being denied tenure at high-prestige law schools at disproportionate rates. While about half of both the men and women law faculty candidates overall were given tenure, schools with a low proportion of women faculty, including a disproportionate share of prestigious schools, granted tenure to women at lower rates (41 percent) than men (51 percent).

In the past two decades, women in legal education have made substantial progress, although they still are not fully represented in leadership positions and are clustered in the least prestigious academic specialties and positions. As of the 2004–2005 school years, women comprised 35 percent of law school faculty but only 25 percent of tenured faculty. They also were 19 percent of law school deans but 67 percent of the assistant deans who generally have staff positions that are not stepping-stones to deanships (ABA,2006).Of the women faculty and deans,11 percent were African-American women, 4 percent were Hispanic, and 3 percent were Asian-American (ABA, 2006).

Angel (2000) documented the continuation of the trend earlier noted in Chused's (1988) study that suggests that within legal education a new caste system is emerging. The majority of legal writing and clinical skills instructors, who usually are not on a tenure track, comprise the new lowest caste in that emerging system, and most of these instructors are women. In both clinical practice and legal writing fields, men are a minority, but they are over represented in tenured or tenure-track positions, while women disproportionately occupy the non tenure contract slots and receive lower pay. For example, women comprise 50 percent of clinical skills teachers. However, 55 percent of the men but only 37 percent of these women clinicians are tenured or in tenure-track positions. Similarly, women comprise 70 percent of the legal writing teachers, but men are twice as likely as women legal writing instructors to be tenured (13 percent versus 7 percent, respectively ;).

Angel's (2000) study also indicates a new trend in law schools and universities: a decrease in the percentage of faculty hired for tenure-track positions and the replacement of tenured faculty with contract faculty. Thus, just as women appear poised to make substantial gains in legal teaching and other academic specialties, they encounter new barriers that disproportionately limit their career opportunities. During the 1990s, the gender balance in law faculty hiring changed to women's disadvantage. In 1992–1993, women made up 50 percent of the newly hired associate professors (i.e., those who were presumably on tenure track). In 1997–1998, they comprised only 39.6 percent of those hired. At the same time, they made up 60 percent of the new lecturers and instructors in 1992–1993 and 66 percent of those hired in 1997–1998 (presumably in contract rather than tenure-track positions), suggesting the growth of the 'women's ghetto' in law school faculties.

As these data's suggest, women and men lawyers have different career paths. A study of Chicago lawyers who graduated after 1970 clearly illustrates the ways these paths increasingly diverge over time. At the start of their careers, women are under-represented in solo practice and small firms and over represented in public sector jobs. These differences grow over the course of the career as women move out of both large and small firms and into non-firm settings in government, legal aid, and corporate work. Conversely, men are less likely to leave large firms and more likely to leave government employment as their careers develop.

These patterns suggest that women chose to leave firms due to inflexible work schedules that create tension between the competing demands of practice and family.

Therefore, the question arises that this should be characterized as an exercise of "choice" or is," in significant part, the product of the dynamics of gender inequality within legal employment" (labeled "gender constraints," which we will explore next. The issue of career patterns and "choices" also differs for white and black women. Simpson's (1996) study of black women lawyers in New York found that of the 42 percent who stated a desire to work in a law firm on completion of law school, only 27 percent found employment with a firm.

3.2.6. LEGAL OCCUPATIONAL CULTURE AND BARRIERS

Research suggests that experiences at the workplace contribute to the gender divide. For one, given the time-demanding nature of firms, women may shy away from firms, leave firms, or forgo partnership opportunities in firms so as to achieve better work-family balance. Gender discrimination in firms may constitute yet another workplace barrier. In addition to bias in hiring and promotion, women may find their abilities questioned and receive less challenging assignments due to gendered assumptions about competence. Further, some find that female lawyers often face unwanted teasing and sexist jokes from their supervisors and colleagues. Catharine Mackinnon's book 'Sexual Harassment of working women' argues that sexual harassment of women at work is sex discrimination in employment. Many women lawyers hesitate from lodging any complain, as they fear that their story will be disbelieved or trivialized. That they will be blamed for the incident.[195]

Though numbers of women in the legal academy have increased, some facts reveal tremendous feelings of marginalization by many women, exclusion from positions of power within their institutions. Many women are in the new of legal writing and clinical teaching; and so they are in lower status positions and do more labour intensive work. Many women do institutional 'caretaking' work: advising and mentoring students, developing student-focused programs, participating as members of the committees within the institution. Their work is, like caretaking work in the home, frequently invisible. Fewer women have chairs or are directors of centers or institutes. Many cannot negotiate higher salaries or positions if they are forced to

---

195 Anleu, Sharyn L.Roach; *Law and Social Change,* Sage Publication, 2000, London, p.178.

'leverage' these matters with outside offers, since they are more frequently locked in geographically by family or caretaking needs.

This modus operandi shows women's subjugation and identifies gender bias in legal education. Using the 2006 Law School Survey of Student Engagement, job preferences and expectations among first-, second-, and third-year law students. Analysis reveals that overall, women are less likely than men to express interest in private firms, and more likely to prefer the public and education sectors. However, there is evidence of a gender convergence as women in elite schools increasingly set aside their non-firm preferences in their expectations, which in turn tend toward large firms. Implications from the findings are discussed in light of gender inequalities in both legal education and the legal profession.

A related body of literature finds that workplace experiences, such as work-family conflict and gender discrimination, play an important role in the sex segregation of lawyers. However, some find that gender differences exist in first jobs, suggesting that gender differences are already apparent at the starting point of legal careers. So far legal profession is concerned; the total number of lawyers increased from 221,605 in 1950 to 857,931 in 1995. Between 1970 and 1990, the percentage of women lawyers in the United States rose from less than 3 percent to 22 percent. This figure revealed women's entry into the profession but not sufficient numbers of women were studying law as their career. In 1995, the practice of law grew from a service activity estimated at $4.2 billion-a-year in 1965 to an estimated $148 billion-a-year in 1999.[196]

Even as female enrollment in law school for the class of 2004 tops 49 percent, a recent report published by the American Bar Association (ABA) concludes that women are still far from enjoying equal status in the profession of law. The most significant change during the last three decades, first among law students and thereafter in the legal profession as a whole, was the growth in the number of women choosing the law as a career vocation. While the number of women in the legal profession has increased dramatically in the United States, research continues to

196 "Preserving the core values of American Legal profession," <www.law.cornell.edu/ethics/mdp1.htm> on 8th December 2008.

document gender differences in career paths among lawyers. According to the report, entitled 'The Unfinished Agenda: Women and the Legal Profession', women in law remain underrepresented in positions of the greatest status, influence, and economic reward. Although women have been a significant presence in the legal profession since the 1970s, they now account for nearly 30 percent of all lawyers and they are on the brink of being a majority of entering law students this fall, they still remain significantly underrepresented in positions of greatest status, influence and economic rewards. This is the conclusion of "The Unfinished Agenda: Women and the Legal Profession," a report released by the American Bar Association Commission on Women in the Profession.[197] In 1984 the total J.D enrollment was 119,847 of which 46,897 were women. The number increased to 47,486 in 1985, 47492 in 1986, 48920 in 1987, 50,932 in 1988, 53113 in 1989 and 54097 in 1990.The data is shown in Table 3.2.Though now 44 percent of all law students are women and it is expected that women will make up 40 percent (estimated) of the legal profession by the year 2010.Even then, the projections are that the legal profession will never be 50 percent women even though women are more than 50 percent of the population. As the report of the American Bar Association (ABA) for Women in the Profession in The Unfinished Agenda (2001, p.5) concluded, "That despite substantial progress towards equal opportunity, the agenda remains unfinished. Women in the legal profession remains underrepresented in position of greatest status ,power and economic rewards. The problems are compounded by the lack of consensus that are in fact serious problems to be dealt with.[198]

The data given in Table-3.2 shows the number of women enrolled for J.D. Degrees from the year 1984-2005. While in Table -3.3 shows the number of J.D degrees awarded to women.

---

197 "Balance and Flexibility are key: Equal numbers don't add up to equal opportunities for many women lawyers,"ABA report < http://www.tba.org/Journal_Tbarchives/jul01/TBJ-jul01-balance.html> on 13th,Sep., 2008.

198 Ryan, Justice C.J; "Women entering the Legal Profession: Change and Resistance,"< http://www.uk.sagepub.com/upm-data/12634_Chapter5.pdf.> on 5thMay2008.

TABLE 3.2

U S A

J.D. DEGREES FROM 1984 - 2004 (Total/Women)

J.D. ENROLLMENT

	1984	1985	1986	1987	1988	1989	1990
Total	119,847	118,700	117,813	117,997	120,694	124,471	127,261
Women	46,897	47,486	47,920	48,920	50,932	53,113	54,097
	1991	**1992**	**1993**	**1994**	**1995**	**1996**	**1997**
Total	129,580	128,212	127,802	128,989	129,397	128,623	125,886
Women	55,110	54,644	55,134	55,808	56,961	57,123	56,915
	1998	**1999**	**2000**	**2001**	**2002**	**2003**	**2004**
Total	125,627	125,184	125,173	127,610	132,885	137,681	140,376
Women	57,952	59,362	60,633	62,476	65,179	67,030	67,438

Source: American Bar Association, <http://www.abanet.org/legaled/statistics/jd.html>

J.D. DEGREES AWARDED

	1984	1985	1986	1987	1988	1989	1990
Total	36,687	36,829	36,121	35,478	35,701	35,520	36,385
Women	13,586	14,119	13,954	14,206	14,595	14,553	15,345
	1991	**1992**	**1993**	**1994**	**1995**	**1996**	**1997**
Total	38,800	39,425	40,213	39,710	39,191	39,920	40,114
Women	16,580	16,832	17,047	16,997	16,729	17,366	17,552
	1998	**1999**	**2000**	**2001**	**2002**	**2003**	**2004**
Total	39,455	39,071	38,157	37,909	38,576	38,863	40,018
Women	17,662	17,516	17,713	18,006	18,639	19,132	19,818

Source: American Bar Association, <http://www.abanet.org/legaled/statistics/jd.html>

The reasons are, women lawyers make less money, and quite often are reprimanded for wearing pants in court. They are told that they do not belong to the bench. On the other hand, a higher percentage of women prefer legal employment in government, in private associations, and in legal aid and public defender offices. The persistence of such sex segregation has implications on gender inequality in the profession. Sex segregation among lawyers not only embodies a form of gender inequality in itself, but also relates to other dimensions of disparities between women and men in the profession.

Women comprise 24 percent of the nation's lawyers. This percentage has doubled since 1985 when it was 13 percent. In the year 1971 there were only 3 percent women who practiced law. The American Bar Association reported that from 1985 to 2000, of all lawyers admitted to practice, 37 percent were women, but from 1995 to 2000, the percentage of women partners in the 250 largest law firms in the United States increased from just 14 percent to 15.6 percent. Women account for only 15 percent of federal judges, 10 percent of law school deans and general counsels and 5 percent of managing partners of large firms.

In 1995, women lawyers comprised only 22.6 percent in private practice, 32.2 percent as government lawyers.21.1 percent of state and local government lawyers, 39.7 percent of private association lawyers and 41.9 percent of the lawyers working in legal aid offices and as public defenders.

The Annual Report of the Attorney Registration and Disciplinary Commission of the Supreme Court of Illinois reports that for 1998 women comprised 30 percent of the total registered attorneys. But in what segments of the profession did this growing number of women lawyers found employment?

The statistics for the classes of 1997 and 1998 indicate that the legal employment patterns of women and men graduates tending to converge were that in judicial clerkships, government and public interest positions, the percentages of women consistently exceeded those of men, while the percentage of men entering law firms exceeded that of women. In 1997 women comprised 14 percent of law firm partners, 19 percent of full professors at law schools, 8 percent of law school deans,

19 percent of federal judges, 20 percent of state civil judges, 22 percent of the American Bar Association House of Delegates Members and 32 percent of the members of the American Bar Association Board of Governors. A slightly smaller percentage of women lawyers (70.9 percent) than of men (74.9 percent) were in private practice. There is a 70 percent higher percentage of women federal judges today than in 1987 (19 percent versus 7 percent), 18.6 percent higher percentage of women judges in state courts of last resort (20 percent in 1997 versus 7 percent in 1986), 144 percent higher percentage of women in the American Bar Association House of Delegates (22 percent in 1997-1998 versus 9 percent in 1987-1988), and the percentage of the women on the American Bar Association Board of Governors went from 3 percent in 1987 to 32 percent in 1997-1998. Growing at a slower rate, one closer to the overall rate of increase of women in the profession, is the 75 percent growth in the percentage of women partners at law firms (14 percent in 1997, up from 8 percent in 1987) and the 46 percent growth in the percentage of women law professors (19 percent in 1997, up from 13 percent in 1990).

In 1999 in the Eighteenth Judicial Circuit, 14.6 percent of the judges were women. There were 3 women out of 15 full Circuit Court judges elected by the people (20 per cent) and 3 women out of 26 Associate judges appointed by the Circuit judges (11.5 per cent).[199]

According to demographic trends compiled by the American Bar Association, by 2005, women were 34.8 percent. The result was that up till 1986 in the United States there were very few women judges in the superior court. There are many women in America who are working for less pay, in public post. Interestingly, in 1991 48 percent of women in private practice were sole practitioners compared to 44 percent of men. The American Bar Association states that being a sole practitioner typically pays the lawyer less money than working in a law firm, although it may also bring more autonomy. In 1991, women practiced at 40 percent of the law firms in the country, more than 2-1/2 times the number in 1980.[200] The largest concentration of

---

199 Ibid.

200 French, Dorothy F; "Facts About Women & the Law,"*DCBA Brief,* October 1999 Issue. <http://www.dcba.org/brief/octissue/1999/art81099.htm> on 6th March2009.

women lawyers is in the United States, where it is estimated that 350,000 women are licensed to practice law out of a total attorney population of 1.2 million.

The article in the Washington Post concluded with the statistic that of the 203 lawyers who had appeared before the Supreme Court of the United States in the 1997 Term, only 14 percent i.e. about 30 lawyers were women. It suggested that this would not change until, down the line, other things changed. At the moment, the clerkships of the Justices of the Supreme Court and of the Federal Courts in the United States are given to women law graduates in the ratio of only 1 to 4 for males. In the top echelons of the Government's legal advisers, it is the same ratio. In the top posts in academe in the United States the position is no better. Yet getting the experience of arguing before the Supreme Court can be an important step in that country on the path to eventual appointment to judicial office. In the US there has been a 16-fold increase in the number of women lawyers since the early 1970s. The Supreme Court and the Court of Appeals in United States of America had one woman judge each.

Legal scholars debate the issues as to women's 'different voice' and the 'sameness' and 'difference' between women and men. However, despite their advances in gaining admittance to law school, women continue to face gender-based barriers once they enter the profession, and partly as a result, they are leaving the profession at significantly higher rates than their male peers are leaving it. Brockman's study of lawyers painted a discouraging picture for women in law. It says "although the legal barriers that historically prevented women from entering the legal profession have been removed, informal and structural barriers that impede women's full participation within the legal profession still exist today."[201] In the US, only 15 percent of federal judges and law firm partners are female, ten percent of law school deans and 5 percent of large firm managing partners. Over time, the legal profession in the United States has been changing in its composition and structure. There are almost 1 million lawyers in the United States in 2001, a three-fold increase in the last

---

201 Krakauer, Lianne, Chen and Charles P; "Gender barriers in the legal profession: implications for career development of female law students," *Journal of Employment Counseling,* June 01, 2003.

three decades. The United States is well known for having more lawyers than almost any other country.[202]

- On average female lawyers earn about $20,000 less than male lawyers in the US, even between those having equivalent positions, experience, and qualifications.
- Studies show that qualified women are only half as likely as men to obtain partnerships.

3.3. BRITISH LEGAL EDUCATION

A number of changes were made to the legal status of women in the 19th century, especially concerning marriage laws. *The Custody of Infants Act* in 1839 gave mothers of unblemished character access to their children in the event of legal separation or divorce.[203] The *Matrimonial Causes Act* in 1857 gave women limited access to divorce. But while the husband only had to prove his wife's adultery, a woman had to prove her husband had not only committed adultery but also incest, bigamy, cruelty or desertion.[204] In 1873, *the Custody of Infants Act* extended access to children to all women in the event of separation or divorce.[205] In 1878, after an amendment to the *Matrimonial Causes Act*, women could secure a separation on the grounds of cruelty and claim custody of their children. Magistrates even authorized protection orders to wives whose husbands have been convicted of aggravated assault.[206] An important change was caused by an amendment to the *Married Women's Property Act* in 1884 that made a woman no longer a 'chattel' but an

---

202 "Lawyers Demographics and Social Structure, Issues Facing the Profession, Democracy in America,"<http://law.jrank.org/pages/18750/lawyers.html> on 6th March2009.

203 "Women in the Victorian era," *Wikipedia*, <http://en.wikipedia.org/wiki/Women_in_the_ Victorian_era> on 15thSeptember 2008.

204 Ibid.

205 Ibid.

206 Ibid.

independent and separate person. Through the *Guardianship of Infants Act* in 1886, women could be made the sole guardian of their children if their husband died.[207]

Universities at first refused to admit women on the grounds that they had been established for men only. In 1869, seven women managed to gain admission to Edinburgh University Medical School - the first women in Britain to be admitted to medical school - but such was the uproar as professors and townsfolk rioted to prevent them from entering the university, that the university reneged on its decision, and cancelled their courses. The Edinburgh Seven, as they are known, took the university to court - and lost. While some professional societies admitted women by the early 1920s, it was 1945 before a woman became a Fellow of the Royal Society. The Foreign Service refused to allow women to take the examinations for the administrative grade until 1947, and Cambridge University held out against giving women degrees until 1949. The story of women in Britain since the Second World War even for a girl born in 1950, for instance, had no equal access to education. But the *1944 Education Act* established the principle of free education for all from primary to secondary, but at eleven plus there were quotas for admission to grammar school.

In 1900 in Western countries there were very few occupations open to women, apart from agriculture. In many countries a large number of women were employed in domestic service. Large numbers of working class women worked in factories, or in the garment industry or in laundries or at various other jobs. From the mid-1850s nursing became a respectable occupation for women. Large numbers of women worked as nurses in the American Civil War, and in England nursing schools were started to give women a proper training. Many poorer women had to do factory work (between pregnancies), or worse still, take poorly paid jobs in service industries (catering, cleaning and so on). Women were increasingly employed in offices in the later part of the century, the invention of the typewriter led to an increase in office jobs for women, as they were found to make better typists than men. When the telephone was invented they were employed as telephone switchboard operators. Large numbers worked as sales clerks in the new department stores. From the 1870s,

---

207 Ibid.

women's colleges were started in places like Oxford and Cambridge, which offered female students an education on a par with that of men, though it wasn't until the 20th century that they gained full acceptance by the universities. As a result only a handful of women could break into professions like medicine, law, and journalism. There were also a handful of women university teachers in 1900, but really only a handful, as very few women went to college then.

The rise of the professions from the late eighteenth century forward, and women's conceptual and actual placement within the private, were both deeply intertwined with the development and differentiation of the European middle classes. The replacement of privilege based on birth with privilege based on merit, often proven through training and examinations formed an important basis for middle-class aspirations to social leadership. Liberal discourse emphasized competition among equal citizens, defined by their independence. This independence crucial to citizenship might be acquired through a general, liberal education that enabled critical thinking, or through ownership of property, or both. Women's lack of independence, in these terms, helped to justify the restriction of their rights: the 'natural occupation' of motherhood tied them to the house and made them 'dependent on the male.' This 'natural occupation' was reinforced through restrictions on women's access to education and employment, which in turn ensured continued dependence on men. An idealization of motherhood contributed to a distinctive pattern of family life among the European middle classes, in which the home was identified as a private sanctuary to be protected from the forces of economic and political competition, and there developed an enhanced association of masculinity with work outside the home and of femininity almost exclusively with the domestic. Middle-class men gained ever-greater access to the professions of law, medicine and teaching throughout the nineteenth century, as more and more of them opted for the higher education that was increasingly a prerequisite for sitting examinations. They joined the organizations that allowed professionals to make various claims on the basis of their social importance. But middle-class women's appropriate full-time occupation, in particular as it related to any conception of its "special importance [...] for society and common weal," was articulated in both scholarly and popular formulations as motherhood and the maintenance of the household. This private role for women was essential to the delineation of a public within which middle-class men could realize their aspirations as 'independent' individuals.

The liberal, middle-class idealization of motherhood and of separate, gendered spheres of activity for the sexes that was used to describe the home as women's proper place paradoxically opened public opportunities to women as the nineteenth century progressed. Motherhood formed the basis of women's first claims to educational access. In a multitude of publications, middle-class women and male allies embraced the idea that women should be properly educated to assume the role of nurturers of the next generation. In the family, wives and mothers wanted a renegotiation of the old order. They argued for a form of democracy in the home where rights and responsibilities would be equally shared. In the work place they wanted equal rights, equal opportunity and equal pay. The lives of my mother and grandmother remained unchanged - they continued to be devoted to their domestic responsibilities.

Mothers needed more than just the most rudimentary or informal education, however, since the middle-class woman's reproductive labour included the reproduction of cultural capital. Freed by servants from the worst drudgery of household work (which she must nevertheless supervise), she was to manage the early education and refinement of her children and direct their assimilation of bourgeois norms and values. In the German states, where formal politics were often inhospitable to liberalism, the *Kindergarten* movement offered an alternative path for the middle-class project of a "conscious and systematic education of a new generation of citizens," and Fröbel emphasized the dependence of this process on women, "to whom God and Nature... pointed out the first educational office in the family." Although the Kinder garden was banned in Prussia during the post-1848 reaction because of its liberal associations, the link between (actual or potential) motherhood and education had been established. There was no question of women serving in any sort of official administrative capacity as they did in France, but they were almost without exception the heads of the private teacher-training seminars attached to Kindergarten.

Similar connections were made in Britain and the Netherlands, where women's opportunities for employment in teaching children were associated with "innate maternal qualities" that might be put to use outside of the individual home. In the British case, women taught girls in private schools as well as in the more often co-educational elementary schools sponsored by religious and colonial societies. Although employment in public elementary education was almost exclusively for men, Dutch women were allowed to teach both male and female pre-school pupils, as well as girls at all levels in private schools.

The connections drawn between actual or potential motherhood and employment in teaching were early manifestations of what historians of women and gender have identified as a malleable ideology of 'materialism' or 'social motherhood' used by women and men across the political spectrum to delineate the proper sphere of women's activities. The popularity of ideas that "exalted women's capacity to mother" and identified specific social tasks for them helped to ensure the success of arguments for expanded education for girls as the nineteenth century progressed, and were one of the bases on which women gained greater access to secondary teaching and other professional opportunities.

Women committed to professional advancement were neither necessarily supportive of, nor supported by women's movements. The interests of women intent on earning a living through legal work could conflict with those seeking to advance women's social status. Even women who themselves wished to practice law could object to legal challenges to exclusion, fearing precedents that would solidify women's exclusion. Further complications included such local exigencies as admission to legal education and university education generally, admission to the bar, reforms of the legal profession, and opportunities for legal work within firms and by women working independently. Several women legal workers who earned legal degrees but never attained admission to the bar. In these respects, the process that opened the legal profession to women shares many features in common with other histories of gender and the professions globally. Women faced obstacles and difficulties in establishing and identifying themselves as professionals, because they were defined into (and often identified themselves with) a feminized private sphere at the same moment when the public was being defined as the symbolic space of both masculine and professional activity. They gained access to the professions by securing access to education, developing a set of discourses to help them transcend the effective boundary between the private and public to demand entry into the professions, and pressing for state intervention on their behalf. Emphasis on the differences between men and women, and the special qualities or characteristics that women might bring to bear in professional activities, was useful in expanding educational opportunities for and opening teaching careers to women. When it came to the field of law, an established profession with a longer tradition of male exclusivity and a closer relationship to the exercise of citizenship, arguments based on gender difference were far less significant in the push for women's access. Rather, arguments about women's particular characteristics and traditional roles were used to suggest their lack of fitness for the legal profession. Emphasis on equality of occupational access between men and women was useful in the eventual creation of opportunities for women in the traditional 'liberal profession' of law.

In 1970, the first British conference of the Women's Liberation movement in Oxford resolved to press for employment legislation. That same year, the Secretary of State for Employment introduced the Equal Pay bill. It was enacted in 1975 known as *The Equal Pay Act 1970*, which prohibits any less favourable treatment between men and women in terms of pay and conditions of employment. It came together with the *Sex Discrimination Act, 1975*. The laws provided a legal framework for change.[208]

The numbers of male university law graduates increased at an average annual rate of 5.4 percent between 1967 and 1978, but the numbers of female graduates increased at 31.2 percent.[209] The Association of Law Teachers (ALT) Survey of Law Schools in 1996 found that of the 40 law schools that responded, 54.45 of undergraduate students on the LLB were female. In light of such a low percentage of women in the law profession in the 1970's and 1980's, it was perceived that gender bias prevailed in law schools, which resulted in few women in the law profession.

---

208 Murray, Jenny; "20th Century Britain: The Woman's Hour," 05-11-2009, *BBC Text Journal*, <http://www.bbc.co.uk/history/british/modern> on 9th Dec., 2009.

209 Abel, Richard; "Comparative Sociology of Legal Professions: An Exploratory Essay," *American Bar Foundation Research Journal*, Vol.10, No.1, 1985, Blackwell, pp. 1-79.

Males outnumbered females on postgraduate academic courses (54.8 percent male). This trend appears set to continue. On graduation, female law graduates face worse prospects than their male counterparts in terms of salaries, the Equal opportunities Commission reporting in August 2002 that, 'Among graduates in 1st and 2nd year, the gender pay gap was widest for female law graduates.' Unfortunately for women law graduates, their subsequent career path is likely to be shorter, less well paid and involves less chance of promotion to positions of seniority than that of men.[210] Professional women still have primary responsibility for both housekeeping and childcare in addition to their professional duties. Men still earn on average 30 percent more than women.

3.3.1. ACADEMIA AND CORPORATE BODIES

The available data from the UK show that while 12 percent of full time professors were women in 2000, in the more segregated subject areas like engineering and technology no less than 97 percent of full time professors were male. In the UK the percentage of women professors in the sciences is less than 10 percent in all subject areas. In some areas this could be explained by a lack of women in the subject area or women's relatively recent entry in substantial numbers in to the field. However, in the biosciences women have constituted over 50 percent of graduates for over thirty years demonstrating that the small number of women reaching top positions may be due to factors other than a lack of female talent.

In United Kingdom in 2003, only 3.7 percent of Executive Directors of FTSE top 100 companies are women and in the USA in 2002 there were 11 women amongst the leaders of Fortune 1000 companies. According to the 2000 Catalyst Census of Women Corporate Officers and Top Earners, women in the USA occupy only 6,2 percent of the positions in business that yield the greatest policy making power.

Both in the United States of America and in United Kingdom, though the numbers of women studying and practicing law has gone up dramatically in the past decade, however women remain concentrated in the lower levels of the profession.

---

210 Kent, Penelope; "Women in Law-A UK and US view," <http://www.womeninlaw.com/newsletter1/kent.htm.> on 6thMay 2008.

Over 80 percent of partners in law firms are male and very few women can be found amongst the judiciary in either country especially at the higher levels.

Lawyers work both in academia, corporate offices and in profession and studies and evidence collected for this study indicate that there may be some differences in the barriers women face depending on which career path they choose. A European Union report on women in industrial research from 2002 shows that there are proportionately far fewer women lawyer working in legal profession (15 percent) than academia (30 percent) in Europe.

The report suggests that the barriers to women lawyers in the profession include a lack of work/life balance policies that allow employees to accommodate family and caring responsibilities and a prevailing culture of patronage, 'old boys networks' and nepotism with non-transparent systems and structures. The career structure in other industry, where it is possible to obtain a permanent position much earlier in the career than, may actually put women in a better position to manage and negotiate career breaks. In certain industries, taking a career break may also be easier than in legal profession. It may be more routine and keeping abreast of the cutting edge and may not be vital. While, there are also a number of companies that have through gender equality policies managed to retain women staff.

Though the trend is that women are joining the profession yet many women leave the profession because it fails to accommodate these diverse demands, creating a self-fulfilling prophesy of failure. A recent Law Society report found that female solicitors are paid substantially less than their male counterparts, and tend to work in smaller, less profitable practices. Across the legal division, women make up 40 percent of new barristers out of which 26 percent of are in independent practice while men representing 74 per cent. Of these, only 8 percent of Queen's Counsels are females. The Equal Opportunities Commission (EOC) explains this tendency in part by reference to the average age of women solicitors holding a practicing certificate (36 years) relative to males (43). . A similar picture pertains at the Bar. It is no surprise therefore looking at the two professions that the figures for the judiciary, the senior judiciary in particular are disappointing. As noted by Lady Justice Arden in a recent address to the Chancery Bar Association in January of this year, since October

2005 no woman has been appointed to the High Court bench. In fact since my appointment in October 2004 out of the 22 appointees, only two were women i.e. just under 10 percent which is roughly the percentage of female high court judges at present. Of those 22 appointments none were from minority ethnic backgrounds. Lady Justice Arden pointed to the Equal Opportunities Commission report, which highlighted that there are 78 "missing women" amongst the 194 senior judges. The report concluded that it will take about 40 years for women to reach an equal number to that of men on the bench. The surprising thing, said Lady Justice Arden, is that there has been this notable lack of progress for women, at a time when there is considerable pressure for diversity in the profession and on the bench. She notes that appointment has to be on merit, but that merit should take into account the different, but equal kinds of contributions that women can make.[211]

In 1957, women lawyers comprised of 1.94percent.In 1967, they were 2.7 percent. In 1971, there was a gradual increase to 3 percent, while in 1977 it rose to 7.33 percent. In 1985, the number of women lawyers increased to 13 percent and in 1987 it was 16 percent. In 1997, it doubled to 32.75 percent. While in 1999, it was 35 percent which is likely to be 40 percent in 2010.[212] The statistics for the Bar is shown in Table-3.3 are as follows:

---

211 Justice Dobbs; Seeches, Association of Women Solicitors, 12th March 2007.<http://www.judiciary.gov.uk/publications_media/speeches/2007/mrs_j_dobbs_120307.htm> on 19th Sep,2008.

212 Morell, Peter; "Women Lawyers: Situation in Britain," <http://en.wikipedia.org/wiki/User:Peter_morrell/women_lawyers> on 19th Sep,2008.

TABLE 3.3

PERCENTAGE OF WOMEN LAWYERS IN UK

Year	Percentage
1957	1.94%
1967	2.7%
1971	3%
1977	7.33%
1985	13%
1987	16%
1997	32.75%
1999	35%
2010	40% (Est.)

Source: Morell, Peter; "Women Lawyers: Situation in Britain," <http://en.wikipedia.org/wiki/User:Peter_morrell/women_lawyers>.

There are far fewer woman judges in England and Wales than in many other jurisdictions throughout the world. Britain's experience with the judiciary is similar to India. Of the judiciary; there are no female lords of appeal in ordinary. Only 6 percent of Court of appeal judges and 7 percent of High Court judges are women; whereas women comprises 19 percent of deputy district judges and 15 percent of district judges .Up to September 2004, 8 percent of the total number of High Court judges in England and Wales were women. At present, just 10 percent of the totals of 108 High Court judges are women, and just over 8 percent of the 37 Court of Appeal judges.

The Law Society of England and Wales also highlighted the lack of women and solicitor appointments to the higher judiciary. Although the launch of the new Judicial Appointments Commission in 2006 which was meant to herald an end to the old "tap on the shoulder" method of recruitment and so-called "secret soundings", the make-up of the judiciary remained as it did in the senior levels, the society said.[213] Up to March 2005, women held 18 percent of judicial posts above tribunal level in Northern Ireland. The number of women holding high legal office in Northern Ireland is low i.e. 18 per cent, compared with other countries

There were 166 women holders of judicial office in Northern Ireland, ranging from County Court judges to chairs of tribunals. There were no women judges in the High Court, nine women in the County Courts compared to 30 male judges; three female full time Resident Magistrates compared to fifteen males and five female deputy Resident Magistrates compared to thirteen males. Out of a total of 63 Queen's Counsel in the province, only five were women. The number of women holding high legal office in Northern Ireland is low compared to other countries.

3.4. WOMEN IN LEGAL EDUCATION IN INDIA

When India gained independence in 1947, its legal profession and legal teaching were not able to play the role they ought, by Western standards. The law was to assist in the form of public law and administrative law, and the legal profession claimed only a small and marginal role in social change. The role of the legal

213 Gibb, Frances; "Arden, Lady Justice: Not enough women Judges," *The Times online*, 4th June 2008, <http://businesstimesonline.co.uk> on 17th Sep, 2008.

profession as a whole was ordinarily restricted to giving advice. India's elaborate written constitution required a wise and effective legal profession, but the flow of talent into the profession did not increase. Before independence, the lawyer had enjoyed some degree of self-determination, had frequently been educated abroad usually in England, and was often prominent in the struggle for independence movement. But after independence the situation deteriorated.

As foreign exchange became scarce, India had to rely increasingly on domestic legal education. Moreover, neither the economic rewards of the profession, nor its social standing, perceived opportunities for contributing to the new and better India. The Legal Profession could not attract young men and women to law. Even now, India lacks a legal profession that understands law as an instrument of economic and social architecture.

In the last two decades; legal education in India has undergone radical changes in its methods of delivery. The concept of full-time law studies was virtually unknown. Full-time law teachers and students were a rare phenomenon; LL.B. degrees were easy to obtain and no noticeable application of the mind was required to graduate, even with distinction. The tradition of legal writing, beyond textbooks, was still nascent. Colonial patterns of legal education, firmly in place for decades, made any alternative way of doing legal education almost inconceivable.

Legal education has now become available to women. Entry into the profession remains controlled at later stages by alternative mechanism. Although women were allowed open access to schools and employment around the turn of the century, on a national level they were not on an equal footing with men in family affairs. The Indian bias against women's education dates back to the colonial period, when only a minority of upper caste and middle class women were allowed access to formal education, and even then, they were confined to separate curricula, often focused on domestic skills and moral and religious education. Chandramukhi Basu (1860 – 1944) was a Bengali speaking Christian from Dehradun, which was located in the (then known as) United Provinces of Agra and Oudh, was one of the first two female graduates of the British Empire. Along with Kadambini Ganguly, she received her Bachelor's degree in Arts from the University of Calcutta in 1883. Miss

Chandramukhi Basu passed from Calcutta University in 1880, as a student of the Free Church Institution (now Scottish Church College) followed by bachelor's degree from Bethune College, an obtained the Master of Arts degree in 1884 at the University of Calcutta.

The year 1896 marks the beginning of a new era in the history of women's education in India when Dhondo Keshav Karve established an ashram for widows and helpless women at Hingne near Pune. 1916: The first women's university, SNDT Women's University, was founded on June 2, 1916 by the social reformer Dhondo Keshav Karve with just five students. In 1917, Annie Besant became the first female president of the Indian National Congress. While in 1919: Pandita Ramabai became the first Indian woman to be awarded the Kaiser-i-Hind by the British Raj for her distinguished social service. In1925, Sarojini Naidu became the first Indian born female president of the Indian National Congress. While in 1927, the All India Women's Conference was founded.

Before 1855 there was no formal legal education for legal officers and lawyers in the country when Sir Erskine Perry, the then Chief Justice of the Supreme Court of Bombay used to lecture on law after court hours. These classes were on a very informal basis and were attended only by a select group of people. A conscious effort was made by a committee to collect funds in order to institute a chair in Jurisprudence at the Elphinstone Institute. This was to be called the Perry Professorship of Jurisprudence, which came to be in 1855. In 1855, Dr. R.T.Reid, (L.L.B. Bar-at-Law and the first Judge of the Small Causes Court, Bombay) was appointed the first Perry Professor and the Government Law School (GLS), was established. The response to the first series of lectures conducted was overwhelming. The Government of India instituted two permanent professorships. The Government Law School was affiliated with the University of Bombay since 1860.From 1855 to 1895 the numerical strength of the GLS grew from 46 to 250 students. However, the first lady to fight for her rights, Ms. Cornalia Sorabjee, in 1897 acquired special permission from the University Senate to sit for the examination. In the past two decades, in India, women have entered the profession in dramatic numbers. But, the Indian bias against women's education dates back to the colonial period, when only a minority of upper caste and middle class women were allowed access to formal education. Even then, they were confined to separate curricula, often focused on domestic skills and moral and religious education. In India, until 1924, no lady students were admitted to the rolls of the Government Law School, as women were then disqualified from being enrolled as legal practitioners in India. However, the first lady to fight for her rights, Ms. Cornelia Sorabjee, in 1897 acquired special permission from the University Senate to sit for the examination. This gender bias was ultimately removed by a resolution moved by Dr. Harisingh Gour in the Legislative assembly on February 1, 1922.

In 1961, the Parliament of India passed the *Advocates Act*, which amended and consolidated the law governing the Indian legal profession. The Act provided for the establishment of an All India statutory body called 'The Bar Council of India'. The Bar Council was made responsible for recognizing Universities whose degree in law would be qualification for a graduate's enrollment as an 'advocate', a lawyer qualified to practice law in all courts and tribunals. In 1965 The Bar Council of India introduced stringent legal education standards - including curricular specifications - designed to prevent the mushroom growth of sub-standard law schools. Since 1951 there has been a steady growth of women in university level institutions and colleges in India. While over the years there has been a steady rise in the proportion of women entering university. The number of women studying law is on the rise... In Mumbai, women form 60-65 percent of students in law colleges. It was 35-40 percent in the early '90s.[214]But the wide gap between women and men entering university persists.

Compared to boys, far fewer girls are enrolled in the schools, and many of them drop out. But, according to UGC records approximately 2, 98,000 law students enroll every year, but if we consider the dropouts and students failing every year, the number of graduates is much lower.[215] So, though women may gain admission in law, but the chances are not continuing the same. Gender discrimination still persists in India and lot more needs to be done in the field of women's education in India. The gap in the male-female literacy rate is just a simple indicator. While the male literary

---

214 Karnad, Raghu; "Women in Law,"24th December, 2007.<http://www.outlookindia.com/printarticle.aspx?236336> on 5th March, 2009.

215 "Legal outsourcing hype: can India deliver?,"*Value Notes Outsourcing Weekly*, Vol. III No. 40, October 06, 2006, New Delhi. <http//: www.sourcingnotes.com/content/view/202/92/> on 5th March, 2009.

rate is more than 75 percent according to the 2001 census, the female literacy rate is just 54.16 percent. A woman can hardly ever choose... She is dependent on what happens to her. She must take meaner things, because only meaner things are within her reach.

Masculinity theories of career stress and the importance of the traditional male pattern of linear progression from the start of one's career to its finish, occur on a full-time basis and without interruption. Using some of the women in the study as examples, the researcher has tried to demonstrate how women's lives do not easily conform to this ideal; the more they depart from this model, the greater the career consequences. Study highlights the influence of large law firms on establishing these expectations, because it is here where norms relating to time are formed and are most heavily policed. Many women lawyers face pervasive limitations of opportunity or encounter obstacles in their chosen profession. Some leave the practice of law altogether, or seek other career avenues.

Radical feminist talked about degradation in a social sense. In a social sense they seem to see degradation as existing over a broad spectrum of society in which everything that men do, from opening doors for women to sexual assault, reinforces their view of men as "dominating." The concept of patriarchy that is prevailing in professional bodies provides for the collective domination of men over women. Feminist writer Alison M. Jaggar describes her view as one in which "almost every man/woman encounter has sexual overtones and typically is designed to reinforce the sexual dominance of men."[216]

Women members constitute 15 percent of the Supreme Court Bar Association and their number is steadily rising. Women make up 50 percent of graduates of the elite National Law School in Bangalore. More and more women are graduating from the law schools as well as from the law colleges spread in different parts of India. Based on the latest estimates, India today has over 500 law schools, 6 million attorneys and up to 200,000 new law students graduating every year. Thus, the numbers of Indians with legal training vary widely, ranging from 1.5 million to as

---

216 "Radical Feminism," < http://www.feministissues.com/radical_feminism.html> on 5th May 2009.

many as 6 million. What is clear is that Indians share with their American counterparts a common business language (English) and the heritage of British common law. Conducted entirely in English, legal education in India follows a structure similar to that in the U.S., typically involving a one, two or three-year diploma or graduate program. [217]

Though, women's representation in most national law schools are on the rise , yet very few women law graduates represent amongst the partners of law firms. They tend to congregate at the lower scale of earnings. Often they are confined to less interesting work. While males push their way forward into partnerships and higher salaries, women tend to cluster just below the glass ceiling. It is not uncommon for them to get favoured pathways to promotion. Discrimination postulates in legal inequality like unequal salaries for similar work, unequal treatment in work, in unequal expectations etc. Especially vital is the control by men in most of the key positions in dominant social structures: like government, state bureaucracies, corporations, professional bodies like law firms and corporate houses.

Men are expected to exhibit masculine behaviours and women to exhibit feminine behaviours, though in practice few people fit their gender stereotypes in all ways and circumstances. The masculine values are the ones valued most highly for positions of power, and people (men or women) in such positions are expected to behave appropriately. At the same time, actual masculine or feminine behaviour patterns are used to justify men holding powerful positions and women remaining in subordinate positions.

The study explores on women, their pressures from inadequate sleep, inadequate time to spend with children and/or husbands, and inadequate time for themselves. These women tell a familiar story: they work as long (or longer) than their partners/husbands on their jobs and are nevertheless the ones with primary responsibility for their children and homes. Although some women attempted to reduce the time crunch by easing their professional life burden, in doing so, they naturally faced a reduction in compensation. The research in conclusion draws that

---

217 "Legal Outsourcing to India," <http://www.delhilaw.firm.in/articlenews/legal_outsourcing_ india.htm> on 7th May 2009.

workplace norms in these firms are heading in the opposite direction to changes promoted by feminists, bar associations, law societies and many advocates of social justice. Despite much marketing and fanfare about their family-friendly policies, many large law firms have steadily increased their billable-hour requirements and their emphasis on open-ended availability. Further, these time norm have slowly seeped into other types of practice.

It is noticed that time is gendered, as men have a great deal more freedom from nonprofessional obligations than women do. The study examines the way the legal profession treats women in great detail, observing that the legal establishment tends to ignore women's family obligations. Access to time "is a critical component of social capital that guarantees professional success", and because women have less time, and hence less "social capital," they are generally found in lower status jobs and receive less pay for their work. Although women's family responsibilities may affect their status as legal professionals, 'discriminatory practices' are primarily responsible for the salary and partnership gaps between the sexes.[218]

While over the years there is a steady rise in the proportion of women entering university, the wide gap between women and men entering university persists. This is greatly reflected when we analyse the access to quality education. In India, the emerging middle class tend to send their boys to private educational institutions to ensure access to higher quality education whereas the girls are sent to the local government-funded school where quality of the education and the relevance of the curriculum may be of doubtful relevance. Lack of legal education has reflected that there has been under -representation of women not only in access to education but also as a faculty in law making institutions. The disillusionment with law in the struggle to end oppression of women and the aspiration of social justice may also be a cause for less number of women opting for law as a career. This is the tragedy with legal education.

The gap in the male-female literacy rate is a simple indicator. While the male literary rate is more than 75percent according to the 2001 census, the female literacy

218 Leiper, McKenzie Jean; *Bar codes: Women in the Legal Profession,* UBC Press, 2007, Vancouver, p. 256.

rate is just 54.16 percent.[219] According to UGC records approximately 2, 98,000 law students enroll every year, but if we consider the dropouts and students failing every year, the number of graduates is much lower. So far around 6, 00, 00 are estimated to enroll every year .While 79,000 law students are estimated to graduate every year. [220] The data is shown in Table 3.4. The data in Table-3.5 reflect decadal growth in Universities and colleges. The highest representation of women was in education. During the year 2000-2001, more than 50 percent of women were in education. This is followed like disciplines like Arts and Medicine. The data on women's enrollment from 1950 to 2000-01 is shown in Table- 3.6.

There were also wide national variations in the type of education. In 1995-96 women comprised 40.6 percent in the faculty of Arts .While in the year 2000-2001 it increased to 44.2 percent. In 1995-96 women comprised 37 percent in the faculty of Science .While it increased to 39.4 percent in the year 2000-2001 In 1995-96 women comprised 39.8 percent in the faculty of Medicine. While in the year 2000-2001 it increased to 44 percent. In 1995-96 women comprised 32.5 percent in the faculty of Commerce and Management. While in the year 2000-2001 it increased to 36.5 percent. In 1995-96 women comprised 16.8 percent in the faculty of Law. While in the year 2000-2001, there was a marginal increase to 20 percent. In 1995-96 women comprised 14.3 percent in the faculty of Agriculture .While in the year 2000-2001 it increased to 17.4 percent. [221] The data in Table -3.7 tell us only about women's entry into university courses. It is thus clear that professional courses like Medicine and Management are more preferred than Law.

---

219 "Women's Education in India,"< http://www.indiaedu.com/education-india/women-edu.html> on 5th Sep.2009.

220 "Legal Outsourcing Hype: can India Deliver?" 6th October, 2007.<http://www.sourcingnotes.com/content/view/202/92/> on 9th Sep.2009.

221 "Salient Observations , Growth in women's enrollment in different faculties," <http://www.insaindia.org/Scienceservice/Chapter%20I.HTML>

TABLE 3.4

LAW STUDENTS ENROLLED EVERY YEAR

Profession	Total Number	Graduates Every Year
Lawyers	6,00,000	79,000*
Engineers	5,20,000	3,50,000
Doctors	6,00,000	18,000
PhD	NA	4,400

*According to UGC records approximately 2, 98,000 law students enroll every year, but if we consider the dropouts and students failing every year, the number of graduates is much lower.

Source: "Value Notes: Reports on Legal Outsourcing Source to India," 6th October, 2007.

TABLE 3.5

DECADAL GROWTH IN UNIVERSITIES AND COLLEGES

Year	University /university level Institutions	Colleges
1950-51	32	695
1960-61	56	1,542
1970-71	102	3,604
1980-81	133	4,722
1990-91	190	7,346
2000-01	256	12,806

Source: "Study and Practice of Science by Indian Women," *Science and Service.* <http://www.insaindia.org/pdf/chapter1.pdf>

TABLE 3.6

DECADAL GROWTH IN WOMEN'S ENROLLMENT

Year	Total	% Women
1950-51	3,96,745	10.9
1960-61	10,49,864	16.2
1970-71	19,53,700	22.0
1980-81	27,52,437	27.2
1990-91	49,24,868	29.2
2000-01	83,99,443	39.4

Source: "Study and Practice of Science by Indian Women," Science and Service, <http://www.insaindia.org/pdf/chapter1.pdf>

TABLE 3.7

UNIVERSITY ENROLLMENT IN DIFFERENT FACULTIES

Faculty	**Year**	**Women**	**Year**	**Women**
Arts	1995-96	40.6%	2000-01	44.2%
Science	1995-96	37%	2000-01	39.4%
Medicine	1995-96	39.8%	2000-01	44%
Commerce/Management	1995-96	32.5%	2000-01	36.5%
Law	1995-96	16.8%	2000-01	20%
Agriculture	1995-96	14.3%	2000-01	17.4%
Others	1995-96	35%	2000-01	37.7%

Source: "Study and Practice of Science by Indian Women," Science and Service, <http://www.insaindia.org/pdf/chapter1.pdf>

In India teacher student ratio vary from 1: 25 to 1:152 in university law departments with an average around 1:50; in law colleges it is worse. In Britain the ratio is 1: 14 almost uniformly in all university law departments. More than 70 percent law teachers in India are par time teachers with 40 percent as having done no research whatsoever.[222] And the contributing factor is the dearth of women in law academia. The percentage of female law faculty has not increased as quickly as the percentage of female law students. This analysis helps us to explore the lives of those at the bottom of multiple hierarchies. To determine how the dynamics of each hierarchy compounds the consequences of another.

a. Total number of students admitted for legal education every year for 2000-01:63,381 (figures beyond the year 2001 are not available).

b. Total number of law graduates admitted to the bar every year in

- 2002: 28,268.
- 2003: 33,657.
- 2004: 46,438.

(Figures for the year 2005 and 2006 are not available).

c. Total numbers of institutions (all inclusive) teaching law as on October 31, 2006: 750.

d. Total number of Government institutions: 153.

e. Total number of Private institutions: 586

f. Total number of National Law School Universities ("NLSU") as on October 31, 2006: 11.

g. Total number of students admitted to the NLSUs in 2006: 936.[223]

Contrary to the popular perceptions and media representations, the bulk of lawyers work does not occur in a courtroom; indeed very little of their work entails preparing for or undertaking litigation. Normally, the tasks lawyers perform include:

---

222 Snyder, Frederick E.and Sairathai, Surakiart; "Third World attitudes toward international law : an introduction," *International and Comparative Law Quarterly*, Vol.38, Cambridge University Press, 1989, pp.440-441.

223 "Report of the Working Group on Legal Education," National Knowledge Commission, India <http://www.knowledgecommission.gov.in/> on 5th Sep.2009.

(a) Offering advice regarding citizens' responsibility, entitlements and rights;

(b) Settling disputes either in or out of courts or other tribunals;

(c) Court work, which entails prosecution or defense of persons accused of criminal offences and representing clients' interests in civil litigation;

(d) Representing clients' – both corporate and individual – interests in various negotiations;

(e) Drawing up legal documents, including contracts, statutes and articles of association for corporations and voluntary organizations.

When the Bar Council of India introduced the five-year curriculum, it did not think that it was going to abolish the three-year LLB programme, which did not attract the right type of students, nor could it give to the students the seriousness of a professional. Therefore, today, mainstream legal education is the five-year LLB. There are some universities or colleges, which are continuing with both the three-year and the five-year courses, to accommodate those who want to study law after their graduation.

The improvements which are contemplated in legal education are difficult to be organised in the three-year curriculum, for two-three reasons: one, the duration is short; two, generally, it is not a residential programme; and three, it is usually offered as a part-time course in the evenings, like in the Delhi University, which offers two evening courses, apart from its morning courses. In a couple of hours in the evening, one cannot impart to students an education, which is skill and research based.

So, the improvements that national law schools have brought about in legal education are: one, to enable the students to understand law in a social context. It is important to understand social realities while studying sociology, political science, economics etc related to law, so that family law, criminal law etc are understood better; through political science, one can understand public law better. That is the integrated knowledge which law is which the national law schools attempted in their five-year curriculum. The second is that given the longer duration and time, they could introduce the concept of clinical teaching, which of course is also attempted in the three year LLB, but with limitations. In the five-year course, there is enough time to give students a project to do in every subject, and teach a larger number of subjects. In national law schools, on an average, about fifty subjects are taught, whereas in any other three-year course, not more than thirty subjects can be accommodated. Given the possibilities of innovation, experimentation and creativity, students enrolled for a five-year LLB are more motivated and have longer time to devote, so the possibilities of quality improvement are definitely higher.

But when the five-year course was started and these innovations were introduced, it had a natural impact on the three-year course as well. So if the three-year course has improved over the last few years, the reason is the national law schools.[224]

Fifth, it is a statistical anomaly that about 50percent of first degree students in many countries in the world are women while the percentage of full professorship usually is below 15 percent (Rees 2001). Therefore, the question must be raised as to why few women are appointed to full professorship. In addition, why women are so under represented in the upper strata of higher education like law despite equity legislation and the increased participation of women in education and in legal profession.

- The faculty of Law has contributed generously in the establishment of Punjab University as one of the attractive educational institutes in India. Punjab University came into existence in 1882 at Lahore, now in Pakistan. The University has more than 55 teaching and research departments and 122 affiliated colleges.[225]
- In 2005 batch, out of 331 students, 115 were girls.
- In 2006, out of the 344 law students, 123 were girls.
- In the current batch of LLB at Punjab University, out of the total strength of 339 students, 106 are girls.

---

224 Prof. Menon, Madhav; *Halsbury Monthly, Lexis Nexis*, April, 2009< http://www.halsburys.in/ emphasise-the- international-law-component.html > on 5th Sep.2009.

225 "Faculty of Law," Punjab University, <http://www.indiaedu.com/admissions/law-colleges/punjab-univ-law.html> on 2nd January, 2009.

- Patna Law College, which is under Patna University, has 11 full- time teachers out of which there is only one women teacher.[226]

- While in West Bengal, in Hazra Law College, Kolkata, there are 8 full time teachers out of which there are only 2 full-time women teachers.

- Jogesh Chandra Choudhary College has 6 full time law teachers out of which 3 are women.

- Surendranath Law College and South Calcutta Law College, two state-aided colleges affiliated to Calcutta University, has less than 10 full-time teachers.[227]

- While the National University of Juridical Sciences has very few women faculty in law though in most cases women faculties are well informed about their subject and good knowledge in departing education.

3.4.1. WOMEN IN THE PROFESSION

In India, there are over eight lakhs practicing lawyers after the United States.[228] Our country has the second largest legal profession in the world. But how are lawyers and the judicial system in India perceived today? It is no secret that the very thought of facing the courts in India leaves the common man with a sense of dread and despair; cases drag on interminably, and justice sometimes seems like an afterthought.

Many students have seldom considered legal Profession as the first choice. Very often, the value of the study of law is not really understood till quite late. Many drift into law either because they are related to some one who is doing well in the legal profession or because they have nothing else to do. They feel that a law degree can help them to get a good job in a commercial organization; or if nothing else, they can enroll themselves as advocates and start practicing. While doing so, many still look for an alternative career because of the initial frustration for not being able to

---

226 "Patna Law College," <http://www.patnauniversity.ac.in/PLC.htm> on 8th March 2009.

227 *Telegraph*, Kolkata, India, 18th March, 2009.

228 "India's Legal System: Can It Be Saved?," http:// www.easternbookcorporation.com/> on 8th March 2009.

make a significant headway at the Bar. Nevertheless, like medicine, engineering, and management, law is also a highly rewarding profession. But the tendency of a good student is to sit in joint examinations of medicine and engineering rather than in law entrance examinations. There are also instances of students getting admitted at the law course to enable them to continue to stay in the hostels, which provide highly subsided board and lodging.

What is necessary is to take a decision to choose law as a career instead of drifting into it as the last resort, and vigorously pursue the course. In fact, the crowd of drifters who could not make a mark in the profession has diluted the quality of legal profession. There are very few women who opt as a career in legal profession. In the state of West Bengal, there are disparities in matter of enrollments of men and women.The tendency is to go for teaching, nursing, medical profession and management.

In the year 2003, Andhra Pradesh had a total of 53,173 lawyers enrolled in the Bar. Out of which 46,660 were men and 6553 were women. Assam and Nagaland had a total of 8,438 lawyers, of which7, 255 were men and 1,183 were women. Delhi had a total of 26, 3,650 lawyers of which 22,500 were men and were women 3,650.The States of Jammu and Kashmir had a total of 2,516 lawyers of which 2,136 were men and 380 were women.[229] Most of the states did not have the data of women lawyers. The available data is given in Table -3.8.

229 "Statement of Total number of Advocates (Men & Women) enrolled with the State Bar Councils as on 31/3/2003," <Barcouncilofindia.nic.in/disk3/number_of_advocates> on 3rd August, 2007.

TABLE 3.8

STATEMENT OF TOTAL NUMBER OF ADVOCATES (MEN & WOMEN) ENROLLED WITH THE STATE BAR COUNCILS AS ON 31/3/2003

STATES TOTAL	MEN	WOMEN
1. **ANDHARA PRADESH** 53,173	46,620	6,553
2. **ASSAM, NAGALAND,** etc* 8,438	7,255	1,183
3. **BIHAR** 86,462	N.A.	N.A.
4. **CHHATISGARH** 11,403	N.A.	N.A.
5. **DELHI*** 26,150	22,500	3.650
6. **GUJARAT** 41,820	N.A.	N.A.
7. **HIMACHAL PRADESH** 4,197	N.A.	N.A.
8. **JAMMU & KASHMIR**** 2,516	2,136	380
9. **JHARKHAND** 2,033	N.A.	N.A.
10. **KARNATAKA** 48,265	N.A.	N.A.
11. **KERALA** 33,894	N.A.	N.A.

STATES TOTAL	MEN	WOMEN
12. **MADHYA PRADESH** 51,323	N.A.	N.A.
13. **MAHARASTRA & GOA** 75,152	N.A.	N.A.
14. **ORISSA** 33,341	N.A.	N.A.
15. **PUNJAB & HARYANA** 38,65	N.A.	N.A.
16. **RAJASTHAN** 34,485	N.A.	N.A.
17. **TAMIL NADU** 41,670	N.A.	N.A.
18. **UTTAR PRADESH** 2, 01,780	N.A.	N.A.
19. **WEST BENGAL** 52,201	N.A.	N.A.
TOTAL		8, 47,015

* As on September, 1999.
** As on 31/3/2001.

•(In some states data's regarding women are not available which is indicated as N.A.)

Source: 'Statement of Total number of Advocates (Men & Women) enrolled with the State Bar Councils' as on 31/3/2003. <Barcouncilofindia.nic.in/disk3/number_of_advocates>.

The legal profession has to meet the requirements of the society, which has entered into the 21st Century. A student of law has to deal with problems of diverse magnitudes and an Advocate has to be trained in professional skills to meet the challenges of globalization and universalisation of law. In spite of the medley of social legislations and the concern of the Indian Constitution for making better the lives of numerous women to have a right 'To live with human dignity as enshrined in Article 21 of the Constitution', women in India still continue to live under stress and strain of male domination that manifests itself in the form of various kinds of cruelties on them. Educationists and social scientists are increasingly veering around the view that persistent gender biases and oppression of women are rooted in post-independence. The struggle for equality and gender justice mounted on all fields and legal profession has been the handmade of dominant social structures.

The analysis in the above foregoing paragraph makes us conclude that there has been an absence of the female viewpoint in the enforcement of adjudicative process. Liberal feminist perspective advocate for reform of the discriminatory practices. Legislation that discriminates on its face between men and women must be reformulated to correct this impact. It is not enough to identify discrimination and recommend reforms. Such an approach should be adopted that equality of women can be achieved through the elimination of discriminatory practices with formal equal treatment.Women are required to participate in all activities while working shoulder to shoulder with men in the society particularly at the Bar.

To summarize, using the US, UK and India as examples, it can be concluded that women are inadequately represented in the higher professional positions.

3.5. A SUM UP

The chapter gives the following findings:

(i) Women required lawsuits against the legal establishment. These suits gradually brought about changes in the legal professional treatment in practice, hiring, and the job market.

(ii) In many countries women have greater difficulties in accessing education.

(iii) Throughout their careers they seem to face greater obstacles than many of their female colleagues in other fields.

(iv) The issues surrounding women in law and legal profession specifically, have however received some attention in recent years and from the available data, case studies and anecdotes it is possible to ascertain that women in face serious obstacles entering into and succeeding in law.

(v) Women were consistently rated negatively. The intensity of feeling against women varied with the size of the firm. However, discrimination showed varying faces to women job seekers, and each form had its consequences. Sometimes women were victim of discrimination and sometimes by the other statutes.

(vi) Prejudices and harassment can discourage women from pursuing or continuing careers in firms. Studies suggest gender discrimination to be not the only a cause of job dissatisfaction among women in firms, but also a significant predictor of women opting out of firms.

(vii) On an average female lawyer earn about less than male lawyers even between those having equivalent positions, experience, and qualifications. Studies show that qualified women are only half as likely as men to obtain partnership.

(viii) Women continue to face gender-based barriers once they enter the profession, and partly as a result, they are leaving the profession at significantly higher rates than their male peers. There are no scientific reasons for this gender gap except with some of the explanations presented earlier along a continuum from blatant (intentional, direct and overt) discrimination to unintentional (covert and sometimes indirect) discrimination.

(ix) International studies have established that men holding leading positions by far outnumbered women. Also men reach leading position faster than women too. From the above data an analysis can be drawn that women were elevated to judgeship at a lower and slower rate than men. In order to achieve real change, a change in attitude in society has to be achieved and not reluctant compliance only.

(x) Increasing number of women are entering into all these professions in similar numbers to men, less than 10 percent of those are wielding the greatest power and influence.

(xi) Women prefer to be mediators than to become judges, which might indicate that some women prefer a less gladiatorial approach to civil litigation.

(xii) Women everywhere in the world play a minor role in decision-making bodies such as quasi-judicial bodies, and extremely few make it to become 'high flyers' either in academia or industry. .

(xiii) The entry of women in the legal profession is a step in their emancipation yet whatever so far has been achieved is not enough.

(xiv) Despite the large numbers of women completing legal training and entering the profession, the numbers of women at senior levels in private practice, at the bar and in the judiciary remain significantly low than those of their male counterparts.

(xv) The main problem of 'leakage' thus occurs even before entry into the pipeline. The gender disparity amongst students is attributed to gender stereotyping that favours males in and factors that restrict young women's access to university education such as early pregnancies, teenage girls becoming mothers by the age of 19, forced or early marriage, a heavier domestic workload for daughters, and preference for son in some communities.

(xvi) While the enrollment of women in University education has expanded, the actual participation of women in practice is slower. The numbers of women studying law at university has remained stagnant at a low level for the past three decades.

(xvii) With the establishment of law schools in many states of India, there has been an attitudinal change towards the legal profession.

(xviii) Yet, professional courses like Medicine, Management /Commerce courses are more preferred than Law.

(xix) Research into social problems into the field of legal profession is at present limited to a few universities.

(xx) While there is the dearth of women in law academia in India, many law colleges do not have the total strength of law faculties.

(xxi) An institution of learning is basically known by its faculty members and also by facilitating the teachings of latest socially relevant and career oriented subjects as per norms of Bar Council of India and the University Grants Commission, more and more faculties are required to fulfill the need.

(xxii) The future ahead awaits most effective role of women at the Bar to eradicate social evils, superstitions, gender bias for motivating women at all levels from village to city.

CHAPTER - IV

PROFESSIONAL HAZARDS OF WOMEN LAWYERS

"The relationship between discourses of secularism and equality, between religion and women mutually constitute. Communities are defined with and through the identity of women while women are defined in through the identity of their communities. It is within this context of mutually constituting discourses that we are engaged in the discursive struggles to articulate the meaning and identity of both community and gender."

- Ratna Kapur and Brenda Cossman
"Communalising Gender/Engendering Community: Women, Legal Discourse and Saffron Agenda"
Economic and Political Weekly, 24th April, 1993

4. 1. AN OVERVIEW

In the previous chapter, we have observed the inequalities, disproportionate p number of women in legal education. In the present chapter we will focus in the professional hazards of women lawyers in Indian context. The researcher examines the reasons for the present situation of women lawyers, including discrimination, harassment, structural and cultural barriers.

Although, women are entering in law schools, yet very few women law graduates represent amongst the partners of law firms. They tend to congregate at the lower scale of earnings. While males push their way forward into partnerships and higher salaries, women tend to cluster below the glass ceiling. It is not uncommon for them to get favoured pathways to promotion. However, women leave the profession at a much higher rate than men, and they are clustered in the lower ranks of the profession. The study includes of the 'broken career syndrome' while the professional hazards has been discussed under the following headings:

Challenges

- Physical disadvantages
- Biological Factors
- Women professional as mothers
- Perception Attitudes towards women lawyers
- Existence of Glass Ceiling
- Networking
- Patriarchal Society

Incorporation of Standards

Lack of Infrastructure

The role of judges

Women as workers in the justice system

Gender Stereotyping

Disparity in Income

Harassment against women

Guidelines and Safeguards

4.2. CHALLENGES

Owing to cultural restrictions and family responsibility, women participation in the formal economy is limited. Some other concerns that affect working women relate to gender discrimination, quantum of payment, safety at work place, working hours and conditions of employment that are sensitive to cultural and religious bondages as well as family responsibilities. Indian legislature has been active on this front. Its main focus is on reducing inequality of any sort, and thereby promoting a fair, non-discriminatory and safe work environment.

Several legislations were brought to improve the working standards of women. One of them were thee *Equal Remuneration Act, 1976* which aims at providing equal remuneration to men and women workers and prevention of discrimination, particularity against women on the ground of gender. It provides that no discrimination should be made in remuneration for the same work or work of a similar nature only on the ground of gender vide Section 4.Further the Act also provides that no gender based discrimination be made while recruiting for the same work or work of a similar nature, or in any condition of service subsequent to recruitment such as promotions, training or transfer vide Section 5.But this act has an exception Under this law, no discrimination is permissible in recruitment and service conditions except where employment of women is prohibited or restricted by the law vide Section 15.

Despite sporadic criticism few progressive changes were made in the laws of the country. But the effect of these legislations could not reach the average women. One of the reasons was neglect in the reform of delivery of legal services. Very few women were enrolled as advocates to argue for their causes. Legal profession was in grip of male bastion. Legal language apparently showed discrimination. The word 'he' includes 'she'. This marginalization of women in legal language was her reflection of her marginalization in real life.[230] The legal language had been gendered which derived from the powerful patriarchal position enjoyed by men. Reforms in legal institutions and processes were thus not easy to accomplish. It required consistent and coordinative effort for a long period After India gained independence, educationists and social scientists viewed persistent gender bias and oppression on women rooted. They suggested that changes should come at the procedural level so that women can benefit from protective and welfare legislations.

It was found that many women lawyers had entered the Bar, but very few had achieved their goals. Many had dropped out unable to cope with the obstacles in the legal profession. They record many unhappy instances of stereotyping, prejudice, harassment and plain unfairness which does little credit to lawyers who have such an influential role in society and who are privileged to play a leading part as guardians of the rule of law and fundamental human rights. Of course, the cited instances represent only a small proportion of the profession. In the legal profession, woman commonly face which reinforces the difficulties are gender bias that persists. There may be

---

[230] Baxi, Upendra; *On being Women, in Mambrino's Helmet Human Rights for a Changing World*, Anand Publication, 1994, New Delhi, p.168.

improvements on the way. But the number and consistency of the complaints are disturbing. No lawyer should accept discrimination or avoidable injustice. Only few star performers with family background have become judges.

If we consider closely the role of lawyers in society, the increase in women's participation in the legal profession reflects important social changes and perceptions about women's role in society. Certain legislation must also provide for appropriate measures to make the life of women easy, particularly when they are employed, by making provisions such as paternity leave. A culture must develop whereby the burden of the family must be shared by both the parents equally. This applies to women who are employed in law firms, law teaching, and legal profession and also in judiciary. In legal profession though women practice independently but it requires long time to work in the Senior Counsels Chamber which otherwise is affected if the husband or the family do not cooperate with her.

Inevitably, many of the cases in the High Courts in India tend to involve big corporate firms and business houses. There are evidences that many of these have a bias towards briefing and engaging women lawyers. They often explain this fact on the basis of the defence that it represents their clients' expectations, not their own. Even senior women solicitors often seem to favour male advocates. It has been seen that women lawyers can provide services more effectively as provided by male counterparts. But such is the general mindset of the litigants. Males therefore represent the ordinary face of the Bar.

Both male and female lawyers face the reality. At least, they appear to revolve around the culture of the legal profession, especially that in the big firms. These are places where extraordinarily long hours of work are the norm. Men and women are expected to stay in the office. Some young women lawyers find difficult to cope with long hours of work. While those who become mothers find it difficult to stay in office where childcare facilities closes after 6 p.m.They have to work in offices, both before going to and after returning from the office. This means to carry out the household chores apart from attending to children and taking care of visitors. As long as there is no understanding and sharing of household work between men and women, the family is solely dependent on the women of the house. It is a kind of deprivation to the women, of leisure or time for pursuit of other interests in addition to reducing the burden of the family cares. Particularly where both the parents of the child are employed, the fact remains that the responsibility of the children is on both the parents and necessarily calls for sharing the burden. But the answer often faces resistance that the child instinctively looks to the mother rather than to the father.

4.2.1. PHYSICAL DISADVANTAGES

Woman's physical structure places her to a disadvantage in the struggle for subsistence. Her physical well-being becomes an object of public interest and care in order to preserve the strength and vigor of the race. This aspect assumes importance when we deal with the women's place at the Bar. Women are always considered as a symbol of sincerity, efficiency, tolerance, patience, and rationality. In spite of this, her success and satisfaction at the Bar is always controversial. She does not have the identity of an advocate as her brother advocate has; the latter identity is more appreciated even though both these segments of the Bar plead at time. This bifurcation of the bar is insignificant for the purpose of over all progress. Woman's physical structure and the performance places her to a disadvantage in the struggle for subsistence and her physical well-being becomes an object of public interest and care in order to preserve the strength and vigor of the race. This aspect assumes importance when we deal with the women's place at the Bar. Women are always considered as a symbol of sincerity, efficiency, tolerance, patience, rationality. In spite of this, her success at the Bar is often controversial. She does not have the identity of an advocate as her brother advocate has; the latter identity is more appreciated even though both these segments of the Bar plead at time.

It needs to be impressed upon the woman, that to begin well is great to win the minds of all which is an accomplishment. In every environment, ultimately, individual make all the difference. The place where the multitudes are at indefinable economic level, satisfaction is a far cry. In such place professional competition evils are always present and these causes raise eyebrows. Even after overcoming these difficulties the colleagues never treat her at par to her excellence. Her success is always treated in the way of sympathy leading to the discouragement of her professional spirits. All these things reflect in the behavioral pattern of the client ultimately ceasing her professional practice.

Due to the limitations of family bar, her inner qualities are curbed down, resulting into an in equilibrium in the professional ethics. Economic insecurity leads to social evil. It is incidental to social change, which is the response to the changing economic & political environment. Ironically the women advocates are fighting for the right to equality, liberty for their clients, from which they themselves are away in the professional practice. No doubt; procurement of work becomes more problematic for women lawyers. A woman cannot be as daring and outgoing as a man.

Instances of physical differences are based on gender while the others are entirely based on conventional, social and cultural differences. Like, many women lawyers complain that they find the masculine social networks alienating. Drinking and tipping that sometimes dominate social life in the top legal establishments is reported as off-putting. Cultural limitations, such as segregation of sexes, the effects of sex role behavior and attitude, make them unable to adopt such practices. In such a world, it is unsurprising that many women feel themselves as strangers.

Legislation that discriminates on its face between men and women must be reformulated to correct this impact. It is not enough to identify discrimination and recommend reforms. Such an approach should be adopted that equality of women can be achieved through the elimination of discriminatory practices. Equality, in this view, is equated with formally equal treatment.

Similarly, it is also not enough to draw attention to the under-enforcement of law, and recommend ways to ensure more efficient enforcement. The emphasis of this approach, which looks to increasing women's access and enforcement through such means as sensitizing the judiciary to women's issues, legal aid, family courts and increased legal awareness of women, if it is effectively enforced, can remedy these problems. Liberal feminist focuses on individual, and in particular on the equal treatment of individuals and demand that laws be reformed to better reflect and promote women's right to full and equal participation in the world around them.[231]

4.2.2. BIOLOGICAL FACTORS

The biological facts put the women in the disadvantages position. As career advancement and work-life balance continues to be elusive for women in the profession of law, the windows of opportunity opens and closes effectively in her late twenties and her thirties if she wants to have family life with children. After early training as a solicitor or lawyer and before it is too late, she must interrupt her career. The length of the interruption may depend on many factors. One of these may be escape from the culture of 'successful' lawyers. This reality has been the subject of casual conversations among women in the profession for many years. Men do not need to interrupt their professional career to have babies. They can work leaving such matters to their spouses or female partners. It becomes hectic for women lawyers and more demanding at the peak of the legal profession. The biological interruption and its aftermath of child caring and rearing, impose on women lawyers who have children are inescapable difficulties which most of their male counterparts do not experience.

In spite of all obstacles in the field some women lawyers have a reasonably high reputation in various aspects of practice, such as dealing with clients, drafting the cases and presentation in the Court. They also get work independently, especially when work comes on the basis of reputation and standing at the bar. The rest are those who cannot boast of such accomplishments as they stick to their patron seniors and hand over the work to be done. The more influential the patron, the greater the amount of work. Experiences show that women lawyers could deal with matters effectively. They have more avenues to excel and to undertake not only legal literacy but to train Para legal volunteers and legal awareness programmers to know their rights and assertion thereof.

---

231 Mukhopadhyay, Maitrayee and Singh, Navsharan; "Challenging the Liberal subject, Law and Gender Justice in South Asia," *IDRC*, New Delhi, 2007,p.124.

Some theorists propose Consciousness-raising as a central element in empowering the client and moving toward the substantive goal of ending the subjugation of women by demonstrating to the courts, among other things, how the law affects women's lives. In addition, feminist lawyers seek to empower their clients through litigation. MacKinnon's concern is to transform power relations through a feminist method, namely consciousness raising. She suggests that consciousness raising enables women to view the shared reality of their condition from within the perspective of their own experience. This grounding in experience permits a critique of the purported generality, disinterestedness, and universality of prior accounts. She seems to suggest that despite women's various experiences women's perspective transcends ideological distortion which will emerge through consciousness rising.[232]

4.2.3. WOMEN PROFESSIONAL AS MOTHERS

Woman lawyers, as mother, may come to realise that there can be other and more fulfilling goals in life than working seven days a week and being at the beck and call of case-managing judges and demanding clients.. Mothers may also select out of their jobs after childbirth because of lack of parental leave, flexible hours, or part-time work options, making it difficult to combine parenting and employment. Alternatively, women may view themselves as overcoming discrimination and stereotypes and working hard to demonstrate their capabilities in order to receive the same, or even fewer. Nevertheless managing multiple roles is highly stressful and often it so happens that women executives develop various health problems like headache, e.g., backache or eye strain. Some of them even fall prey to depression because of their inability to manage everything at the same time. However, a psychologist points out that the mindset of working women is changing and often each additional role brings increased self - esteem leading to a feeling of physical and mental well-being. Organizations, too are lending a helping hand to encourage them. A Human Resource professional says, "We offer flexi - time policies to all our female employees, help out in paying bills and have crèche facilities for their kids in our company premises." Times surely are changing. Rewards refer to this as 'raising the

232 Anleu, Sharen Roach; *Women in the legal profession-Theory and Researc,* Sociology Department, the Flinders University of SA, p.196. < http://docs.google.com/viewer.>on 3rd March 2010.

bar' for women in law such that a "unique and exceptional set of standards is imposed."[233]

But, along the way, however, many still find that they face pervasive limitations of opportunity or encounter obstacles in their chosen profession. All these lead us to conclude that the women can be described as a social collective. This dilemma not only treats women as a substance but also as a kind of entity in which some specific attributes inhere.

One classifies a person as a woman who has the essential attributes of woman characteristics which all women share: something about their bodies, their behaviour or dispositions as persons, or their experience of operations. This approach conceptualizes women as a collective and states attributes of a biological female. The content of these structures varies enormously from one social context to the next. Saying that a person is a woman may predict something about the general constraints and expectations she must deal with. But it predicts nothing in particular about who she is, what she does, how she takes up her social positioning and professional roles etc.[234]

Some leave the practice of law altogether, or seek other career avenues. The 'broken career syndrome' and the increasing number of women who opt for part-time work is said to put them out of favour with clients who want their lawyers at their beck and call twenty-four hours a day. As for the rest, in solicitors firms, at the Bar and in the judiciary, what is in need is a healthy dose of realism, more open minded discussion, more flexibility, to put an end of stereotyping women lawyers as second class. In the law schools, women gain more than their share of the top prizes. When they ultimately reach that central podium, women shine or they fade according to their talents and the merits of their clients' cases.

---

233 "Managing multiple roles," < http://www.paycheck.in/main/women-paycheck/articles/copy_of_managing-multiple-roles> on 10th March2010.

234 Young, Iris Marion; *Intersecting Voices: Gender as Seriality: Thinking about Women as a Social Collective,* Princeton University Press,U.S.A.,1997 pp. 12-13. <http://www.jstor.org/pss/3174775>.

4.2.4. PERCEPTION AND ATTITUDES TOWARDS WOMEN LAWYERS

Considering the less desirable working conditions and blocked career advancement, are women more likely than men to leave law practice? Research reveals that women are overrepresented in the exodus from law, suggesting what some writers term the 'flight from law'. Nelson's (1988) study of lawyers revealed that women are more likely to leave firms before making partner than are male associates. The turnover of women was highest among earlier cohorts of women. Of women associates hired from 1971 to 1975, only 35 percent remained in 1984 compared with 48 percent of all associates. The differential turnover declines with the next cohort; of those entering law from 1976 to 1980, 42 percent of women remained in 1984 versus 51 percent of the total cohort. Despite the improvement over time, the differential remained substantial throughout the period (Nelson 1988). Spurr & Sueyoshi (1994) analyzed two cohorts of U.S. lawyers (one cohort entered law firms between 1969 and 1973 and the other between 1980 and 1983). They found that over the entire sample period, women are considerably less likely to be promoted and slightly more likely to leave the law firm without being promoted. In contrast to Nelson's (1988) study, Spurr & Sueyoshi (1994) found little change in the gender differential of the turnover hazard, with the gap increasing slightly across cohorts. These new forms of discrimination, because they are so subtle and complex, are also more pernicious. Law firm principals often still believe a woman who takes advantage of a flexible work schedule or maternity leave should be accorded less respect than a male lawyer who works full-time. This is no less a product of bigotry than the 20th century notion that women are too emotional to practice law, or vote.[235]

In a longitudinal study of lawyers in Ontario, Kay (1997) found that women move out of law practice 60 percent more quickly than men and that small law firms appear to be the least successful in retaining female lawyers. Further, in a survey of Quebec lawyers, Kay (2002) found that women are more likely than their male colleagues to be actively searching for new employment outside the legal profession. Recent studies of law firms in the United States show that 9 percent of women had departed their firms within 16 months of being hired and that more than half (55

235 Kay, Fiona and Gorman ,Elizabeth; "Women in the Legal Profession,,"*Annual Review of Law and Social Science,*Vol. 4: December 2008,pp.299-332.

percent) had departed within four and one-half years of their start dates. What explains sex segregation among lawyers?

Research suggests that experiences at the workplace contribute to the gender divide. Although 50 percent of women coming out of the law schools are now women, yet 15 percent are equity partners and only 5 percent as managing directors.[236] There are a far lower percentage of women who are partners in large or mid-size firms. The reasons of not having women in the legal firms are clear. Firms listed the qualities quite unrelated to professional task. Women candidates with rural background were considered undesirable by law firms by varied sizes in all parts of the country. Women were consistently rated negatively. The intensity of feeling against women varied with the size of the firm, however. Discrimination showed varying faces to women job seekers, and each form had its consequences. Sometimes women were victim of discrimination and sometimes by the other statues. In view of the generally negative attitude toward women lawyers it was found to be randomly scattered across the spectrum of jobs offered by the legal profession.

For one, given the time-demanding nature of firms, women may shy away from firms, leave firms, or forgo partnership opportunities in firms so as to achieve better work-family balance. Such prejudice and harassment can discourage women from pursuing or continuing careers in firms: studies suggest gender discrimination to be not only a cause of job dissatisfaction among women in firms, but also a significant predictor of women opting out of firms. Generally negative attitude toward women lawyers was found to be across the spectrum of jobs offered by the legal firms.[237]

Although research has documented turnover among women lawyers, particularly from private practice, only a handful of studies have explored the factors precipitating the decision to leave. Brockman (1994) surveyed lawyers who had left the profession in British Columbia and found that the concerns expressed by women

236 "Flight of Female Lawyers in Canada, Mirrors US Exodus of Counsel," *Legal Practice and Management Report,* Vol.28, No.9, 2009. <http://www.bowmanandbrooke.com/CM/Publications> on 3rd March 2010.

237 "The Mission, Process and Report of the Special Committee: The Appraisal of the American Legal Profession in the year 2000," <http: //www.law.cornell.edu/ethics/mdp1.htm.> on 5th March 2009.

who had left legal profession include difficulties associated with combining family life and practice. Laband & Lentz (1998), analyzing Wave II (1990) of the ABA's National Survey of Career Satisfaction, found that sexual harassment and discrimination were triggers among women lawyers for lower overall job satisfaction and a greater intention to voluntarily exit their current employment context. In contrast, Wallace (2001) found in her interviews and survey of Calgary, Alberta, lawyers that women have a stronger desire to continue practicing law than men. Wallace further found that the presence of preschool children was not important in affecting lawyers' desire to leave law, a finding that is contrary to various studies suggesting that young children amplify the time demands and pressures of practicing law, especially for women. Walace suggests that her findings may reflect the growing use and ability of lawyers to pay for childcare and domestic services that may help alleviate childcare demands.[238]

There still remains a stereotypical attitude about women, held by both men and women. These attitudes are rarely disclosed or discussed. Some of them concern how women should dress, speak and engage with or manage others. Aggressive or abrasive qualities are not encouraged in women, yet are respected or accepted in some men. A woman lawyer has to do a job ten times better than her male counterpart. If a woman argues in a high pitch, she often gets to hear, "Do not get hysterical." "But if a man argues in the same tone, judges accept it as something normal."[239]

Women may be perceived as fragile or weak and their judgment or competency as a legal practitioner may be questioned as a result. Even matters such as height, voice pitch and tone and age impact upon attitudes to women. Such stereotypical assumption or view about women will amounts to less favorable treatment when linked to an adverse employment decision. Sex stereotyping has been defined as a process whereby decision-makers apply or impute various personality attributes and characteristics about women and measure other women by those standards.

---

238 Kay, Fiona and Gorman, Elizabeth; "Women in the Legal Profession," *Annual Review of Law and Social Science,* Vol. 4: December 2008, pp.299-332.

239 Sinha, Bhadra; "Few women judges in higher courts," *Hindustan Times*, 16th July 2007.

A further explanation for women's departures from law concerns violations of trust in the workplace. Kay & Hagan (2003) found in their surveys of lawyers that women were more likely to be excluded from important files, and this experience of being placed on the periphery of firm practice significantly increased women's subsequent intentions to quit the legal profession. Partnership ensured a greater degree of security and formal recognition of status, reducing women's probability of leaving law firms. But for men, it was not so much partnership as power, specifically authority and autonomy to delegate legal work and to direct policy-making decisions within the firm that reduced their inclinations to leave the firm.

Gender differences further surfaced through the impact of job satisfaction. Consistent with the differential values argument, Kay & Hagan (2003) found that whereas the intent to leave the firm for men was influenced by their satisfaction with firm promotion opportunities, pay, job security, and benefits, for women plans to leave the firm were more strongly influenced by lack of intrinsic rewards, including limited opportunities to demonstrate legal skill and to attain a sense of accomplishment through the practice of law. Dissatisfaction in law practice takes its toll, manifesting itself through a loss of legal talent from the profession—a loss more often incurred by women's attrition from law practice.[240]

According to the report, women face their strongest opposition to change in the culture of big law firms not only from the old lawyers but also from young male lawyers who are most resistant to the partnerships and other flexible working arrangements that are often needed to find a space for women in senior legal practice. Hence, lack of equal opportunity for women lawyers in the big firms puts them in disadvantage position. Gaining equal opportunity will require a new balance between professional work and personal lives. Any change will have to confront deep-seated work practices in the law. All sorts of unconvincing excuses have been offered over the years for these practices. Women it was said were shorter in stature and might not be seen. They have high-pitched voices that did not carry in Indian courtrooms. What an unconvincing excuse that is, second only to the old excuse that there are insufficient female toilets to allow the appointment of women judges. Then it is said

---

[240] Kay, Fiona and Gorman, Elizabeth; "Women in the Legal Profession," Annual Review of Law and Social Science, Vol. 4: December 2008, pp.299-332.

women have fewer mentors than their male counterparts. They find it more difficult to break into the big time. Judges too are sometimes blamed for insensitivity, as for example in pressing the hearing of cases beyond the normal court hours without regard to the needs of women advocates, in particular, to attend to their family responsibility. Yet if complaint is made about such practical problems, women advocates may be denounced as grizzlier who would not, or could not, face up to the practical necessities of life in a gruelling profession.[241]

Women's careers are confronted with choices that most men's are not. As a result of this commitment, combined with fewer advancement opportunities, law firms and corporate legal departments are more likely to lose their female lawyers. Fortunately, this is preventable if employers attempt to make a change. Until women are granted equal opportunities in the legal profession, employer retention of women will become increasingly more challenging and sacrificial.

4.2.5. EXISTENCE OF GLASS CEILING

Recent discussion suggests the existence of dual career structures and 'glass ceilings', restrict women's opportunities for promotion. For example, in the United States, women who take advantage of flexible working hours, maternity and child care provisions offered by some law firms may be disadvantaged in promotion decisions and relegated to the 'mommy track'. Many others decide to leave because of incompatibility between motherhood and law. Changes in the structure of the profession are benefiting men more than women. Aggregate statistics showing women's greater participation in the legal profession obscure gender segmentation within the occupation. A simple comparison of men and women according to broad areas of practice and employment obscures differences in the types of work they perform in different organizations or within the same organization, for that matter.

Glass ceiling is an invisible barrier that determines the level to which a woman can rise in a practice. It prevents women from occupying leadership positions in the practice. It is generally based on attitudinal or organizational biasness. There are

---

241 Kirby, Justice Michael; 'Women in the Law - What Next?' <http://www.hcourt.gov.au/speeches/kirbyj/kirbyj_vicwomen.htm>.on 2nd July 2008.

many signs that make the glass ceiling visible in the organizations. A major sign of the same is the difference in compensation of women. Women practitioners are paid far less that their male counterparts.

Another indicator of the glass ceiling is when women's advancement is hampered by the corporate culture. For example, corporate policies and practices can maintain the status quo by keeping men in positions of corporate power. Stating that women outperform in care taking qualities while men outperform in taking charge qualities, is how the corporate vindicate this biasness. Despite better performances, women receive less approval and recognition from their male bosses and are slower to be promoted. Such stereotypes act as main reasons of why women fail to reach to the top in an organization.

An increasing number of women are proving that when it comes to taking up the corporate challenges, they have much more than just a pretty face to show. However, there are factors that hamper their growth within the organization. Firstly, work-life balance challenges impact women's advancement and, if not dealt with at the right time, may contribute to the glass-ceiling phenomenon. Assumptions are often made regarding women's availability to do a job without interference from family responsibilities. Secondly, higher roles ask for higher commitments, which may include working more than 40 hours of work per week. Those who put in longer hours generally rise faster, leaving those behind who are unable to dedicate more hours to work due to family responsibilities.

There are stunning statistics which elude the corporate world. According to a recent study, only 26.1 percent of the listed companies (392 of 1,500 firms) have a woman on their boards. Out of the 278 directors on the BSE Sensex companies, there are only 10 women directors. Apart from this, women executives in India earn 40 percent less than what men earn over their entire career. Even when compared to global counterparts, corporate India stands below average. Over 77 percent of the 200 largest companies in the world, as ranked by Fortune, had at least one women director on their board as of 2006. Only 36 percent of Indian companies have women holding senior management positions as compared to 91 percent of companies in China. These figures force us to ponder on how successful women have been in breaking the glass ceilings.

Another issue is the double bind that women face when it comes to leadership behavior. The research shows that when a woman is assertive and takes charge, people often react negatively, but if she fulfils the prescribed stereotype of being a kind and gentle woman, she may be regarded as a poor leader. These factors often act as obstacles thereby barring women from climbing up the corporate ladder.

Finally, women's entrepreneurial success in smaller companies has been ignored and appears to carry less value in comparison with senior roles in traditional and larger corporate settings.[242]

4.2.6. NETWORKING

Networking is a very important aspect of progressing in a Legal career especially those who practice in the Bar. However women may find it difficult to break into networks that are strongly male dominated because they do not feel welcome there, because they do not have the time for socializing after regular work hours or are less able to travel to attend conferences because of other competing commitments. Women judges and women lawyers attribute male-domination of the judiciary in large part to the exclusion of women from the networks that influence judicial appointments. Women lawyers attribute the small number of women appointed to bench and bar committees to the exclusion of women from formal and informal selection processes. A large proportion of women lawyers believe that men have a better chance than women to be promoted to law firm partnerships and to equivalent positions in public law organizations.

4.2.7. PATRIACHAL SOCIETY

Radical feminism is a philosophy emphasizing the patriarchal roots of inequality between men and women, or, more specifically, social dominance of

---

242 "More women CEOs in India than U.S.," *siliconindia news bureau*, Monday, 30th November 2009,<http://www.siliconindia.com/shownews/India_conservative_More_women_CEOs_in_Ind ia_than_US-nid-63352.html>on 4th May,2008.

women by men. Radical feminism views patriarchy as dividing rights, privileges and power primarily by gender, and as a result oppressing women and privileging men. It is also believed that irrespective of their sex, caste or religious placements, the people who indulge in gender injustice are under the influence of patriarchy. The problem in the patriarchal society is not only on the ground of biological functions but also the misinterpretation of values prescribed to males and females. It is absolutely agreeable that because of our society's patriarchal nature, women status is lower than men. When we look into the problems we can find some other reasons other than this but the character of patriarchy is involved in some or the other to every reason. Gender inequalities have been created in the household's affairs and in the societies and are commonly portrayed as among the most oppressed. Majority of them are grounded in both poverty and patriarchy. Patriarchy limits women's ownership and control of property and other economic resources including the products of their own labour. Based on this analysis Kapur and Crossman noted the following: "Though there has been a decadal growth in women's enrollment but within the framework of constitutional law, equality rights have not always been receptive to women's claims. Dominant understandings of gender differences often operate to preclude any substantive interrogation of this disadvantage."[243]

Patriarchal societies propagate the ideology of motherhood which restrict women's mobility and burdens them with the responsibilities to nurture and rear children. The biological factor to bear children is linked to the social position of women's responsibilities of motherhood: nurturing, educating and raising children by devoting themselves to family. "Patriarchal ideas blur the distinction between sex and gender and assume that all socio-economic and political distinctions between men and women are rooted in biology or anatomy" (Heywood, 2003: 248).Gender like social class, caste, race or religion is a significant social cleavage and it is important to analyze it to understand social inequalities, oppressions and unequal relationship between men and women. It has been explained by feminist scholars / thinkers/ writers who believe that the theory of 'sexual politics' and 'sexism' are conscious parallels with

---

243 Cossman, Brinda; "Gender Equality and the Dilemma of Difference," 28 *Osgoode Hall L. J.* 303 (1990), Hein Online, < http://heinonline.org/> on 4thFebruary2010.

Since in the Indian context questions of cultural identity, difference, plurality and diversity have been important, some Indian feminists in their effort to counter attacks of being western have turned out to "Hindu iconography and Sanskrit idioms denoting women's power, thus inadvertently strengthening communal identity that Indian, Hindu and Sanskrit are synonymous." Flavia Agnes critiques such feminist groups.[244] Maitrayee Chaudhuri also argues that in India the battle for recognition of 'difference' had to be worked out independently without the accepted terminology of today's western feminism or multiculturalism. "Within the Indian sub-continent there have been infinite variations on the status of women diverging according to cultural milieu, family structure, class, caste, property rights and morals" (Thapar, 1975). Therefore despite several debates and discussion on Indian women's movement there have been no clear ideological lines drawn and no major trends have emerged.

In fact, the women's issues taken up in the women's movement since 1975 have arisen out of the movement itself and have been taken up by women's groups representing all ideologies and tendencies. The effort to characterize the specificity of women's oppression and to analyze the links with other forms of social oppression is more an ongoing theoretical research rather than an ideological dividing line. In India almost all feminists agree that women's movement has to be linked to broader movements against all kinds of social oppression. While in the West there have been a wide variety of feminist positions, from those stressing male power and sexual dominance to 'Marxist –Feminist' positions stressing social production, in India it has been mainly the Marxist who have dealt with the issue of women's oppression and subjugation though there have been varying approaches.[245]

4.3. INCORPORATION OF STANDARDS

Several bar reports have identified some other difficulties faced by women advocates. These included the incorporation of standards of equal opportunity in the professional rules of the Bar. There are sometimes reports of obscene conduct and even harassment targeted at young women lawyers. An old curmudgeon may mean no

---

244 Agnes, Flavia; *Law and Gender Inequality*, Oxford University Press, New Delhi, 1999, p.67.

245 Ray,Suranjita; "Understanding Patriarchy," University of Delhi, Delhi.pp.2-5. <du.ac.in/course/material/ug/ba/hrge> on 7th March 2010.

great harm by telling a young women lawyer that she is nice to look at professional parties or playing the role of home maker. But such personal behaviours would not be something he would dare attempt with male counterparts. Reports of such harassment come from time to time to the attention of the judges, mainly from the young female associates who are shocked that, for peace-sake, the targets all too often accept such behaviour without complaint.

Apart from this, several bar reports have identified many of the difficulties faced by women advocates. It collected a number of practical suggestions. These included the incorporation of standards. They also included support for women advocates by relief from fees for chambers and clerks during absence because of pregnancy. A major step forward in this area would be the provision of a tax deduction for working mothers who can only keep up their earning capacity by paying for childcare. This would seem a reasonable contribution for society to make if we are serious about responding to the constant loss of highly trained female professionals. Their departure from the workforce comes at an economic cost to the country. Making it easier for women lawyers to stay in work is in the country's interest. Pregnancy leave is not enough. Children make unrelenting demands for many years after birth. Most of those demands fall on women. If they are professional women, the need for childcare is no luxury.

'Dobbing' is alien to the professional culture of the law. It has also been reported that male lawyers try to cut humour about female colleagues and others. There are lawyers who constantly crack jokes. However, to litigants courtrooms are deadly serious places. It is a place for litigants who visit their counsels to be taking their problems seriously. A little humor can help. Humor amongst colleagues can certainly help in private dialogues. Humor has its place. In a professional world, whatever the stresses, people are expected to control their conduct in such matters. But there are some things in life, including important decisions, which are serious, solemn and have to be taken as such.[246]

---

[246] Kirby, Justice Michael; "Women in the Law - What next?,"<http://www.hcourt.gov.au/speeches/kirbyj/kirbyj_vicwomen.htm> on 2nd July 2008.

In the male-dominated society, the attitude that the girl child be denied the right to be born, has to undergo a fundamental change. While law can be remodeled from anti-woman stance, society has to move to sincere action beyond mere tokenism of reservation of seats for women in panchayats, municipalities and even in Parliament. The hard task is social transformation by which a girl is given an equal opportunity of survival and development so that she becomes an adult partner in the country's development. Courts can only show the way but ultimately it is public opinion that must uphold the rights of women.

Despite the large numbers of women completing legal training and entering the profession, the numbers of women at senior levels in private practice, at the bar and in the judiciary remain significantly low than those of their male counterparts. Discrimination occurs, not merely because women are actively excluded from senior positions, but because of various social pressures and preconceived notions about women and how the legal profession operates. To date, very little has been done to develop methods to assist the profession to identify and then eliminate practices that may operate as barriers to women's equal participation From being perceived as a last resort for those who failed to get admission elsewhere, law has now become a career that needs preparation even at school-level both for men and women. Practical side of legal education, such as visiting advocates' offices, studying court diaries, case bundles, dealing with actual clients and court visits should be given better attention by education planners were women lawyers should be more focused.

In the other wings, for e.g. in judiciary, there are many in the Bench who consider women as subordinate to men, women as instruments of man's comfort and pleasure. They cannot accept anything contrary. So when they see a woman filing a petition for maintenance or seeking shelter from the husband who batters her, they immediately become hostile to her. More so, if a woman's organization is seen as supporting her case, the anger raises more and the resentment towards that woman's action of reaching out to a court becomes obvious. It reflects in the pronouncements from the dais so that the men in the court smile and sneer while women are made to feel belittled and harassed. In such atmosphere, legal proceedings continue to be prolonged. In the process women lose hope

If a woman does not measure up to the standards, then she may be perceived negatively which is in violation of the guidelines set forth in the Directive Principles of State Policy. These are not enforceable by any court, but are considered fundamental in the governance of the country.

The Directive Principles of the State Policy makes provisions with regards to women:

Article 39

Article 39 enjoins the State to direct its policies towards securing all citizens without discriminating between men and women,

- Equal right to access adequate means of livelihood. [Article 39(a)]
- Equal pay for equal work. [Article 39(d)]

To become very good in the law, like surgery, one needs to have a lot of experience to rise at the top. Unless a women advocate breaks the barriers, she will not get that experience. She will remain a comparative outsider though being in the profession.

Law has a major role in transforming political thoughts into reality. On the one hand there has to be legislation and on the other hand its implementation and enforcement. While our Parliament responded with amendments to the Constitution and new laws, the judiciary responded by defining discrimination of various forms operating against women. Here it is important to remember how discrimination has been defined in the Convention on the Elimination of all forms of Discrimination against Women (CEDAW) document. Discrimination against women shall mean any distinction, exclusion or restriction made on the basis of sex which has the effect or purpose of impairing or nullifying the recognition, enjoyment or exercise by women, irrespective of their marital status, on a basis of equality of men and women, of human rights and fundamental freedom in the political, economic, social, cultural, civil or any other field. Thus the equality to be achieved has to be substantive equality and not simply formal. In form there is equality but substantively discrimination.

4.4. LACK OF PROPER INFRASTRUCTURE

The practice of law is based on the assumption that a lawyer has the freedom to devote long hours to research. Particularly in the early years of their career, lawyers are also expected to show a great deal of flexibility and willingness to take up briefs wherever opportunities arise around the world. At least in academia, men and women are often well into their thirties by the time they get their first permanent position. In Legal profession, the ages from twenty five to thirty five are seen as key in establishing a reputation through appearance in cases, and it is a period when lawyers are expected to devote maximum time to give positive results and establish themselves on their own right. As these are also considered to be prime childbearing years, such a career structure poses immense difficulties for those who also have coinciding domestic or family responsibilities and do not have a partner who stays at home to take care of them For an example, there are more than 7,000 women lawyers practise in Delhi High Court and the trial court comprising from the four districts of Tis Hazari, Karkadooma, Rohini and Patiala House. Besides, there are women judges, magistrates, judicial officers and administrative staff, many of whom have small children. But the lack of crèches had resulted in a skewered male-female ratio in the legal profession.[247] This apparently shows lack in fractural facilities – a very basic need for working women.

The existing court buildings are grossly inadequate to meet the existing requirements. The conditions particularly in small towns are pathetic. A visit to one of these courts would reveal the space constraints faced by them, overcrowding of lawyers and litigants, lack of basic amenities such as regular water and electric supply and the unhygienic and in sanitary conditions prevailing therein.

The Sixth Central Pay Commission recommended the Government to frame policies to keep women fulfill family responsibilities. Thus, Child Care Leave was granted to women employees of the Central Government having minor children below the age of 18 years, for a maximum period of 2 years (i.e. 730 days). This can be availed during their entire service, for taking care of up to two children whether for

---

247 Sarda, Kanu; "Delhi High Court to get Crèche for Lawyers' Tiny Tots," 20th, July 2008. <http://www.thaindian.com/ >on 25th july 2998.

rearing or to look after any of their needs like examination, sickness etc.[248] But women in Legal profession are denied of such leave.

Although many professions share the demanding schedules but experienced by young women lawyer, the combination of pressure and insecurity that characterizes the legal profession during the years when most people are starting families, means that women wanting to work and progress in law may face even greater obstacles than working women in other professions. Generally women lawyers tend not to have partners who stay at home, therefore combining a career with raising a family leads to far greater career interruptions and lack of mobility for women compared to men. This has negative effects for women's ability to compete with men in terms of productivity and networking and this impedes their career progress.

The laws must also provide for appropriate measures to make the life of women easy, particularly when they are employed, by making provisions such as provision and a culture must develop in our society whereby the burden is shared by both parents equally. The absence of this freedom militates against the economic empowerment of women, with many other deleterious consequences. Besides, effect of employment in adding to the economic independence of women, outside work is also causally important for women in making better 'deal' in intra-household distributions. Needless to say, women's work at home can be back-breaking, but it is rarely honoured or even recognized and certainly not remunerated, and the denial of the right to work outside the home is rather a monstrous violation of women's liberty. It reflects even today. Ordinarily the prohibition may work more implicitly through the power of convention and conformity. Quite often there may not even be a clear sex ban on women seeking employment, and yet women reared in the traditional values may be quite afraid to break with the traditions and to shock others. The prevailing perceptions of normality and appropriateness are quite central to this question. In this highly competitive world, working women juggle many responsibilities demanded by their various roles. Striking a balance between their work and family roles is essential for the physical and mental well being of female

---

[248] "Major Legislation," <http://www.paycheck.in/main/women-paycheck/women-legislation/women- legislation/women-legislation-5> on 5th May 2008.

employees. It is high time that judiciary addresses their needs so that they can easily overcome this role conflict.

Many women lawyer see themselves as having to choose between having a family and a successful legal career. Further, for those young aspirants with no proper office, there are little chances of earning enough money to finance her through the cases they might plead. In effect, for a young women lawyer earnings become difficult in early years of practice coupled with raising a family compared with other young women in other profession. However, there remains concern about the extent of discrimination against women in the legal professions. Whilst women are entering the legal professions in increased numbers they are leaving in disproportionate numbers suggesting that a career in law is not a friendly career for women or women with children. Women in the law, of course, face the same problems that affect all working women in relation to pregnancy, child care, sexual harassment, concentration in particular areas of work and so on.

Article 41, 42 & 43 of the Constitution provides for:

- Right to work. (Article 41)
- Provision for just and humane conditions of work and maternity relief. (Article 42)
- Living wage, decent standard of life and full employment of leisure and social and cultural opportunities, for workers, including women workers. (Article 43), yet there are many District and Family Courts which do not have proper toilets for women, nor proper canteen for refreshment, nor any medical facilities.[249]

One of women lawyer remarked, "Before I had children, I worked 100 hours a week with my male counterparts. When their wives had babies, they continued to work those hours. 'When I had babies I couldn't logistically, nor did I want to although I did want to be just as successful'. This is a big turning point for a lot of women. Day care and flex time and financial help make a difference but the bottom

---

249 "Family Courts in Varanasi, A Case Study," *Published by National Institute of Public Cooperation and Child Development*, New Delhi, p.13.

line is that you simply don't put in as many hours as a typical male. This starts to make a big difference by the time one is ready to make tenure; many women have just gotten tired of the balancing act and their own perception that time wise they will never catch up with their male peers. Legal profession is a driving, demanding field, and if you can't row the men often say get off the boat. Many women thus get off and drop the profession finding it hard to survive.

Comparatively women who are Central Government employees (those directly under GOI) are governed by the *Central Civil Service (Leave) Rules, 1972.* Under the rules, female employees are entitled to maternity leave for a period of 180 days for their first two live born children. During maternity leave employees are paid equal to the pay drawn by them immediately before. The Central Government in 1999 by notification under Central Civil Services (Leave) Rule 551 (A) made provisions for paternity leave for a male Central Government employee (including an apprentice and probationer) with less than two surviving children for a period of 15 days to take care of his wife and new born child. He can avail this leave 15 days before or within 6 months from the date of delivery of child. If such leave is not availed within the period, it shall be treated as lapsed.[250] This freedom is denied in many cultures and this attitude in itself is a serious violation of women's liberty and gender equality. Hence women practitioners are sufferers not only in matters of money but also loose clients during the period of absence.

Studies have shown that many women do not return to law as career after taking a break to have children. Even a break could be a problem as there is a tendency of not being in touch in the profession which becomes competitive day by day by the entry of young entrants. A further problem related to the difficulties of combining a career and family relationships, frequently mentioned in this study, is the so-called 'two body problem'. This refers to the tendency for women lawyer to be married to a fellow lawyer from the same or similar discipline who tends to be older and hence likely to be more advanced in his career. In a situation of limited career options the woman is more likely to follow her more senior partner to a new

---

250 "Latest Central Government Orders for India Government employees,"< http://hubpages.com/hub/Latest-Central-Government-Orders-for-India-Govt-employees> on 5th May 2009.

location, to the detriment of her own career. Limited career options in many areas of law can cause particular problems for women. Opportunities to practice a career in law, business or medicine may be found in most large towns and cities around the world. But what happens if the partner shifts to a smaller place where it is often carried out in a limited way. The greater the specialization of the lawyer the more likely it is that advancement can only be obtained by relocating to a different area or even country. This tends to affect women's careers more than men's especially when family ties are involved.[251]

A number of studies show that single childless women also face discrimination and isolation in the workplace and they are often no more successful than other women. The unmarried mother also reinforces our cultural understanding of proper motherhood means. In this sense she is a type of women rather woman. Yet she simultaneously operates in the discourse as women because she always invokes the proper place of man. Therefore man is the solution, he signifies the stability, legitimacy and mastery which is not only absent in her but inverted. The married mother like the childless women is therefore also quintessential women because she represents all those values which invert the desirable characteristics of Man.

At this point it may appear that my concerns are with the symbolic. However, my interest extends beyond this because my purpose in mapping the development of the "unmarried mother" and "childless mother" are to throw light on the dominant regime of meaning which already treats these women as problematic and destabilizing.[252]

The workplace culture seems, in terms of discrimination and the unfavorable male dominated environment for women, to be an equally important issue to tackle as the way in which legal careers are organized around the image of lawyer as dedicated individuals who are able to rely on supportive spouses to free them to pursue their

---

251 "Why women,"<http:// sites.ias.edu/sig/system/files/pdfs/Women_in_Science.pdf> on 4th April 2009.

252 Smart, Carol; "The Woman of Legal Discourse', *Social & Legal Studies,* Vol. 1, No. 1, 29-44 (1992) Sage London ,< http://sls.sagepub.com/cgi/pdf_extract/1/1/29> on 4th April 2009.

careers. The male bias of the workplace culture, career structure and image of law has not always been recognized by the legal community.

One interesting point to come out of the study of the is that even male advocates are now finding it more difficult to find a domestic partner willing to put up with the hours that, until now, have been standard to the life of a top lawyer. Eighty percent of the lawyers surveyed in Kolkata said that their wives were the principal carers for their children. Not one of the female lawyers surveyed had such a partner. Perhaps the pressure for a change in the work routine of advocates will come about not because of more women lawyers but because males find it more difficult to gain the domestic support that they took for granted in the past. A radical change of outlook is necessary to come to that conclusion.

4. 5. THE ROLE OF JUDGES

The judges should always take particular care to provide appropriate protection to women victims and witnesses against intrusive and oppressive questioning or treatment in court. Questions should designed be asked in such a manner as not to degrade the self respect of the victims. Thereby promoting comprehensive assistance to victims. This is especially in matter of rape cases and domestic violence. Article 8 of the European Convention on Human Rights (set out in Chapter 1.6) protects private life. As representatives of public authority the judges are bound to ensure that during the court process unjustified interferences in a person's private life are not permitted by questioning or otherwise.[253]

4. 6. WOMEN AS WORKERS IN THE JUSTICE SYSTEM

All the main agencies and regulatory bodies concerned with administering the justice process have equal opportunities policies. The guiding principle...in selecting candidates for judicial appointment is that appointment is strictly on merit. Decisions

253 "Guidance Note on National Human Rights Institutions and Transitional Justice," *UN Office of High Commissioner Human Rights*, 27th September, 2008 p.26.

on merit are based on assessments of candidates against the specific criteria for appointment. Extraneous matters such as a candidate' chambers or firm are immaterial.

Solicitors and their staff must deal with all persons with the same attention, courtesy and consideration regardless of race, colour, ethnic or national origins, sex, creed, disability or sexual orientation. Solicitors must not discriminate on grounds of race, colour, ethnic or national origins, sex or sexual orientation, and must not discriminate unfairly or unreasonably on grounds of disability, in the selection, treatment or promotion of staff.

However, there remains concern about the extent of discrimination against women in the legal professions. Whilst women are entering the legal professions in increased numbers they are leaving in disproportionate numbers suggesting that a career in law is not a friendly career for women or women with children.[254]

4. 7. GENDER STEREOTYPING

'Gender stereotyping', like other forms of stereotyping, assumes that women's lives follow certain patterns and a departure from that is 'abnormal' or presumed against. For this reason, assertive women or women who otherwise do not match the female stereotype might be challenging too many men and women.

It is easy to fall into stereotyping as a short-cut to make sense of what appears in front of us. Great care should be taken to avoid the trap of stereotyping. It may often be discriminatory and, in certain circumstances, has been found to be unlawful under the *Sex Discrimination Act 1975 of England (Hurley v Mustoe [1981] IRLR 208)*, where an employer assumed a woman would be unreliable because of child care obligations and therefore had a policy of not employing women with young children). As the Equal Opportunities Commission (EOC) has stated: 'stereotypes pigeon-hole boys and girls, men and women into fixed roles and behaviors that deny individual

---

254 "Women and Equality: Equal Treatment Bench Book," *Judicial Studies Board*, March 2004,p.18

aspirations.'[255] Whilst much has been achieved in recent decades to secure greater equality for women, gender inequality remains a significant feature of both public and private life for women and men.

Such inequality is reflected in traditional ideas about the role of women and men and, though they have shifted over time, the assumptions and stereotypes that underpin those ideas are often very deeply rooted. Indeed, they so permeate our view of the world that they often appear to reflect no more than 'common sense'. Thus, it seems innocuous to assume that a woman will have children, look after them and accordingly take a break from paid work (if indeed she ever takes it up) to accommodate the family. However, such assumptions and stereotypes can and often do have the effect of seriously disadvantaging women. It does not take a great deal of thought to recognize the impact of such assumptions on the profession.

4. 8. DISPARITY IN INCOME

Women account for around 15 percent of the Indian work force and 70 percent of all women of working age are in paid work (though this figure varies to 71 percent) Of those women who are employed, 43 percent work part-time (as compared to around 9 percent for men). The pay gap between women and men's earnings persists, notwithstanding that the *Equal Pay Act, 1970* came into force nearly 30 years ago.[256]

The Equal Remuneration Act, 1976 aims at providing equal remuneration to men and women workers and prevention of discrimination, particularity against women on the ground of gender. It provides that no discrimination should be made in remuneration for the same work or work of a similar nature only on the ground of gender vide Section 4.

Further the Act also provides that no gender based discrimination be made while recruiting for the same work or work of a similar nature, or in any condition of service subsequent to recruitment such as promotions, training or transfer vide Section 5.But the Act has an exception that under this law, no discrimination is permissible in

255 Ibid p.3.

256 <http://www.eurofound.europa.eu/eiro/2001/04/feature/uk0104126f.htm.> on 6th August 2009.

recruitment and service conditions except where employment of women is prohibited or restricted by the law. (Section 15).[257]

Indeed, in 2003 it was reported that the gender pay gap had actually widened in 2002 (to 18.8percent from 18percent in 2001). Women who work part-time continue to earn less than 60percent of the average hourly rate for full-time men and this figure has barely changed for a quarter of a century. As well as receiving lower pay, part-time workers are also disproportionately excluded from other benefits, for example, pensions and sick pay, and this impact most significantly on women.

Research in 2000 indicated that over a lifetime a woman loses over £200,000 in earnings simply by virtue of being a woman. It has been indicated that almost a third (29percent) of the gender pay gap is attributable to women being paid less simply because they are women, more than 50 percent of the remainder (26 percent, 15 percent and 12 percent respectively) resulting from differences in the length of women's full-time work experience, from the more interrupted nature of women's working lives and from women's greater tendency to work part-time. Only a relatively small proportion of the gap (13 percent) was attributed to occupational segregation and a minimal 6 percent to differences in educational attainment. This demonstrates that the causes of unequal pay, although gender related, are more complex than merely differences in treatment based on sex. The pattern of women's lives as compared to conventional working patterns is such that conventional pay systems and merit systems can disadvantage them. The gender pay gap was even wider in weekly earnings (25 percent) because men work longer hours than women on average and was more likely to receive additional payments, such as overtime.

There has been virtually no change in the full-time gender pay gap since the mid-1990s. Women working part-time earned only 59 percent of the average hourly earnings of men who worked full-time. This gender pay gap of 41percent has hardly changed since 1975. In most major occupational groups and industrial sectors, average hourly earnings were higher for men than for women. But the width of the gender pay gap varied considerably. Amongst occupations, it was widest for

257 <http://www.womenpaycheck.in/main/women-legislation/women-legislation-8> on 3rd May 2009.

managers and administrators than amongst industries, in banking, insurance and pension provision. The gender pay gap was wider for married/cohabiting people than for single people and for those with dependent children than for those without them. There was a wide gender pay gap at every qualification level including for graduates.[258]

4. 9. HARASSMENT AGAINST WOMEN

Sexual harassment has been defined and explained as: "Unwanted conduct of a sexual nature, or other conduct based on sex affecting the dignity of women and men..." This can include unwelcome physical, verbal or nonverbal conduct. A range of behavior may be considered to constitute sexual harassment. It is unacceptable if such conduct is unwanted, unreasonable and offensive to the recipient; a person's rejection of or submission to such conduct is used explicitly or implicitly as a basis for a decision. The essential characteristic of sexual harassment is that it is unwanted by the recipient, that it is for each individual to determine what behavior is acceptable to them and what they regard as offensive. Sexual attention becomes sexual harassment if it is persisted in once it has been made clear that the recipient as offensive regards it, although one incident of harassment may constitute sexual harassment if sufficiently serious. It is the unwanted nature of the conduct, which distinguishes sexual harassment from friendly behaviour, which is welcome and mutual. Women's learned physical helplessness (inability to fight back), vulnerability and sexual submissiveness (rapability), the exclusion of women from control of financial resources (financial deprivation) and the social isolation and 'privatization' of women in the role of wife and homemaker are all elements of legitimate desired marriage relationships. The result is she is not accepted as an individual professional. Thus women are not only the most frequent victims, but they are also the appropriate victims.

Sexual harassment entails sex discrimination, as the recipient's gender is "the determining factor in who is harassed". Conduct of a sexual nature or other conduct based on sex affecting the dignity of women and men at work offends a principle of

258 "Women and Equality: Equal Treatment Bench Book," *Judicial Studies Board*, March 2004, pp.4-18.

equal treatment for men and women. Such conduct, including conduct of superiors and colleagues, constitute an intolerable of violation in the dignity of workers. Survey conducted within the bar in the year 2008 helped in gauging the seriousness of the problem of harassment. The responses are given in Table – 4.1.

TABLE 4.1

WOMEN LAWYERS AND JUDICIAL OFFICERS

Country	Year of Survey	Women lawyers surveyed	Responses
India	2008	In the metropolitan district of Kolkata	Of the women surveyed, none divulged the pressure of sexual favours or unwanted dates, sexual remarks etc. Rather they denied. Most of them were aware of their rights related to sexual harassment. There were redressal mechanisms for such cases available in the Bar Council of West Bengal and punishment for the same. Many women lawyers who were interviewed usually dismiss the idea of aspiring to the judiciary. Some women who had developed a good practice were not inclined to aspire for judgeship. Though their background were from prominent professional families.
India	2007	In the district of Patna	No complaints of sexual harassment were divulged. Though some remarked that there might be rumours of sexual harassment.
India	2008	Judicial officers in the district of Kolkata	None acknowledged that they were unwanted favours in the matters of posting and promotion. Most of them acknowledged that efficiency, sincerity, integrity, hard work and merit are the criterion for promotion. But many of the women judicial officers were favoured in matters of posting as they wanted to live with their husband as far as possible.

Source: Survey done in High Court of Kolkata and Patna.

At present there is no specifics legislation in India to deal with sexual harassment of women at workplace except for *The Indecent Representation of Women (Prohibition) Act, 1987.* It prohibits indecent representation of women through advertisements or in publications, writings, paintings, figures or in any other manner. Although it is not known to have been used in cases of sexual harassment, the provisions of this act have the potential to be used in two ways. First, if an individual harasses another with books, photographs, paintings, films, pamphlets, packages, etc. containing indecent representation of women'; they are liable for a minimum sentence of two years.

Second, a 'hostile working environment' type of argument can be made under this act. Section 7 (Offences by Companies) - holds companies where there has been 'indecent representation of women' (such as the display of pornography) on the premises guilty of offenses under this act. (Cognizable, bailable offense; with a minimum sentence of two years).[259] *The Sexual Harassment of Women at their Work Place (Prevention) Bill, 2006* is pending approval form both the houses of Parliament. The bill once passed aims at providing legal protection to women at workplace against any kind of sexual harassment ranging from staring to rape.[260] Sexual harassment remains a problem for women both at work and outside of work. It is difficult to put a figure on the extent of sexual harassment inside the workplace or out because it often goes unreported.

Sexual harassment of women in the workplace became a subject of National Human Rights Commission (NHRC) consideration during the years from 1990-2009. The National Human Rights Commission (NHRC) instituted a committee to investigate harassment of women in the legal profession and asked universities to establish complaint committees immediately. The commission suggested the creation of a telephone hot line for complaints, initially starting in New Delhi, and gave advice to the media on reporting incidents of harassment against women.[261]

---

259 "Existing laws in India which can be used in cases of sexual harassment," <http://www.nwmindia.org/law/bareacts/sexualharassment.htm> on 6th January 2010.

260 "Sexually harassed at work?," < http://dfl.wageindicator.org/home/india/sexually-harassed-at-work> on 8th January 2010.

261 "Crime and Society," < http://www-rohan.sdsu.edu/faculty/rwinslow/asia_pacific/india.html>. on 9th January 2010.

In addition, women employees suffer discrimination in a variety of other ways. Employment rates, for example, are lower than those of those of men. Further, minority women and those belonging to the backward class and scheduled tribes have not surmounted the basic obstacles facing all women. Like all women, women of minority are grossly under represented in the top jobs category and have a high rate of unemployment though reservation has been given to scheduled caste and scheduled tribe. Hindu women of Bangladeshi origin, by contrast to other Indian families had to face lot of struggle due to partition. And women of Pakistan origin are strongly discouraged by their families and communities from undertaking work at all because of their purdah. While women belonging to the scheduled caste and those belonging to the minority section who do work are often poorly paid and highly exploited, particularly if they are home workers in an industry. It is also crucial to recognize the extent to which the statistics obscure class divisions internal to groups.[262]

Moreover, women have a different life's experience. They sometimes have a different way of looking at problems. The real loss in the lack of female advancement in the legal profession is not just the frustration of particular women's careers. It is not simply the economic loss that is inherent in failing to promote to the full the highly refined economic talent of a trained lawyer. The biggest loss, it seems to me, lies in the failure to bring the skills of women to bear on the administration of the law. Women bear many of the enduring burdens of life. They are better at it because those burdens are usually foisted on them and they just have to make the best of things. Whilst one must not stereotype men or women, it is my experience that women often see legal issues from a different perspective. That perspective should be available in full proportion to the judiciary, the bar and the legal firms, corporate lawyers, the law schools, and government departments of India. It needs to be available to the whole community that the law serves. Only a change in the mindset could bring about gender-sensitivity in the administration of justice. Although there have been notable gains for women globally in the last few decades, gender inequality and gender-based inequities continue to impinge upon girls' and women's ability to realize their rights and their full potential as citizens and equal partners. In fact, for every right that has been established, there are millions of women who do not enjoy.

---

262 "Women and Equality,"< www.jsboard.co.uk/downloads/etbb/edwomen_and_equality.doc> on 12th January 2010.

Till today, only 39 percent of girls and 64 percent of boys get education in Bihar, Rajasthan, Uttar Pradesh and Madhya Pradesh. If women teachers were increased chances are that girls in rural areas would continue to study. As girls get enlightened, they will raise better families.[263] But lately we find in legal education that the number of women enrolling to study law is increasing day by day. Once again, to cite the example of Punjab University, in the current batch of LLB, out of the total strength of 339 students, 106 are girls. In 2006, out of the 344 law students, 123 were girls. In 2005 batch, out of 331 students, 115 were girls.[264] The same situation we find in Bihar, West Bengal and other state of India as discussed in the earlier chapters. These days, women law students, after completing their degree prefer to join corporate firms which offer a good financial start, comfortable work environment and a bright future.

4. 10. GUIDELINES AND SAFEGUARDS

In India, it has been only six years since sexual harassment was for the first time recognized by the Supreme Court as human rights violation and gender based systemic discrimination that affects women's Right to Life and Livelihood. The Court defined sexual harassment very clearly as well as provided guidelines for employers to redress and prevent sexual harassment at workplace. While the Apex Court has given mandatory guidelines, known as Vishaka Guidelines, for resolution and prevention of sexual harassment enjoining employers by holding them responsible for providing safe work environment for women, the issue still remains under carpets for most women and employers.

The Supreme Court of India has for the last two decades been making many bold innovations in administering what it calls 'substantial justice'. The guidelines that the Supreme Court has laid down in the case of *Vishakha versus State Of Rajasthan (1997) 6 SCC 241* are to be followed.[265] These guidelines encompass a

---

263 Legal Rights of girl child in India, < http://www.indianchild.com/girlchild/rights-of-girl-child.htm>on 24thMarch2011.

264 Ohri, Raghav; *Not many women practise law,* Express India 19th March2001< http://www.expressindia.com/latest-news/not-many-women-practise-law>On24thMarch2011.

265 *Vishaka and others v State of Rajasthan and others*, A.I.R. 1997Supreme Court 3011.

comprehensive definition of sexual harassment, directions for establishment of a complaint mechanism and the duty under which employers are obligated to obviate any such act. Here the study focuses on some of the notable recent judgments in the realm of 'gender justice':

1) *Vishakha versus State Of Rajasthan;*
2) *Apparel Export Promotion Council versus A K Chopra (1999)*[266] *and*
3) *Gita Hariharan vs. Reserve Bank of India (1999),*[267]
4) *Upendra Baxi v. State of U.P., (1987),*[268]
5) *Mackinnon Mackenzie & Co. Ltd. v. Audrey D'Costa, (1987)*[269]

In all these cases, the Supreme Court of India invoked and strongly relied on the provisions of international instruments, ostensibly to fill the void in the domestic law related to the rights of women. This represented a significant departure from the Court's earlier stand in keeping with the traditional rule. With more women coming out to work, suffering harassment at the hands of male colleagues at the work place endured by women due to their inherent modesty, fear of loss of job, absence of redressal machinery, the Supreme Court formulated guidelines in *Vishaka* v. *State of Rajasthan, (1997) 6 SCC 24)* in the absence of any legislation in addition to rights available under the *Protection of Human Rights Act, 1993.*

Vishaka was a public interest class action and came up before SCI at the instance of certain social activists and NGOs seeking to prevent sexual harassment of working women in all work places. Their grievance was that while working women remained vulnerable to this, neither the legislature nor the executive government was taking any effective preventive measure in this behalf. So the plaintiffs approached Supreme Court of India for the enforcement of the Fundamental Rights of the workingwomen as guaranteed by the Constitution.

---

266 *Apparel Export Promotion Council vs. A.K Chopra,* AIR 1999(2) SC 625; 1999 (1) SCC 759;

267 *Gita Hariharn vs. Reserve Bank of India and Ors.,* 1999 (2) SCC 228

268 *Upendra Baxi v. State of U.P.,* AIR 1987 SC 191

269 *Mackinnon Mackenzie & Co. Ltd. v. Audrey D'Costa*, (1987) 2 SCC 469

In this landmark decision to court Chief Justice J.S. Verma gender equality includes protection from sexual harassment and right to work with dignity, which is a universally recognised basic right. In other words of Dr. A.S. Anand, C.J., "There is no gain saying that each incident of sexual harassment at the place of work, results in violation of the fundamental right to gender equality and the right to life and liberty – the two most precious fundamental rights guaranteed by the Constitution of India." Vishaka guidelines apply to both organized and unorganized work sectors and to all women whether working part time, on contract or in voluntary/honorary capacity. The guidelines are a broad framework which put a lot of emphasis on prevention and within which all appropriate preventive measures can be adapted. One very important preventive measure is to adopt a sexual harassment policy, which expressly prohibits sexual harassment at work place and provides effective grievance procedure, which has provisions clearly laid down for prevention and for training the personnel at all levels of employment.

In *Upendra Baxi v. State of U.P., (1987) 2 SCC 402,* the Supreme Court ensured minimal hygiene, shelter, providing nutritional and medical facilities to women under State protection. The courts' approach to defense of 'morally loose woman' in rape cases has undergone a radical change.

The Constitution guarantees gender equality and the right to life and liberty in Articles 14, 15 and 21 and also provides for the Fundamental Right of each citizen to practice any profession or to pursue any occupation, trade or business, vide Article 19 (1) (g). There exists a Fundamental Right to Judicial Remedy in the event of violation of any of these Rights. Constitution of India lays the foundation for women centric and other related legislations that protect women in workplace. (All laws enacted have to be within the constitutional framework.) It embeds in itself such provisions mainly by way of fundamental rights. Constitution of India promotes equality of gender and at the same time urges the state to provide protection to those sectors that are vulnerable.

Below mentioned Articles in the constitution of India focuses on women and their constitutional rights.

Fundamental Rights

Article 14

Article 14 of the constitution of India enunciates the general principle of equality and prohibits the state from denying to any person, equality before the law or equal protection of law. The underlying principle of Article 14 of the Constitution of India is that "like should be treated alike and not that unlike should be treated like."Article 14 of the Constitution of India prohibits class legislation but permits reasonable classification.[270]

Article 15

- ***Article 15 (1)***

  Article 15(1) of the Constitution protects the rights of citizens, as it prohibits the state from discriminating against any citizen on grounds of gender amongst other grounds like race, religion, etc.

- ***Article 15 (2)***

  Article 15(2) prohibits any citizen from being subjected to any sort of disability, liability, restriction or conditions on grounds of gender. This is with regards to accessing the public places like restaurants, shops, etc. It is also effective while utilizing facilities of public utilities like wells, roads and such other places which are wholly or partly maintained by or out of State funds or dedicated for public usage.

- ***Article 15 (3)***

  Article 15(3) empowers the State to make special provisions in favour of women and children. (For example, reservation of seats for women in public bodies, free primary education for children, etc.)

- ***Article 16***

  Article 16 of the Constitution, states that there shall be equality of opportunity for all citizens in matters relating to employment or appointment in any office under the State. Also, no citizen shall be held ineligible or discriminated against on grounds of gender.

---

270 Kant, Anjani; *Women and the law,* APH publishing, 2003, New Delhi, p.160.

Fundamental Duties

Article 51A

- ***Article 51 (e)***
  Article 51A (e) imposes on every citizen by way of fundamental duty the responsibility to renounce practices derogatory to the dignity of women.

- ***Article 39(e)***

- ***Article 39A***
  Article 39A makes provision for providing equal justice and free legal aid to all the citizens.

Rule 18(4) of the Indian Foreign Service 9 Recruitment, Seniority and Promotion) Rules, 1961which required permission before marriage and denial of right to employment to married women for panel employees was declared discriminatory by the Supreme Court on the ground of sex and thus violative of Article 14 of the Constitution. The Court upholding the principle of equality of status put the female employee at par with men.

In most of the judgments, the Supreme Court of India has pointed out that it is the responsibility of the legislature and of the executive government to ensure that the working women could live with dignity and carry on their respective vocations in a safe environment. This requires suitable legislation and the creation of a mechanism for the enforcement of the rights of women. If the legislature and the executive failed to perform their duties the Court said that it had to assume an active role to administer gender justice when required.

But the question is: Has the legislature achieved its objective?

In this context, the Supreme Court of India looked for inspiration to the Beijing Statement of Principles of the Independence of the judiciary in the LAWASIA region. These principles were accepted by the Chief Justices of Asia and the Pacific at Beijing in 1995 as the minimum standards necessary to maintain the independence and effective functioning of the judiciary. According to the Supreme Court of India, the Objectives of the judiciary as mentioned in that Statement include:

a) Ensuring that all persons are able to live securely under the rule of law

b) Promoting within the proper limits of judicial function, the observance and attainment of human rights and

c) Administering law impartially among persons and between persons and the State.

The Supreme Court of India also adverted to the provisions of 'Convention on Elimination of All forms of Discrimination against Women' (CEDAW) which required the States Parties to take all appropriate measures to eliminate discrimination against women in the field of employment, as the right to works is an inalienable right of all human beings. Under the Convention, equality in employment can be seriously impaired when women are subjected to gender specific violence, such as sexual harassment in the workplace.

CEDAW defines sexual harassment in comprehensive terms: it includes unwelcome sexually-determined behavior, sexually-colored remarks etc. Such conduct can be humiliating for the working women and may constitute a health and safety problem. It is discriminatory when the woman has reasonable ground to believe that her objection would disadvantage her in connection with her employment, or when it creates a hostile working environment.

The Government of India ratified the CEDAW Resolution on 25th June 1993 and had also made an official commitment at the Fourth World Conference on Women in Beijing undertaking to formulate and put into operation a national policy on women and to take other measures as required under the said instrument. At the time of Vishaka, however, the legislature had not made any law to give effect to CEDAW Resolution and as such there was a void in domestic law, said the Supreme Court of India. Against this background the Supreme Court of India declared, "It is now an accepted rule of judicial construction that regard must be had to the international conventions and norms when construing domestic laws when there is no inconsistency between them and there is a void in the domestic law. Therefore in the absence of enacted law to provide for the effective enforcement of the basic human right of gender equality and guarantee against sexual harassment at workplaces, the

Court should lay down the guidelines and norms to be duly observed at all workplaces or other institutions, until legislation is enacted for the purpose."

The Supreme Court of India then went on to set down elaborate guidelines and norms for the prevention of sexual harassment at the place of work and laid out the duties of the employers or other responsible persons in this behalf. Comprehensive measures for the safety and protection of working women, against overt or covert acts or conduct amounting to sexual harassment, as defined by the by the CEDAW were rescinded. Also, provisions were made for punitive and disciplinary actions in appropriate situations, including the development of a complaint mechanism, the formation of Complaint Committee and the adoption of measures for adequate awareness campaign and holding of workers meeting for discussion and dissemination of information, etc. The Supreme Court of India made it clear that this should be treated as the law declared by the Court as the law of the land under Article 141 of the Constitution.

While Vishakha was a Class action, in another case of *Apparel Export Promotion Council vs. A K Chopra (1999) 1 SCC 759,* the employer of AEPC had taken disciplinary action, leading to termination of service of A K Chopra. He was a company officer who had been found guilty of causing sexual harassment to Ms. X, a stenographer. By sexual remarks and conduct soliciting sexual intimacy he took taking of his advantage of his superior position. By implication, he had caused Ms. X to believe that her objection would be disadvantageous to her in her employment and adverse consequences might result if she did not consent to such advances or sought to resist the same. However, Chopra was directed to be reinstated in service by the High Court, being the first court of judicial review, on the ground that at the most he had only attempted to commit the offense but had not actually done it. When the matter was brought on for further appeal the Supreme Court reacted sharply.

In its judgment the Supreme Court again invoked international Instruments and observed that they cast an obligation on the Indian State to gender-sensitize its laws and the courts are under an obligation to see that the message of the international organizations are not drowned by inaction and neglect. The Court held that on the basis of the CEDAW declaration, sexual harassment is a form of sexual discrimination projected through unwelcome sexual advances, request for sexual favors and other verbal or physical conduct with sexual overtones, whether directly or by implication, particularly when submission to or rejection of such conduct by the female employee was capable of being used for 'effecting' the employment of the female employee and unreasonably interfering with her work performance and had the effect of creating an intimidating and hostile working atmosphere for her. And eventually the case was dismissed, eventually the case was dismissed.

In *Gita Hariharan vs. Reserve Bank of India (1999) 2 SCC 228* the gender justice question arose as to whether the mother of a minor child could be regarded under the Guardianship statute, as the 'natural guardian' of the child when the father was alive. The statute law on the subject was to the effect that the natural guardian of a minor is the 'father and after him the mother'. This was always taken to mean that if the father was alive, he would be the natural guardian, and only after his death the mother can be the natural guardian. But SCI felt that such an interpretation would lead to unfair discrimination against the mother and would amount to a breach of gender equality as guaranteed by the Constitution and international instruments. Supreme Court, therefore read down the provision of the statute, and construed the words 'after him' following the word 'father' to mean, that the mother would be the natural guardian even during the life time of the father, if the father was absent from of the scene of the minor either due to his own indifference or by choice or when he was physically absent or when he is unable to perform the duties of guardianship for any disability or did not want to, due to an understanding with the mother, or when he had no objection to the mother being the guardian.

In 1987 in *Mackinnon Mackenzie & Co. Ltd. v. Audrey D'Costa , (1987) 2 SCC 469* the Supreme Court intervened to ensure that a Confidential Secretary in a private firm got the same pay as a male steno's in the firm. Differential ages of retirement between foreign and Indian Air Hostesses in the case of *Lena Khan v. Union of India (1987* [271] was removed. The plea that such a step was taken to avoid violation of British law was firmly repelled by the Supreme Court declaring that Air

---

271 *Lena Khan v. Union of India* (1987) 2 SCC 402

India must comply with Article 14 and if need be, walk out of the country which makes it impossible to abide by the ideals of our Constitution.

In 1982, in *Air India v. Nergesh Meerza (1987)*,[272] the Supreme Court refused to fix different ages of retirement and in preventing them from having children.

All the above decisions have been widely hailed. But they remain controversial, as it only appeared to have justice done in paper.

To allow women to take up employment or hold elective offices and inherit property is not yet socially accepted wholeheartedly. We have the duty, therefore, to educate our society, to bring awareness as to the need for such laws or the necessity for women to take up employment which in fact results in empowerment of women. Unless there is social acceptability of a law the effectiveness thereof would be in serious doubt as, for example, in the last century the *Child Marriage Restraint Act* was passed and still in certain areas in this country, even today child marriages take place. So also the Constitution abolished untouchability and several enactments have been made to give effect to the same but still the same is practiced in a virulent form all over the country, which is a matter of shame.

These two instances clearly point out that law alone cannot tackle social problems and a lot of awareness is required among the public before such laws are accepted or such laws are promoted. Therefore there is a great need for us to go to the villages and educate people at different levels of the need and efficacy of such laws so that there may be social acceptability and success of the same. As long as there is no empowerment to women, no society can progress. Indeed in any culture where there has been progress of women, there has been overall economic development, longevity has increased, population control and nutrition level has enhanced.

No doubt, democracy provides equal opportunities for all to take up any profession. Isn't my right were being affected? Women as free citizens, and constituting almost half of the population, are only theoretically able to redress their

---

272 *Air India v. Nergesh Meerza* (1987) 2 SCC 469

grievances through democratic means. Due to socio-economic reasons and cultural patterns they are not effective players of the game of democracy. The disadvantages of democratic process make it imperative that a pro-woman and anti-subordination interpretation of Constitution and laws shall be made. In a patriarchal social construction, where power dictates freedom, lack of power on the part of women because of their position as incomplete agents in democratic participation is likely to marginalize their freedom. This is reflected in Legal profession. Women are entering in the Legal profession, yet, the numbers don't add up to gender equity for women lawyers. On average, women earn less than male lawyers. A lot of judges and lawyers are not comfortable with women lawyers. Networking and mentoring are important in finding clients and jobs, but women still face roadblocks in these areas For the women attorneys, like other professionals, a major concern was balancing family life with the demands of a career.

Eventually, women will reach a point in the field of law that they will receive equal opportunity, along with the guidance and aid that is imperative in reaching their success in both the professional and personal aspects of their lives. The movement however has made only incremental changes in the past decade. These are serious issues that need to be given more attention and hopefully will make some sort of a difference for all women in the legal profession

In 1970, when Hon'ble Ms Justice Manju Goel became the first woman to join the West Bengal Judicial Service she recalls and said that "her posting as District Judge was not quite happy." When she joined the West Bengal Judicial Service, she recalls and said "her posting as District Judge was not quite happy." "The High Court of Calcutta promptly posted her to Murshidabad, a place separated by an eight hour train journey from the city of Calcutta where she lived. Many male officers who had joined the service with me were retained in Calcutta and other convenient places. The idea behind posting her was a positive effort to discourage (if and discriminate), women from joining the Judicial Service."[273] But, in another instance, a few years back the High Court of Andhra Pradesh recruited ten women Additional District

---

273 < www.aptel.gov.in/members/manju.html>

Judges from the bar as the High Court found that it did not have a sufficient number of women judges in the Andhra Pradesh Higher Judicial Service. A growing preference for women judges or at least a move to encourage women to join the judicial services – becomes apparent when the two incidents are seen in comparison to each other. The initial hesitation to post women officers on the criminal side has long been forsaken.[274]

Thus slowly, women have fully justified this legislative measure, as they have not been found in any manner inferior to men in intelligence, integrity or professional competency.

All the wings and layers of government - legislature, executive and judiciary at central, state and local levels - have the responsibility towards empowerment of women in the light *of* Article 15(3) read with Article 12 of the Constitution. Although Article 15(3) is an enabling provision that authorizes the state to make special provision for women, the discretion conferred there under shall be exercised without fail, and be exercised reasonably. It is also fundamental duty of every citizen to renounce the practices derogatory to the dignity of women.[275] Thus social and individual responsibilities for feminist cause are contemplated in addition to democratic so to countervail this lacuna and make freedom worthwhile to women; empowerment emerges as the true method of freeing women. Thus instead of uncritical reliance on democratic forces, appropriate technique of interpretation can rescue their interests.

Another approach is purposive interpretation, which tries to elicit and focus on the reason or spirit behind the constitutional provisions and law. By looking to the values of the right, social needs, competing interests and policy alternatives, the development of policy-oriented jurisprudence expands the ambit of rights. For example, the court reasons that right to life means right to live with human dignity

---

274 Higgins, Tracy; "Democracy and Feminism," *110, Harvard. Law Review*,pp 1676-1685

275 Article 51A (e), Constitution of India.

and all those interests essential to this constitute essential parts of this right.[276] To conform to the aspiration reflected in the term 'protection' in the marginal note to Article 21 it is essential that access to those conditions that make life livable with human dignity is part of right under Article 21. If at workplace atmosphere with potential for sexual harassment exists, positive responsibility of the state and employers to remove such atmosphere and create sense of security is the method of protection. The term 'protection' in the clause 'equal protection of the laws' under Article 14 as viewed by Granville Austin, "seems to place upon government the positive responsibility to give the have-less access to those rights they previously have been powerless to exercise."[277] With an array of Directive Principles of State Policy which have great relevance in women's welfare,[278] purposive interpretation is a seminal tool for the cause of constitutional feminism. It is appropriate to see how the Indian constitutional experience evinces the working of constitutional feminism.[279]

4.11. A SUM UP

A perusal of the chapter gives the following findings:

(i) This marginalization of women in legal language was her reflection of her marginalization in real life.

(ii) Whereas the increasing number of women are unable to cope in the first phase of profession. It puts them out of favour with clients who want their lawyers at their beck and call twenty-four hours a day.

(iii) Women as lawyers face difficulties associated with combining family life and practice of law and problems of discrimination specifically in career advancement.

---

276 Francis Coralie Mullin v. Administrator, Union Territory of Delhi, (1981) 1 SCC 608: 1981 SCC (Cri) 212.

277 Granville Austin; *Working a Democratic Constitution*, Oxford University Press, 1999, New Delhi, p. 669.

278 Articles 39(*a*) to (*f*), 42, 43, 44, 45, 47 and 51 of the Constitution of India.

279 Bhat, Dr P. Ishwara ; "Constitutional Feminism : An Overview,"(2001) 2 SCC (Jour) 1.

(iv) Society owes a special responsibility to women as mothers, safe bearing and rearing of children is an obligation that must be shared by the mother, the father and the society.

(v) The contribution made by an active house maker to the management of a family should be accepted as economically and socially productive and as essential for national development.

(vi) The study assesses some theoretical explanations of gender inequalities that persist across legal profession in hiring, remuneration, promotions, and other professional opportunities in law.

(vii) In this connection, the researcher examined women's responses to their experiences and women's impact on the law and the profession.

(viii) Some of the conclusions are based upon the study of around 50 women lawyers of different ages and from diverse social and cultural backgrounds who practice law across this state in many areas of practice. The stories they tell are personal and highlight not only the consequences of motherhood to their careers, but also the internal struggles they faced pursuing successful careers while balancing the demands of motherhood.

(ix) This deeper look into the hearts of these women provides important insight into why career patterns of women in the field of law are different than career patterns of men which concluded that the advancement of women in the legal profession continues to be undermined by insufficient accommodation for parental responsibilities.

(x) Marriage and motherhood should not become a disability preventing women from fulfilling their full and proper role in the task of national development for which society including women themselves must accept their due responsibilities.

(xi) Several bar reports have identified some other difficulties faced by women advocates. Reports of such harassment come from time to time mainly from the young female associates who are shocked but most often accept such behaviour without complaint.

(xii) It can have a devastating effect upon the health, confidence, morale and performance of those affected by it. The anxiety and stress produced by sexual harassment commonly leads to stress, being less efficient at work, or leaving their job to seek work elsewhere.

(xiii) These acts have led to degradation in the legal profession as they set forth wrong behaviors and affect the career of a woman. Therefore, there is still long way to change the values and thinking of tradition bound people of countries like India.

(xiv) The studies indicate the attitudes, environmental problem and difficulties in securing work. There is a feeling of resentment towards the competence of lawyers.

(xv) The study investigates some of the judicial decisions of the Supreme Court of India, which reveal the discriminative and oppressive working conditions of women in general including women in legal profession.

(xvi) The departure of women professionals from the Bar male is a great loss to the legal profession and an economic loss to the family and to the country.

(xvii) India has witnessed many social changes post independence. Today, women have come out of homes and established an identity of their own in different areas of work. Though most Indian adult women make an economic contribution in one form or another (including housework, working in family land etc.), much of their work is not documented.

(xviii) The problem women still face in the workplace, regarding equal salary and advancement opportunities, will not change over night. There are certain things that can be done that may aid, at least partially, this situation.

(xix) Social awareness is necessary to attain goals envisaged in the Constitution or other statutes and to transform 'de jure' equality to 'de facto' equality as equality of women is a basic condition of social, economic and political development of the nation.

CHAPTER – V

WOMEN LAWYERS AROUND THE WORLD

"Nature has tempered women as little for the judicial conflict of the courtroom as well as for the physical conflicts of the battlefield........"

-Chief Justice C.J.Ryan

Wisconsin Supreme Court

Cited in Epstein, 1993, p 269

5.1. AN OVERVIEW

Women are entering the legal profession in increasing numbers and permeating the profession, but the study in the earlier chapters reveals segregation along gender lines. As they advance their careers, they have either to compete with men and win power on merit or choose an alternative route to professional success and fulfillment that involves balancing or integrating work and domestic commitments.

After looking into the oppressive and discriminating attitude of people towards women in the legal profession including the male lawyers and judges. However we have noted some progressive decisions of the Supreme Court to remove in equal treatment to women in our country. In this chapter, we will note the position of women lawyers around the world which has been discussed as follows:

Oceania countries

Australia

New Zealand

North America

Canada

South America

Venezuela

Argentina

Peru

South Africa

European Countries

Italy

France

Germany

Belgium

Finland

Norway

Finland

Croatia

Serbia

Russia

Asian Countries

Japan

Korea

Philippines

Nepal

Muslim Countries

Qatar

United Arab Emirates

Egypt

Afghanistan

The nature of problem worldwide

A Sum up

Worldwide, there has been a marked increase in the number of women attracted to law. As of 2005,women represented virtually half (48 percent) of all law students in the United States(ABA, 2006).Similarly the number of women lawyers have in Canada and Australia in the last 25 years have mushroomed.[280]

5.2. OCEANIA COUNTRIES

AUSTRALIA

In Australia, the first step was taken when the Senate of the University of Sydney opened its doors to women in 1881 which culminated in the *Women's Legal Status Act of 1918,* and in 1921 she was admitted to the Bar. The proportion of full-time women advocates varies between the States. The highest proportion at the separate Bar is in Victoria (16 per cent). Most States comprise about 12 percent. In Western Australia it is 8 percent. They now comprise 50 percent of law graduates. Yet they are seriously under-represented in legal partnerships. Their salary levels show a gap when compared to male counterparts. Lawyers' Weekly recently described the differential as 'alarming'. In legal firms many women still appear to hit a glass ceiling in Australia. On average, Australian women lawyers earn $20,225 less a year than males'; progress in legal profession is slow.

The proportion of women law graduates has gradually risen over the past 20 years. The position of New South Wales seems to be probably better than most parts of Australia. In 1984, the percentage in New South Wales was 33 percent. In 1990, it had risen to 46percent. Now, it hovers at 50percent. This change in the gender composition of the legal profession promises, ultimately, a remarkable change in its self-image and in the way it goes about its work. The same percentages are reflected in the admissions to the College of Law. In 1984 it was 36 percent. In 1990, it was 47 percent. In 1994 it reached 50 percent for the first time.

In seventy years, the proportion of women actually admitted to the legal profession in New South Wales has gone up most significantly. In 1920 it was 0 percent. In 1984, it was 31 percent. In 1990 it was 43 percent. Now, as with legal graduates, it hovers at 50 per cent. Interestingly, there is a shift in the sectors in

---

[280] Ryan, Justice C.J; "Women entering the Legal Profession: Change and Resistance,"p.119.< http://www.uk.sagepub.com/upm-data/12634_Chapter5.pdf> on7th March 2009.

which women lawyers are working. In 1984, 79 percent were employed in the private sector of the legal profession. This had dropped to 72 percent in 1988. In 1994 it was fewer than

That there is a barrier in respect of the top legal appointments seems beyond doubt. An analysis of the employment of women lawyers in government posts in New South Wales showed that 13 percent of all male employees had made it to the top grade, only 5percent of women made that grade. Sixty seven percent of the women find themselves at the bottom grade whereas only 45 percent of men are there. The same pattern appears in the appointment of academics in New South Wales. Sixteen percent of all male academics have professorial or equivalent rank. Yet only 6 percent of women have attained that position. The proportion is reversed at the lowest (tutor or associate lecturer) status: 16 percent of women and only 5 percent of men.

As to the top of the pile, the judiciary, the situation is even less encouraging. In 1970 the statistic was an easy one to remember. The proportion of women in judicial office in New South Wales was zero percent. In fact, it was not until 1962 that a woman (Miss Roma Mitchell of Adelaide) was appointed to the rank of Queen's Counsel. It was not until 1965 that the same woman was appointed to judicial office in the Supreme Court of South Australia. In 1970, Justice Mitchell was still the only woman judge appointed to a superior court of our country.

In 1980, in New South Wales 2 percent of judicial officers were women. Now the percentage is getting closer to 10 percent. The position has improved somewhat in the intervening quarter century. Now the percentage is getting closer to 10 percent. According to the Australian Law Reform Commission, the position across Australia is marginally worse. At the time of its analysis in 1994, about 7 percent of all federal judgeships were held by women. About 6 percent only of State judicial officers nationwide were women. The position has changed a little with the recent appointment of the first women judges to the Supreme Courts of Victoria and Western Australia. But there are still many courtrooms in our country where women advocates must go and, unlike Kathryn Tucker in the Supreme Court of the United States, they cannot look up to the bench to find the reassurance of a woman holding judicial office and exercising it with professionalism and skill.

According to the Australian Law Reform Commission, the position across Australia is marginally worse. At the time of its analysis in 1994, about 7 percent of all federal judgeships were held by women. About 6 percent only of State judicial officers nationwide were women. The position has changed a little with the recent appointment of the first women judges to the Supreme Courts of Victoria and Western Australia.[281]While in 2004, women comprised just fewer than 50 percent of law students compared to only 20 percent in 1970 (Thornton 2004).[282]

NEW ZEALAND

Although women never were barred from law practice in New Zealand, they were only 9 percent of law students in 1981. Two years later they were 35 percent of law graduates at one university and were expected to be half of all lawyers with less than seven years of experience by 199 Following a UK survey which showed that just over 14 percent of women made partner in the top 50 law firms there, a similar survey by New Zealand legal newsletter Law Fuel showed that at New Zealand's top firms 17 percent of women are made partner.[283]

5.3. NORTH AMERICA

CANADA

Canada opened the floodgates when it grudgingly admitted Clara Brett Martin to membership in 1897.Although the number was not large but by 1923, 27 of the 35 women had entered the profession. Of the 100 admitted in 1939, more than the half had entered the profession. Women entering the profession had increased slightly in the forties and fifties. There were 73 women lawyers in Ontario in 1941 and 107 in 1951.World war ii took men away from the Law Schools and firms and women were

---

281 Kirby, Michael;"Women Lawyers-Making A Difference," Speech delivered in Women Lawyers Association of New South Wales,18th June,1997.< http://www.hcourt.gov.au/speeches/kirbyj/kirbyj_womenlaw.htm> on 2nd Jan.2008.

282 Ryan, Justice C.J; "Women entering the Legal Profession: Change and Resistance,"p.113. <http://www.uk.sagepub.com/upm-data/12634_Chapter5.pdf> on7th March 2009.

283 "Glass ceiling for aspiring female law partners", ***Business news,*** 4th February, 2010.<http://tvnz.co.nz/business-news/glass-ceiling-aspiring-female-law-partners-3348333> on 7th March 2010.

encouraged to fill office needs, although they rarely appeared in courts. In 1961, there were still only 162 women lawyers in Ontario. In 1960s and 1970s brought the beginning of major change of both men and women.[284] Male students doubled between 1962-63 and 1980-81, while the number of female students increased twenty-four times. The changing role of the universities and of women reduced social barriers to law and made it possible for women to enter the profession in rising numbers. Women now represent approximately 35 to 40 percent of new entrants in virtually all provinces.[285] In the 1981 census, that woman appeared to be entering male-dominated fields of studies such as business, engineering, medicine and law in greater numbers. In Canada, 26 percent of the federal judiciary are women; with one-third of judges at provincial level. In 2003, women represented 53 percent of the law school graduates.[286] But in the last decade women have been leaving law, particularly from private firms, at two to three times the rate of their male counterparts, Given that only 16 percent of senior lawyers in Canada are female, one of the biggest challenges for women working their way up is not seeing role models who look like them or who understand what they're experiencing. Women mentoring women is seen as one solution.[287]

There seems to be a higher proportion of women lawyers in French than in English Canada, which would parallel developments in Europe. Is there some worldwide conspiracy to keep the profession predominately male, or have we collectively reached the 'peak' of women's interest in the legal profession?

Female representation in Northern Ireland compared to some other overseas jurisdictions is even worse. These differences may be explained by the varying status of the profession across cultures. Many students in Europe and South America study law part-time while working at some other job. This extended period, lasting as long as seven to ten years, frequently is interrupted by other employment opportunities,

---

284 Hagan, John, Hagan, Fiona; *Gender In Practice, A study of Lawyers Lives*, Oxford University Press, London, 1995 pp. 9-10.

285 Abel, Richard, 1 and Lewis Philipp, S.C; "Feminization of Legal Profession," *Lawyers in Society*. Beards Books, 2005, Washington D.C.p.206.

286 Ryan, Justice C.J; "Women entering the Legal Profession: Change and Resistance,"p.113. <http://www.uk.sagepub.com/upm-data/12634_Chapter5.pdf> on7th March 2009.

287 CanWest, Valerie Berenyi; "Female lawyers fighting sexism,"News Service,6th November,2009.

financial pressures, and changes in family structure (marriage and children). The fact that female enrollment has stabilized at an almost uniform rate of 35 to 40 percent is difficult to explain.

5.4. SOUTH AMERICA

BRAZIL

In Brazil, where law represents a liberal education for the Elite, women were about 25 percent of law graduates in 1980. With respect to statistics, the number of women practicing law is increasing. In Brazil women are 46 percent of all legal aid attorneys, who earn the lowest salaries, and 20 percent of public prosecutors. Because poverty makes the courts inaccessible to most people, police chiefs (who are law graduates) settle many disputes. Women constitute only 6 percent of police chiefs (Falcão, 1988).[288] While in Brazil, women are 24.6 percent of law graduates but only 20.9 percent of legal professionals. These decisions are more particularistic, on the basis of factors such as personal affinity, and generally less on the basis of factors such as personal affinity, and generally less visible.[289]

VENZUELA

In Latin America, culture delayed women's entry to law school. The first woman received her degree from the Universidad Central de Venezuela in 1936. She wasn't able to vote until Venezuela granted suffrage in 1947. A review of women's participation in legal profession in Latin America shows that although the percentage of female lawyers and judges is high compared to countries in the North, ranging from a third to half of the workforce, there are barriers to women's career progression that prevent them from reaching positions of power and influence. In Venezuela and Peru there are higher numbers of women judges, in criminal and family courts, with few above the courts of first instance.

---

288 Abel, Richard.l and Lewis Philipp, S.C; "Feminization of Legal Profession," *Lawyers in Society*. Beards Books, 2005, Washington D.C.p.213.

289 Barzaghi, Allessandro: *The Legal Profession in Italy: From Law School Practice.* <http://www.scu.edu/scjil/global/BarzaghiArticle.shtml.> on7th March 2009.

PERU

In Peru, Janet Tello Girali is an appellate level judge. When she started as a legal assistant 20 years ago at the Supreme Court in Lima, there was a courtroom that women were not allowed to enter. In 1998, to dispel the widespread suspicion that judges were corrupt, Judge Girali helped found an association of judges dedicated to proving judges could be fair-minded and independent. Today she has formed another association, which is training judges to be more sensitive to gender issues.[290]

The story in Asia and Africa is much the same, with many nations resisting higher education for women or their admission to the bar. Women now have access to the legal profession in most nations. So the challenge continues. However, the increase of women in legal education in many countries has occurred at the expense of the working class. Despite democratization of the university, law students, including women, remain solidly middle- or upper class in most countries.[291]

ARGENTINA

A study of women lawyers in Argentina highlights a common problem facing women lawyers in countries where opportunities are scarce. Because of the scarcity of work it is important for young lawyers to spend more time in senior's chamber. This is more difficult for married women than it is for married men, unless the couple can both benefit from such a move. When they do not it is usually the woman who gives up on her career. In Argentina successful women lawyer tend to be either single or married with no children, a tough choice echoed in anecdotal evidence from women around the world collected for this study. Law is almost everywhere, and its application is in all fields, still it is a predominantly male profession and perceived as a 'masculine' endeavour. Even though this may be slowly changing, the image of law portrayed in the media and the lack of women in policy and decision making positions , in judiciary means that it is seen as a 'man's world' deterring many young women aspirants who might have thought of choosing law as a career. Compared to professions such as advertisement, medicine, media, and film industry, that are

---

290 Mathis, Karen J : "Status of Women in the Legal Profession around the World" <www.womeninlaw.com/newsletter2/mathis.htm> on 9th March 2009.

291 Abel, Richard L., and Philip S. C. Lewis, editors, *Lawyers in Society: An Overview*. Berkeley, Calif: University of California Press, 1995. < http://ark.cdlib.org/ark :>

increasingly portrayed in the media as comprising both successful men and women, little seems to have changed in the portrayal of the average lawyer, especially those involved in legal research, as predominantly middle aged and male. The women who do opt for a career often find themselves in a male dominated work environment facing very real discrimination although it may be subtle and sometimes even unintentional. Studies show how such a work environment can result in women's marginalization within the legal community and a feeling of isolation.

SOUTH AFRICA

Navanethem Pillay was the first woman to start a law practice in Natal Province, South Africa, in 1967. She met all obstacles in her path to becoming a lawyer and in her criminal practice concentrated on crimes of violence against women and children. She went on to serve as an acting judge on the High Court of South Africa, and then became the president of the International Criminal Tribunal for Rwanda in 1995. She has been selected this year to serve on the International Criminal Court in The Hague. Interestingly, of the six candidates elected to the ICC, only one was a man![292]

5.5 EUROPEAN COUNTRIES

Italy and Brazil, for example, display high attrition rates during law study because entry is easy, Law Schools are free or very inexpensive in Italy but students has to incur high opportunity costs in delaying earning capacity for as long as seven years, unassisted by practice which is in the common law countries.[293] Practical legal education actually occurs in costly "crammer" courses, often established by private entities (and offering low-paid employment for law graduates).In 1950, France had 23 percent of law students .While in 1960, the number decreased to 13 percent and in 1970 it again increased to 24 percent .But decreased to 16 percent. Similarly, the law students in Germany comprised 10 percent in 1950 but declined to 13 percent in 1960. It further declined to 7 percent in 1980 and 6 percent in 1991.There was not much of

292 Mathis, Karen J; "Status of Women in the Legal Profession around the World,"<http://www.womeninlaw.com/newsletter2/mathis.htm> on 5th March 2009.

293 Santa Clara Journal of International Law <http://www.scu.edu/scjil/global/Barzaghi Article.shtml>

fluctuation in Italy. Though Spain had 31 percent in 1950 of law students .It declined to 22 percent in 1991.The data's are shown in Table-5.1. In Continental Europe, where law is an undergraduate degree, women represented 37 percent of German law students, 54 percent of French, 35 percent of Belgian, and 54 percent of Norwegian, as of 1983.[294]

---

[294] Abel, Richard.l and Lewis Philipp, S.C; "Feminization of Legal Profession," *Lawyers in Society*. Beards Books, 2005, Washington D.C.p.207.

TABLE 5.1
PERCENTAGE OF UNIVERSITY STUDENTS IN LAW
(COUNTRY – WISE)

	1950	1960	1970	1980	1991
France	23	13	24	16	
Germany	10	9	9	7	6
Italy	16	19	9	14	15
Spain	31	18	10	17	22

Source: Richard Abel, and Philipp S.C Lewis; Women in Legal education, *Lawyers in Society: an Overview*, p.206.

ITALY

In 2002, women graduating from Italian law schools were 60 percent of the total. Among lawyers younger than 30 years old, women represented 51.7 percent of the total, and this percentage is going up every year. Among older lawyers, things change: women lawyers over 40 years old are only 16.4 percent of the total. This shows that in the past, the legal profession was seen as men's business. Of the global population of lawyers, women represent today a respectable 33.7 percent. Statistics show that many women drop out of the profession after 5 to 6 years, due to difficulties in trying to match family and profession. Women are also virtually not represented in bodies governing lawyers and make considerably less money than their male colleagues.

Italy has a plethora of lawyers, not as many as the United States, but still a very high number. According to recent information, practicing lawyers right now in Italy reached 1, 50,000.[295] The figure is quite amazing, considering that Italy is a Country with 57 million people. This means that 2.5 individuals out of 1,000 are lawyers.

France, for instance, has 39,000 lawyers, for roughly the same population. This means a more balanced per capita number of 0.7 lawyers out of 1,000 individuals. Many may object that comparing lawyers in different countries is like comparing oranges and apples, because every country has different rules for accessing the practice of law in a broad sense. Even conceding a margin of error, the final conclusion remains the same: many licensed lawyers barely make a living, and end up to make ends meet by being ambulance chasers.

If legal education generally has become more available to women, entry into the profession remains controlled at later stages by alternative mechanism. Although women were allowed open access to schools and employment around the turn of the century and suffrage on a national level in 1933, they were not on an equal footing with men in family affairs. Men were automatically heads of households, and married

---

295 Santa Clara; *Journal of International Law* <http://www.scu.edu/scjil/global/Barzaghi Article.shtml> on 8th March 2009.

women were legally subordinate to their husbands. Under the constitution of 1988, women became entirely equal to men for all legal purposes.[296]

GERMANY

In Germany as in many other countries, women were only admitted to the university law schools in the beginning of twentieth century, more precisely between 1900 to 1909.In 1912, the first women passed the first state examination in law. In 1991out of 9635 candidates who passed the first examination 4115 were women (42.7 percent). In the same year, out of 7806 candidates who passed the second examinations, 2914 were women (38.6 percent).[297]

In Germany, women prefer public sector jobs because the civil service, particularly the judiciary, permits part-time work and allows maternity leave for many years with guaranteed reentry to the same job. Women currently represent 28 percent of judges in practice training and 30 percent of all probationary judges (those with less than three years' experience). Unfortunately, these jobs are becoming less available as the economy slows. Since women experience difficulty in obtaining jobs in private corporations many are becoming advocates. In 1983 they represented 36 percent of advocates (Blankenburg & Schultz, 1988).

FRANCE

In France, which has career judges, more than 54 percentof the judiciary is women.

BELGIUM

In Belgium, by contrast, where judges are less numerous and even more prestigious, women are less well represented. They constituted 14.5 percent of the judiciary in 1982, and only 3.5 percent at the highest level, but 20 percent of the bar. Women made up less than 5 percent of law graduates employed in banking and other

---

296 Lewis, Jone Johnson; "Encyclopedia of Women's History," <http://womenshistory.about.com/ library/ency/blwh_brazil.htm.> on 5th March 2009.

297 Schultz Ulrike, Shaw, Gisela; *Women in the Worlds Legal Profession,* Hart Publishing, Oxford and Portland, 2003, Oregon, p. 277.

commercial spheres but 23.4 percent of law teachers and 35.6 percent of advocates. They represented only 3.5 percent of notaries—a highly prestigious and remunerative office in Belgium—but 80 percent in the Soviet Union, where the functions are more bureaucratic and ministerial. Women represented 35 percent of law students but 50 percent of law graduates seeking work, which suggests higher levels of unemployment. Fifty percent of all Belgian women attorneys work in Brussels, perhaps because lifestyle is more anonymous in the city (Huyse, 1988). In contrast, French women lawyers are over-represented in suburban practices serving working-class populations and underrepresented in prestigious commercial Paris practices (Boigeol, 1988).

NORWAY

In Norway women are underrepresented in litigation partly because the role is viewed in Norway as requiring 'aggressive' and 'defiance'. They are overrepresented in the lower ranks of the central government. Women in private practice handle two-thirds of all personal relations clients, while men handle three-fourths of all matters involving property (twice as many men as women reported having consulted a lawyer: 27 percent vs. 13 percent).

FINLAND

In Finland, the first women law graduate was Agnes Lundell in1906. Between 1906 -1948 only100 women took a Law degree in Finland. The dramatic expansion of the university system of the late 1960s had the impact in 1970s which affected legal education. In 1980s with the impact of the labour market, the share of women in legal profession continued to grow rising from 28 percent to 42 percent in the course of the 1990s and reaching 43 percent in the year 2000.[298] Lately, 46 percentof judges are women.

CROATIA

Since 1994, courts in the Republic of Croatia have limited the right to free legal aid. In 1995, the government eliminated this right altogether. As a result, free

298 Ibid. p. 389

legal representation is only available through members of the Bar Association who agree to take a case on a *pro bono* basis. People eligible for *pro bono* work must be 'socially underprivileged' as defined by the Bar Association, and produce supporting documentation. Many women who do not meet the definition of "socially underprivileged" are nonetheless unable to afford a lawyer. Often these women do not have the skills necessary to represent their own interests and to protect their rights.[299]

Recently Croatia has one woman judge.IkaSaric is a Judge in the Appeal Court in Rijeka, Croatia. She became a judge of first instance and then was transferred to the Appeal Court. Judge Saric is admired by women lawyers of Croatia for her strength, character and high ethical standards.

SERBIA

There is no specific data available on the proportion of women lawyers in Serbia.Peposava Karamarkovic was the President of the Supreme Court of Serbia since 1991. In 2000, Judge Karamarkovic was dismissed from the bench by the Milosevic regime. She was re-appointed to the Supreme Court as its President after the regime's downfall. Her judicial reform initiatives are substantial. She is a courageous leader of the legal reform movement in Serbia, a standard bearer for judicial integrity, and a woman lawyer.[300]

RUSSIA

Women make 46.9 percent of the employed population in Russia. The greatest proportion of working women is in public health service and education. The principle for equal pay for equal work are in the constitution but men prevail among leading positions and dominate among well paid and so their average pay is higher than women.[301]

299 < https://litigation-essentials.lexisnexis.com/> on 8th March 2009.

300 "Serbian Supreme Court: President of the court", <http://www.vrh.sud.rs/code/navigate.php?Id=81> on 10th September 2009.

301 "Interesting Facts about Russian women and Women Rights in Russia," Submitted by Administration, published on 14th August, 2009.<http://www.waytorussia.net/WhatIsRussia/Women/Facts.html> on 8th September 2009.

In Russia, attorney Elena Mizulina served as a criminal law professor prior to being elected in 1993 to the Federation Council, which is the upper chamber of the Russian Parliament. She has since served as the Deputy Chairman of the Committee on Constitutional Legislation and Judicial Issues of the Federation Council. Working closely with CEELI, the ABA's Central and Eastern European Legal Initiative, Deputy Mizulina tirelessly worked for the passage of the Russian Criminal Procedure Code. This landmark Code moves Russia forward significantly in the area of criminal justice reform.

5.6 ASIAN COUNTRIES

JAPAN

In Japan women continue to represent a small fraction of law students. In Japan this is attributed to the persistence of traditional beliefs that men should be breadwinners and women should perform domestic chores at home. Although coeducation has been the official policy since the late 1940s, women frequently are educated in single-sex schools. Although 95.5 percent of girls entered high school in 1984, compared to 92.8 percent of boys, only 12.6 percent of women attended four-year universities and colleges, compared to 36.4 percent of men. Increased sexual equality can be attributed to international pressures, most notably the United Nations Convention on the Elimination of All Forms of Discrimination of 1979, to which Japan was a signatory, and to Japan's desire to be seen as a 'progressive' nation. Japanese legal education system is driven more by examination than by formal schooling. The profession of barristers, known as bengoshi, is highly regulated, and the passage rate for the bar exam is around three percent. Prospective attorneys who do pass the exam must take it three or four times before passing it and a number of specialized "cram schools" exist for prospective lawyers. After passing the bar exam, prospective barristers undergo a one-year training period at the Legal Research and Training Institute of the Supreme Court of Japan. During this period, the most capable trainees are 'selected out' to become career judges; others may become prosecutors or private practitioners.

In 2004, the Japanese government passed a law allowing for the creation of three-year law schools .The 2006 bar examination will be the first in Japanese history to require a law school degree as a prerequisite. In the past, although there has been no educational requirement most of those who passed the examination had earned undergraduate degrees from "elite" Japanese universities such as the University of Tokyo or Kyoto University. Since 2004, the J.D. degree is also awarded in Japan, the only civil law country to do so, where it is known as Homu Hakushi.[302]

KOREA

Similar to the Japanese legal education system, the legal education in Korea has been driven by examination. The profession of barristers, is highly regulated, and the passage rate for the bar exam is around five percent. Prospective attorneys who do pass the exam usually take it two or three times before passing it and a number of specialized 'cram schools' exist for prospective lawyers. After passing the bar exam, prospective barristers undergo a two-year training period at the Judicial Research and Training Institute of the Supreme Court of Korea. During this period, the most capable trainees are 'selected out' to become career judges; others may become prosecutors or private practitioners.

In 2007, the Korean government passed a law allowing for the creation of three-year law schools .According to the new law, the old system of selecting lawyers by examination will be phased out. The U.S.-style law schools will be a sole route to become a lawyer.[303]

Law degree programs are considered graduate programs in the Philippines. As such, admission to law schools requires the completion of a bachelor's degree, with a sufficient number of credits or units in certain subject areas.

---

302 "State Master," – Encyclopedia: Juris Doctor <http:// www.statemaster.com/encyclopedia/Juris-Doctor> on 8th September 2009.

303 *Wikipedia,* <http://en.wikipedia.org/wiki/Legal_education> on 8th March 2009.

PHILLIPENES

Graduation from a Philippine law school constitutes the primary eligibility requirement for the Philippine Bar Examinations, administered by the Supreme Court during the month of September every year.[304]

NEPAL

The Supreme Court in Nepal recently has appointed its first female judge: Ms Sushila Singh Shilu, who will serve for a two-year term as a member of the court where she has been working as a lawyer for several years. She joins just with five other female judges in Nepal, with all the others presiding over lower courts. Women comprise only a small percentage in most areas of Nepali professional life.[305]

Yet, even today, female judges are most often found in the courts of first instance and their numbers and percentages decrease as you climb up the judicial hierarchy. The percentage of women reaching partner status has remained stagnant or even declined in most nations. Women continue to face barriers in law firm environments that undervalue their work, misread their commitment, and thwart effective mentoring

While there has been a notable increase recently in the number of applications by women for judicial office, many women do not apply, or may not do as well as men, for a range of reasons that are remediable.

5.7. MUSLIM COUNTRIES

In Muslim dominated countries, male lawyers are opposed to women being appointed as judges and say if at all; they should be restricted to family courts. For them, a woman is emotionally and physiologically not geared to fit in the role of a judge since the job demands a balanced disposition. Historically, Islamic religion in the world is opposed to having females as judges, he said. There are verses in the

304 "Law School," *Wikipedia*, <http://en.wikipedia.org/wiki/Law_school#Philippines.> on 12th March 2009.

305 <http://BBC/News/South AsiaNews.bbc.co.uk/1/hi/world/southasia >on5th March 2010.

Holy Quran and some Hadith (Traditions of the Prophet) against women being appointed as judges, many Muslims held this view. But Muslim women lawyers are critical of their male counterparts and opine that females should not being allowed to become judges are biased.

A judge has to base his or her decision on points of law and evidence, so where is the question of emotion and physiology being involved in it. There is no reason why women cannot become judges? In Qatar, women have proved their worth in every conceivable field, so why they shouldn't be allowed to enter the judicial profession?

The question is whether women can become judges or hold the high public post has been supported by Muslim scholars by sound reasons. A few points will help us to understand the mood of the Islamic Sharia and polity. What we find in the Islamic Sharia is that women are absolved in a number of responsibilities and obligations without least affecting their 'rights'. It has a high importance attached to the bearing and upbringing of the offspring. Proving for the household expenditure in a Muslim family is the sole responsibility of a man, as husband, as father, as son to the mother, as brother for unmarried and divorces sisters. This is so even for women more specifically the wife. Why then under normal circumstances should she seek a job, including being a judge?

QUATAR

Women are showing excellence in almost every field in Qatar and walking shoulder to shoulder with men, but dispensing justice is not their cup of tea. "It is entirely the male's domain", though, they support the idea of women judges in the family courts," Women are physiologically not geared to be in a judge's role since their performance can be affected during menstrual cycle, pregnancy and delivery,"are the normal belief.

The Peninsula was seeking the views of the legal fraternity on whether women should be appointed as judges in the Qatari courts after media reported that United

Arab Emirates recently had decided to have females in the profession, which triggered a debate. Some of the views were taken.[306]

According to some male protagonist even if a woman is picked as a judge, her performance would be good for a limited period. "It's rare to have a female judge with a stable track record." Some of the men are not opposed to women being inducted as judges but quickly referred to the family courts where women have more important role for them. While some lawyers think that in criminal courts, female would not be able to fit in as a judge though there are enough signs indicating that women may soon begin entering the judicial profession. The number of women lawyers is increasing and, recently, a female has been picked as a Public Prosecutor.

UNITED ARAB EMIRATES

The United Arab Emirates inspite of such opinion prevailing hopes to amend a law and allow women to become federal judges and prosecutors[307]

If approved, the move would make the United Arab Emirates the second Gulf Arab country to allow women to become judges, the English-language daily said. Muslim region see women's primary role as being in the home.[308] Although many Arab women lawyers have represented clients (mostly women) in family matters, women judges of most Arab countries do not preside over family courts. These courts apply religious law, which historically has prohibited women from holding judicial office.

AFGHANISTAN

In January, 2003 for the first time in Kabul, Afghanistan launched Afghanistan's first association of female judges. Funded by the United Nation's Development Fund for Women (UNIFEM), the Afghan Women Judges Association

---

306 Saeed Mohamed; "Mens verdict: No women judges," *The Peninsula,* 8th Jan. 2008. http://www.thepeninsulaqatar.com/Display_news.asp?section=local_news&month=january2008 &file=local_news2008010822652.xml on 17th March 2010

307 Piper, Elizabeth, "UAE seen hoping to allow women judges," Dubai, 6th Jan.2008, Business News, 2008

308 Ibid.

(AWJA) aims to ensure the active participation of female judges and lawyers in the judicial system, as well as to promote quality and reliable legal advice for vulnerable Afghan women countrywide. Despite the Afghan Women Judges Association having experienced women judges and lawyers, had never been given the opportunity to assume higher positions.

There are currently some 50 female judges in Afghanistan, most of who work in Kabul. Because of security and some unsuitable traditional matters, women judges cannot work in the provinces. There was only one female judge in the northern province of Ballista. There are infrastructure challenges; poor court facilities in Afghanistan that reflects the country's broken infrastructure. For example, most courts are not located in separate buildings and share space with other agencies. The judges often do not have desks so they carry their folders with them wherever they go. There are no women's bathrooms in these buildings so the judges must wait until there are no men present to use the facilities. In crowded courtrooms, judges waiting to hear their cases often find themselves seated next to defendants. The hallways are always dark, because the country has limited electricity.

Women would have to work harder to prove the efficient and effective role they could play in judicial affairs if public perception were to change, particularly in rural areas.

EGYPT

In Egypt, the move follows a decision by the SJC in 2003 to allow the appointment of women, for the first time, as adjudicators in the nation's courts. Rights activists, meanwhile, praised the new postings, noting that Egypt traditionally lagged behind many of its Arab counterparts in terms of female judicial participation. The decision was supported by Egypt's state-appointed Grand Mufti, Sheikh Ali Gama, who ruled that the appointment of women to judicial positions did not contradict Islamic precepts.

In mid-March, the SJC accepted 124 applications from female candidates, with the stipulation that applicants must have previous experience working in judicial agencies. After extensive examinations, 31 were chosen to preside over family courts (although one, citing personal reasons, turned down the posting). "This latest victory ... means that everyone is beginning to recognise women's rights and women's potential," Hanan Abdel-Aziz, one of the newly appointed judges, told the state press at the time.

The move is not without precedent. In 2003, a woman, Tahani el-Gebali, was made a justice on the Supreme Constitutional Court by presidential decree, officially making her the country's first-ever female judge. Unlike the new batch of female judicial appointments, however, el-Gebali's position entails handing down rulings on legislation rather than on individuals.[309]

An UK scientist describes being one of the few women in her work place: "When you talk to younger women they will often say that they have no problems at work and that they get along with their male peers very well. But the change happens when you reach your thirties and people start settling down. You suddenly find that you are not 'one of the guys'. On top of that you get the bantering, big brother teasing type stuff, which is not meant to exclude or offend but still it affects you. I liken it to a gentle jabbing in the arm with a finger. It doesn't hurt and there is no evidence of harm, but as time goes on it starts to get sore. It undermines confidence and wears you down and before you know it you have started modifying the way you behave in the workplace. It's a time when a lot of women start to feel isolated." Similar issues have been stated in the legal profession in earlier chapters.

5.8. THE NATURE OF PROBLEM WORLDWIDE

Over and over, as the statistics are tallied, the picture remains the same:

- In Mexico only 15 percent of law degrees went to women in 1965; by 1997 it was 47 per cent.
- Chile raised from 23 percent in 1992 to 40 percent in 1999.
- By 1998, 60 percent of Venezuelan law students were women.

---

309 Morrow, Adam and Moussa, Khalid; "Female Judge Appointments Stir Controversy,16th Apri,2007,Cairo. <http://ipsnews.net/news.asp?idnews=37358> on 6th Sep.2008.

- The same is true in Hong Kong.
- In the UK, in 2001 59 percent of students enrolled in undergraduate law courses were women and in 2000/01. 48 percent of pupil barristers were female, as were 59 percent of trainee solicitors.
- In 1999, female students constituted 57 percent of undergraduate law students in Australia
- Croatia is in the minority of nations, where as much as three quarters of the law students are women and more than 50 percent of the profession is female.
- In Germany, females account for, on average, a quarter of the nation's lawyers.
- In Nigeria the ratio is 60 percent female to 40 percent male.
- In 1999, 29 percent of the practicing legal profession in Australia was women and of these 16 percent were partners or sole principals.
- The situation in Africa is as varied as the nations and cultures of that great continent. In Nigeria where senior advocates are the equivalent of QCs in the UK, few women have risen to this level. Women continue to face severe challenges in the profession. Two women who have struggled and succeeded are Dorothy Ufot and Hauwa Ibrahim. Their practice settings are quite different but they have both experienced the sting of discrimination in Nigeria.
- Some believe that the women in Latin America have faced greater barriers to advancement than their peers in America and Europe.
- A study of women in Argentina found the inequity in wages discouraged Argentine women from working, especially because the inequality became more pronounced as age and qualifications increased. Some of the available data on women lawyers around the world confirmed the impression that women receive the least prestigious jobs specifically for the legal sector. Despite women earning their law degrees yet have to continue their struggle.
- In Mexico, the Barra Mexicana has 1977 members, 11 percent, are women.
- In Venezuela, the top six law firms has only 17 women .

5.9. A SUM UP

This chapter fives the following findings:

(i) The broad line of distinction between male and female is unconstitutional, and drawing lines among sexes is unnecessary. What is apparent is that there is a glass ceiling and women find it is difficult to breakthrough.

(ii) Women in many countries now constitute half or more of the workforce and they can be found in all professions. Yet, more analyses show that women's participation tends to be highly concentrated in only quite a narrow range of legal profession.

(iii) Women are clustered in the lower echelons of professional hierarchies while elite positions are by and large the reserve of men. This horizontal and vertical segregation means that female dominated occupations tend to be those with lower standing in terms of career opportunities, income and prestige.

(iv) In the Soviet Union women are well represented in the public health service.

(v) As in other countries, however, the majority of women work at the lower levels, as notaries, investigators, and assessors (Matveev, 1977/78).

(vi) The proportion of women in the legal professions is higher in socialist countries partly because those administrative jobs are less prestigious than the commercial work and litigation performed by lawyers in capitalist nations.

(vii) The proportion of women in the legal profession is smallest in Japan. In Japan women represent about 10 percent of those who pass the extremely difficult bar examination. Fewer than ten women are prosecutors, and only about fifty are judges, most at the lower levels (district and family court) (Kamiya, 1986). These data suggest that traditional gender roles remain very strong in Asian cultures.

(viii) In India, in 1981 women represented 2.7 percent of the Indian bar. Even upper-caste women in the Punjab encounter structural barriers and are expected to interrupt their careers to bear and raise children (Sethi, 1987).

(ix) Although relatively large numbers of women work in the judicial system in Morocco, they suffer 'humiliation' at home and have failed to act collectively to challenge a legal regime in which "polygamy, repudiation and unequal inheritance are daffy practice," for fear of the repercussions at home.

(x) In Muslim countries, women are largely excluded from the important spheres of politics and religion. Those who work at all are encouraged to remain in the 'social-cultural' sectors of their professions—the arts, education, medicine, and some segments of the civil service (Memissi, 1986).Very few women could reach the higher echelons of judiciary.

CHAPTER-VI

WOMEN IN JUDICIARY

"Empowering women is the most effective tool for development as well as for poverty reduction. Women, who are educated and have been given a chance, have proved that they excel in their professions and careers. Educated and enlightened women can look after families better, make societies compassionate and make nations progressive"

- Smt. Pratibha DeviSingh Patil

The President of India

At the Sixth South Asia Ministerial Conference, Beijing

17th January, 2008

6.1. AN OVERVIEW

In the earlier chapter, after looking into the legal profession in general, we have studies about the position of women in judiciary .In this chapter the researcher will focus into the representation, working conditions of women in judiciary in India. In discussing the role of women in judiciary, the researcher has also mentioned contribution of women in judiciary and referred some important reality. That though there is no discrimination against women in the judicial system in India, yet there is not very many women in the higher echelons of the judiciary. The analysis done from the available data shows some discouraging phenomena and the causes have been discussed under the following heads:

Disproportionate representation

Factors for in adequate Representation

- The Colonial legacy.
- Impact on women.
- Participation in Decision making.
- Disproportionately Engaged in Cases.

- Employment Sector.
- Economic Development.
- Education.
- Work force Participation.
- Injustice to women.

A peep into the profiles of the High Courts.

- Allahabad High Court
- Andhra Pradesh High Court
- Bombay High Court
- Calcutta High Court
- Chhattisgarh High Court
- Delhi High Court
- Gauhati High Court
- The Gujarat High Court
- Himachal Pradesh High Court
- Jharkhand High Court
- Jammu and Kashmir High Court
- The Karnataka High Court
- Kerala High Court
- Madhya Pradesh High Court
- Madras High Court
- Orissa High Court
- The Patna High Court
- Punjab and Haryana High Court
- Rajasthan High Court
- Sikkim High Court
- Uttarakhand High Court

Family courts in India

- An analysis of the Family Courts

  Launched without proper planning

  Lack of experience

  Less number of women judges

Lack of uniform rules

Non enforcement of rights

Unsatisfactory working conditions

The family courts are not easily accessible

Complex procedures

The Juvenile Justice Board.

A Glance into other services

Judicial reforms: New initiatives taken by the government

- Computerization of Courts
- Fast Track Courts
- Mahila Courts
- Newly created High Courts / High Court Benches
- Filling up Vacancies of Judges

A critical analysis

A Sum Up

In 1944, Asima Chatterjee became the first Indian woman to be conferred the Doctorate of Science by an Indian university. On August 15, 1947, following independence, Sarojini Naidu became the governor of the United Provinces, and in the process became India's first woman governor. In 1951, Prem Mathur becomes the first Indian women commercial pilot of the Deccan Airways. While in 1953,Vijaya Lakshmi Pandit became the first woman (and first Indian) president of the United Nations General Assembly. In the past, women's chances to become judges were slim hence judiciary had under representation of women. Her promotion to the Kerala high court in 1959 made her the first woman judge to make it to a high court.[310] was the first woman Chief Justice of a High Court in India, the first woman Judge of the Delhi High Court, the first woman to top the Bar examinations in London: Leila Seth has led a full life.

But lately, the increased presence of women in legal profession and the increasing entry of women in judicial service are bringing more civility to the profession. According to the 2001 census (at the last count) the population of India

[310] Singh, Sach Kanwal; "Courting Justice: Looking at India's justice dispensing system,"<worldsikhnews.com/5%20August%202009/Courting%20Justice.htm> on 1/02/10.

was 1,028,737,436 - more than a billion, of which 496,514,346 was female.[311] The total population of the country stands at 1,129.9 million (July 1, 2007 est. CIA).[312] According to a report published in India today, 'In 1950, there were 14 women pursuing higher studies per 100 males in India. The ratio is now 68:100 (Report of Consultative Committee of Parliament, 2006).' So, the ratio is definitely getting better, although the actual number of women who go on to become graduates is only 12,136,839.[313]

The proportion of women in the judiciary remains low in India, especially when compared with most countries of Europe. Prior to 1999, the Court of Justice had had one woman member until Ireland appointed Fidelma Macken in late 1999, and Germany appointed Ninon Colneric and Austria appointed Christine Stix-Hackl Advocate General in 2000.The 1995 U.N. meeting in Beijing was a catalyst for the demand for balanced participation of women and men in decision-making processes within the E.U., and it coincided with Sweden, Finland and Austria joining and championing the cause of gender equality. In 1999, the Commission published a report on women in the judiciary and women lawyers began to organize across Europe. The situation is a little different in other countries. For instance, according to the Office of the Commissioner for Federal Judicial Affairs in Canada, as of December 2008 the Canadian Supreme Court has four women out of a total eight judges. Furthermore, nine out of 30 judges in its federal court are women. In UK this year, the selection of a large number of woman judges to the high court raised to about 15 percent of the total strength. Even China is known to have a large number of woman judges. There were several interesting findings regarding women judges in between 1980 to 1990. They were:

(1) the lack of politicking and networking available to women judges and women seeking to become judges;

---

311 "State of Indian Women,"*CIOSA*, 18th November 2008'.<http://www.ciosa.org.in/index.php?option=com_content&task> on 6th Feb.2009.

312 Kaur,Jaspreet., "An Overview of Indian Demographics and its Implications on Market Planning," <http://www.indianmba.com/Occasional_Papers/OP160/op160.html.> on 7th Feb. 2009.

313 <http://www.anniezaidi.com/2008/01/womanhood-circa-2008-aka-kis-namaakool.html> on 1st Feb.2010.

(2) inappropriate interactions that take place in courtrooms; and

(3) the difficult act of balancing family life with the demands of a legal career

The first review of Judge Strength of High Courts was undertaken in 1995 and the approved strength of Judges in 18 High Courts was fixed on the basis of the revised guidelines laid down by the Supreme Court of India. The approved strength on December 31, 1998 was 618 comprising 498 permanent Judges and 120 Additional Judges. After the triennial review in 1999, the approved Judge strength was increased to 655 consisting of 514 permanent Judges and 141 Additional Judges.

But empirical studies have show that women did not attain judgeships. In the Supreme Court with 1 out of 25 male Justices, women had taken just 1 percentage in1997. On 4th May, 2001, there were altogether 20 women judges in the High Courts and Supreme Court of India. Of them, one women judge was in the Supreme Court of India out of a total sanctioned strength of 26 judges. In 2003, there were 17 women judges out of a total of 514 judges in the Supreme Court and High Courts in India.[314] The data is shown in Table 6.1.The approved strength of Judges in High Courts was 719 and the actual strength was 521 as shown in Table 6.2.[315] Because of the shortage of judges, there are huge pendency of cases in Supreme Court, High Courts and Subordinate Courts.[316] The data is shown in Table 6.3. In the year 2006; there were only 38 women judges in the higher judiciary.[317] The data is shown in 6.4. While in 2007, only 39 women judges were working out of the sanctioned strength of 689 as provided by the Ministry of Law and Justice.[318] The data is shown in Table 6.5.

The Indian judiciary continues to turn a Nelson's eye to gender parity despite the government making a concerted bid to raise women's representation in parliament and state legislatures to 33 percent. With only 42 woman justices in 21 high courts

314 "India, Ministry of Statistics and Programme Implementation, Central Statistical Organisation (2003):Women and Men in India 2002," *Department of Justice*, Ministry of Law and Justice and Company Affairs, New Delhi, *Centre for Women studies*, Combatore.

315 "Strength of Indian judiciary and lawyers," <http://hslsa.nic.in/Justice.pdf> on 2nd April 2009.

316 Lahoti, Justice R.C; "Speech on Law Day," (2005) 2 SCC (Jour) 1.

317 "Parliament debates: Women Judges in High Courts," Press Releases, published on 16th August, 2007.

318 "Ministry of Law and Justice," *Press Releases,* 16th August 2007, <http://pib.nic.in/release> on 2nd April 2009.

and none in the Supreme Court, women are inadequately represented in the country's judiciary. The official figures reveal that currently out of the total number of 630 judges working in 21 high courts of the country, merely 52 are women – a figure that works out to around 8.25 percent of the total. Compared to the total sanctioned strength of 895 judges in the high courts, the number of women judges working there further falls to an insignificant level of 5.8 percent in 2010.[319] As per official figures, the Supreme Court shares its dubious distinction with several high courts, including those of Jammu and Kashmir, Chhattisgarh and Himachal Pradesh. In the entire history of six decades, only three women were able to make it to the apex court as judges – M. Fathima Beevi in October 1989, Sujata V. Manohar in November 1994 and Justice Ruma Pal in 2006.

We can thus infer that women judges represent a very small proportion of those who, as advocates or solicitors, have been chosen for public service. So what explains this insularity?

319 *Published in News Views*, 7th March, 2010, < http://news-views.in/women-less-than-10-percent-of-indias-higer-judiciary-march-8-is-international-womens-day/> on 7th March 2010.

TABLE 6.1

NUMBER OF JUDGES BY SEX IN SUPREME COURT/HIGH COURTS ON 17.01.2003

Name of the court	Number of Judges		
	Female	**Male**	**Total**
Supreme Court	1	24	25
High Courts			
Allahabad	1	69	70
Andhra Pradesh	2	32	34
Bombay	3	49	52
Calcutta	1	41	42
Chhattisgarh	-	4	4
Delhi	1	27	28
Guwahati	-	12	12
Gujarat	1	30	31
Himachal Pradesh	1	5	6
Jammu & Kashmir	-	11	11
Jharkhand	-	12	12
Karnataka	1	31	32
Kerala	1	25	26
Madhya Pradesh	1	23	24
Madras	1	30	31
Orissa	-	12	12
Patna	1	23	24
Punjab & Haryana	1	30	31
Rajasthan	1	25	26
Sikkim	-	2	2
Uttaranchal	-	4	4
Total	**17**	**497**	**514**

Source: India, Ministry of Statistics and Programme Implementation, Central Statistical Organization (2003). Women and Men in India 2002. New Delhi, *Centre for Women studies,* Combatore.

Note: Department of Justice, Ministry of Law and Justice and Company Affairs.

TABLE 6.2

STRENGTH OF JUDGE IN 2005-06-A GLANCE

Name of the court	*Approved strength*	*Actual strength*	*Vacancies*
Supreme Court of India	26	25	1
High Courts	719	521	198
Subordinate Courts	13,204	11,103	2101

Source: Strength of Indian judiciary and lawyers, <http://hslsa.nic.in/Justice.pdf>

TABLE 6.3

PENDENCY OF CASES AS ON 30-6-2004

Supreme Court of India	29,315
High Courts	32,24,144
Subordinate Courts	2,53,50,370

Source: "Speech on Law Day," Justice R.C. Lahoti, (2005) 2 SCC (Jour) 1.

TABLE 6.4

WOMEN JUDGES IN SUPREME COURT & HIGH COURTS ON 17/5/06

Courts	**No. of women Judges (As on 17/05/2006)**
Supreme Court of India	1
Allahabad High Court	4
Andhra Pradesh High Court	2
Bombay High Court	5
Calcutta High Court	1
Delhi High Court	4
Guwahati High Court	1
Gujarat High Court	3
Karnataka High Court	1
Kerala High Court	1
Madhya Pradesh High Court	4
Madras High Court	4
Patna High Court	3
Punjab and Haryana High Court	3
Rajasthan High Court	1
TOTAL	**38**

Source: Parliament debates: 'Women Judges in High Courts', Press Releases, published on 16th August, 2007

TABLE 6.5

WOMEN JUDGES IN HIGH COURTS ON 16/08/07

Sl. No.	Court	Sanctioned Strength	No. of Judges in position	No. of Women Judges	No. of male Judges	Vacancies
	SUPREME COURT	26	26	-	22	04
	HIGH COURTS					
1.	Allahabad	95	76	04	72	19
2.	Andhra Pradesh	39	31	02	29	08
3.	Bombay	61	53	05	48	08
4.	Calcutta	50	42	02	40	08
5.	Chhattisgarh	08	06	00	06	02
6.	Delhi	36	32	05	27	04
7.	Gauhati	23	23	01	22	00
8.	Gujarat	42	30	03	27	12
9.	Himachal Pradesh	09	09	00	09	00
10.	Jammu & Kashmir	14	09	00	09	05
11.	Jharkhand	12	09	00	09	03
12.	Karnataka	40	36	01	35	04
13.	Kerala	29	27	01	26	02
14.	Madhya Pradesh	42	41	04	37	01
15.	Madras	46	44	04	40	02
16.	Orissa	20	14	01	13	06
17.	Patna	31	31	04	27	00
18.	Punjab & Haryana	40	35	01	34	05
19.	Rajasthan	40	37	01	36	03
20.	Sikkim	3	01	00	01	02
21.	Uttaranchal	9	09	00	09	00
TOTAL		**689**	**595**	**39**	**556**	**94**

Source: Ministry of Law and Justice, Press Releases, Thursday, August 16, 2007, <http://pib.nic.in/release>

6.2. FACTORS FOR DISPROPOTIONATE REPRESENTATION

6.2.1. THE COLONIAL LEGACY

Firstly, in terms of continuity, the judicial institution was the least affected in the transition from the 1935 Government of India Act to the Constitution. This meant that many of the traditions, rituals and privileges that constructed judicial insularity were uncritically carried forward The black coat, gown and the band are the most visible testimony to this. The colonial legacy also includes the structure of the language used in the courtroom – legal documents continue to be drawn in archaic English from the Victorian era. All of this is compounded by the attitude of the higher judiciary in protecting their privileges.[320] Despite the relative lack of transparency, the process of selection and upward mobility in the judiciary is very much political. But this insularity has also meant that as an institution, the judiciary has not managed to keep pace with the evolutionary processes of the other branches of government. The most obvious evidence for this would be the gross under-representation of women in the higher judiciary.

The under-representation of women in judicial office has led to calls for greater female representation based on an argument that women offer a different voice from that of men. This argument has largely foundered, and a more recent rationale rests on the need for diversity in the judiciary. However, the disadvantage experienced by women applicants to judicial office is rooted in deeply entrenched structural discrimination and exclusion, imbricates in the constitution of the judge, judging, and judicial authority as male, masculine, able-bodied, and class-privileged. Arguments for wider representation in judicial office need to address more effectively how the judge, judging, and judicial authority are constituted.

6.2.2. IMPACT ON WOMEN

The judiciary is unable to comprehend the social flavour of the legislations passed by Parliament and the state legislatures," since it has inadequate representation

---

[320] Kunhu, Bobby; "Ostrich on the Bench," 25th November, 2009. <http://www.sacw.net/article1249.htmlon3rd> 3rd March 2010

from "weaker sections" of the society, referring to disadvantaged castes and classes, and women. Women have been treated differently and unjust to them in many sectors in India. Some of important sectors where they are concerned more are given below and these are the fields where we can make efforts and strategies to improve so that it will bring changes and increase the status of women.

6.2.3. PARTICIPATION IN DECISION MAKING

Participation of women in the decision making bodies whether at home, workplace or community is marginal, never reaching even 25percent of the total population of women in India. At the same time women are seen as the bearers of Indian tradition and culture. Without enabling women to exist as citizens with judicial and economic power is it possible for them to safeguard the tradition and culture of this country? The poor judicial participation of women in India is largely the due to the consequence of the fact that the upbringing of girls does not equip them for roles and responsibilities as judges. The societal construction of image for women as motherhood, dependent and faithful wives, and homemakers makes it difficult them to turn out actively in the political sphere and represent themselves as responsible citizen of the citizen. That is why despite representing nearly 50percent of the Indian population, less than 6.5 percent of the Indian women are found as High Court judges.

6.2.4. DISPROPOTIONATE ENGAGEMENT IN CASES

One of the reasons being the trend that they are disproportionately engaged in shorter cases and cases involving family disputes and criminal law. Men still get the lion's share of big, important cases. Men are not stereotyped as especially suitable for any branch of legal practice. Women lawyer's still report instances of the alienation at the Bar akin to that their sisters find in the big firms. Although active hostility has probably diminished, there are still reports of alienating game play and barriers to entry into the mainstream of advocate's practice. Women are less likely to be briefed regularly then men. Amongst the ten largest Indian law firms it can be said that 91 percent of the briefs goes to male barristers. Some government departments have an unblemished record of never briefing a female advocate, hence very few women get a good standing as government pleaders which is a step behind of elevation to the bench.

That, as women progressed through their careers, their jobs becomes increasingly difficult because of the subtle and largely unconscious bias against women within It found evidence of clear differences in salary, resources and response to outside offers, with women lawyers consistently receiving less than men despite equal professional accomplishments.

Junior women lawyers feel that their most common concern being the extraordinary difficulty of combining family and work. However as their careers progressed they became increasingly marginalized and excluded from positions of real power. Women became increasingly aware of the unevenness of the playing field as they progressed through their careers. All sorts of unconvincing excuses have been offered over the years. As a result, female lawyers were less likely to be promoted than men; they had shorter contracts in legal firms and receive less recognition and feedback within the workplace. Female practitioners with the requisite years' experience were less likely to be elevated to the bench.

6.2.5. EMPLOYMENT SECTOR

The male-female superior-inferior hierarchy along with certain norms, values, practices and beliefs are still prevailing in the employment sector. In other words, a seperordinate-subordinate hierarchy is established on the basis of sex differences, whereby males have represents the outside world and women represents only in the household work. On the face of things; one would expect that the life as an independent lawyer would be easier. They are the women who want to escape the glass ceiling to escape to the Bar. There, they hope, they will advance on their merits. Skills of analysis and communication are not determined by gender. They are partly inborn and can be improved and refined, if only the opportunities offer. Yet if one looks at the Bar in India, it remains, overwhelmingly, a male preserve. The proportion of full-time women advocates varies. Bar is such a congenial place, offering equal opportunity for women, then why does this branch of the legal profession attract such a small proportion of women when for recent years women have represented about 40percent of the nation's law graduates? Part of the explanation is the time it takes to correct the old disproportions.

In the big legal firms women still cluster below the glass ceiling and if amongst the advocates they still lack the speaking parts in bigger cases. At Bar senior advocates argue cases and therefore women advocates are hardly in the limelight. These are influential factor to judicial appointment in higher judiciary. Both male and female candidates for positions are screened by a dominated Bar. Secondly, the absence of women from the judicial screening panels is often cited as an influential factor in judicial appointments. The high road to the highest courts will remain, for the foreseeable future, largely a male preserve. Some will say that we should not be too concerned about these facts. After all, the judiciary is a technical job, merit is the sole criterion for appointment and it matters not who performs the role of the judge. The law is not just another business. The bench is not just another workplace. Judges of our legal tradition have choices that they make in interpreting the Constitution, the Acts of Parliament and the common law. It is important that women should be brought to bear fully in the exercise of those choices. ?

In the High Court the average is about 6 per cent. In the Family Court it is around per cent. In the District Court around 2 percentapproximately. In the magistracy the proportion is higher and perhaps this is because of the more open procedures of recruitment and selection that apply. That is a real breakthrough for the judiciary. Upholding a service rule that preferred women in recruitment to public employment to the extent of 30 percent of posts, the Supreme Court stated in *Government of A.P. v. P.B. Vijay Kumar (1995) 4 SCC 520*: "To say that under Article 15(3) job opportunities for women cannot be created would be to cut at the very root of the underlying inspiration behind this Article. Making special provision for women in respect of employments or posts under the state is an integral part of Article 15(3)."[321]

---

321 Singh, Justice Yashpal; "Women Empowerment: Gender Justice-A Legal Panorama," , http://www.allahabadhighcourt.in/../Gender_Justice_-_A_Legal_Panorama. > on 6thMarch 2010.

6.2.6. ECONOMIC DEVELOPMENT

According to 1992-93 figures, only 9.2 percent of the households in India were female-headed. However, approximately 35 percent of the households below the poverty line were found to be female-headed.[322]

6.2.7. EDUCATION

Though it is gradually rising, the female literacy rate in India is lower than the male literacy rate. Compared to boys, far fewer girls are enrolled in the schools, and many of them drop out. According to the National Sample Survey Data of 1997, only the states of Kerala and Mizoram have approached universal female literacy rates. According to majority of the scholars, the major factor behind the improved social and economic status of women in Kerala is literacy. Education is an instrument for liberation and freedom but is far behind the touch of women with 48.3 percent (2003 est.) compare with male with 70.2 percent. In case of India, even the educated women with graduate and post graduate are unable to stand economically independent. In some cases, it is true that education is valuable only to the extent that it enhances their value in the marriage-market. They are bound by the societal imposed duty on them for being a faithful daughter, sister, and wives.

Under Non-Formal Education programme, about 40 percent of the centers in states and 10 percent of the centers in UTs are exclusively reserved for females. As of 2000, about 0.3 million NFE centers were catering to about 7.42 million children, out of which about 0.12 million were exclusively for girls. In urban India, girls are nearly at par with the boys in terms of education. However, in rural India girls continue to be less educated than the boys.

According to a 1998 report by U.S. Department of Commerce, the chief barrier to female education in India are inadequate school facilities (such as sanitary

---

322 "Women in India," *Wikipedia.* < http://en.wikipedia.org/wiki/Women_in_India> on 6th Feb.2009.

facilities), shortage of female teachers and gender bias in curriculum (majority of the female characters being depicted as weak and helpless).[323]

6.2.8. WORKFORCE PARTICIPATION

Contrary to the common perception, a large percent of women in India work. The National data collection agencies accept the fact that there is a serious under-estimation of women's contribution as workers. However, there are far fewer women in the paid workforce than there are men. In urban India Women have impressive number in the workforce. As an example at software industry 30 percent of the workforce is female. They are at par with their male counter parts in terms of wages, position at the work place. But this is only restricted to metropolitan cities.

6.2.9. INJUSTICE TO WOMEN

There are various reasons of leading injustice to women Different scholars view different views on this. The study of women's work force in a society involves a complex of multi dimensional thoughts. Women have been marginalized in every walk of life. According to liberal feminist, society remains structured in ways that favours men and disfavours women in the competitive race for the goods with which our society rewards us power, prestige and money. They are against the excuses or justification used to keep women in a lesser place. They argue that society should not only compensate for past injustices, but also eliminate socio-economic as well as legal impediments to women's progress today. This gender parity is clearly reflected in Indian society. Women are always at a disadvantage in every field. In the field of judiciary their presence is virtually absent at the higher level, where the real power lies. Indian women are getting less pay for the same work than men.

In most Indian families, women do not own any property in their own names, nor do they get a share in their parental property.Due to weak enforcement of laws protecting them, women continue to have little access to land and property. Due to weak enforcement of laws protecting them, women continue to have little access to land and property. In fact, some of the laws discriminate against women, when it

---

323 <http://in.answers.yahoo.com/question/index> on 7th January 2010.

comes to land and property rights.[324] Based on an analysis of women's, Martha A. Chen observed that "women seldom control either through ownership or use rights. With very few exceptions, women do not own land, the primary means of production."[325]

These relative deprivations women suffer in assess to productive resources and ownership and control of land, despite legal provision and ignorance of their legal right could be traced to be some important reasons. The other primary reasons seems to be old attitudes and values towards women's position which not only deprive equal assess to ownership and control but also discourage and disapprove redressal in courts of law for equal rights to property.

The Hindu personal laws of mid-1956s (applied to Hindus, Buddhists, Sikhs and Jains) gave women rights to inheritance. However, the sons had an independent share in the ancestral property, while the daughters' shares were based on the share received by their father. Hence, a father could effectively disinherit a daughter by renouncing his share of the ancestral property, but the son will continue to have a share in his own right. Additionally, married daughters, even those facing marital harassment, had no residential rights in the ancestral home. After amendment of Hindu laws in 2005, now women in have been provided the same status as that of men. Thus it took long time to bring women in the Hindu scheme of inheritance and succession and to assert the rights of ownership of property.[326] Thus, if women were not given ownership right till 2005 and had no economic independence, how would they make their presence feel in the legal profession?

6.2.10. WOMEN IN THE COURTROOM

As participants in the justice process, women are entitled not to be disadvantaged by reason of their status as women if they have recently given birth, or caring for children. Similarly, women and men who have dependent children may

---

324 "Women in India," *Wikipedia*, <http://en.wikipedia.org/wiki/Anna_Chandy> on 2nd May2009.

325 Chen, Martha A; "Women's work in Indian Agriculture by Agro Ecologic Zone," *JSTOR, Economic and Political Weekly,* Vol.24, No.43, 28th Oct.1989. <http://www.jstor.org/pss/4395524> on 2nd May2009.

326 Sarkar, Lolita and Sivaramayya; ***Women and Law, Contemporary Problems,*** Vikas Publishing House Pvt House, 1996, New Delhi, p.169.

have child care responsibilities, which make conventional sitting hours difficult or impossible for them. Such responsibilities should be accommodated as far as possible. It is unlikely to help in the achievement of justice if a witness or party is late or distracted by reason of concern over childcare. With sensible listing and case management such responsibilities should be readily accommodated.

6.2.11. WEAK LEGAL PROTECTION

India the largest democratic country in the world prescribed guarantees the protection of rights and status of the citizens of India irrespective of their social status, caste, class, sex etc. The makers of the Indian Constitution were very realistic in their expectations and that explains the various safeguards that they built into the Constitution to protect the rights of the marginalized and vulnerable groups in society. But there the question is as far as women are concerned do this our legal system is justifiable or not?

Every seventeenth person in India has a case going on in the courts; six percent population in India is affected by litigation; on an average, more than 10 percent of the population of Punjab and Haryana is affected by litigation. In fact, this number is higher than the national average; the total number of cases pending in Indian courts: 2.5 crore, out of which the total cases pending in subordinate and High Courts is 286 lakh.

These are some of the facts which were brought to light by Ashwinie Kumar Bansal, governing council member of International Centre for Alternate Disputes Resolution (ICADR). The report was submitted by Kumar at a seminar on 'ADR: Arbitration, Mediation and Conciliation' held at Law Bhawan, here.

In his report, Bansal has highlighted certain facts highlighting the dearth of judicial strength and the huge number of pending cases.

As per Bansal's report:

- The total institution in the High Courts was 16 lakh cases and total disposal was 15 lakh cases in 2006. Hence, the institution of new cases exceeded the actual disposal of cases. The overall institution continues to exceed disposal. High Courts have increased their annual disposal by 50 percentsince 1999.

- Total judges working in India (subordinate and High Courts) = 12,364. There is one judge for 83,000 Indians.

- Institution of civil cases in the High Courts was 11 lakh in the year 2006 as against the disposal of 10 lakh cases. The institution of criminal cases in the High Court in the year 2006 was 5 lakh as against disposal of 6 lakh cases. For the first time in the last eight years, disposal of criminal cases by High Courts exceeded the institution.

- Total pendency (civil and criminal cases) in subordinate courts has increased from 204 lakh at the end of 1999 to 257 lakh at the end of 2005. But it has reduced to 249 lakh in the year 2006.

- Total Advocates in India is 8.47 lakh. There is one advocate for 1,200 Indians.

- Institution of civil cases in the subordinate courts in 2006 was 40 lakh cases against disposal of 40 lakh. There are 72 lakh civil cases pending at the end of 2006 in various subordinate courts in India.

- Institution of criminal cases in subordinate courts in 2006 was 116 lakh as compared to 118 lakh cases. Thus, disposal of cases is more than the institution of new cases in 2006. There are 176 lakh pending criminal cases in the end of 2006. As many as 52 lakh cases involving petty offences were pending in the magisterial courts as on December 31, 2006. The annual disposal by subordinate courts increased from 124 lakh in the year 1999 to 163 lakh in the year 2005 and to 158 lakh in 2006.

Comparison of Indian and foreign judicial scenarios

- The population and judges ratio in India is 13.5 judges per 10 lakh people as compared to 135-150 per ten lakh people in advanced countries.

- At present, in India, the ratio is 13.5 judges per million of population whereas it is about 58 judges in Australia, 75 in Canada, 51 in UK and 107 in United States.

- The Madras High Court is in the lead in terms of speedy disposal of 648 cases on an average each day. Tamil Nadu is followed by Uttar Pradesh where the Allahabad High Court (Lucknow and Kanpur benches put together) dispose off 445 cases everyday.

- Sikkim High Court is the only HC to have total three judges sitting on the Bench, which is the total sanctioned strength; it has the pendency of about 50 cases, which is the lowest number of pending cases in a HC

- A total of 40,243 cases are pending in the Supreme Court of India as on January 31, 2007.

- The number of cases pending in the Punjab and Haryana High Court were around 2.6 lakh and old cases (in the courts for two years and more) are around 1.7 lakh. In the same period, the number of pending cases in the subordinate courts is around 11.8 lakh. This means, on an average, more than 10 percent of the population of Punjab and Haryana is affected by litigation. It is higher than the national average.[327]

6.3. A PEEP IN TO THE NUMBER OF WOMEN JUDGES IN THE HIGH COURTS

Allahabad High Court

The Allahabad High Court was originally founded as the High Court of Judicature for the North-Western Provinces at Agra on March 17, 1866 by the *Indian High Courts Act of 1861* replacing the Sader Diwani Adalat. The location was shifted to Allahabad in 1869 and the name was correspondingly changed to the High Court of

---

[327] Ohri, Raghav; Expressindia.com. <http://www.4jat.com/jat_community_article.asp?jat_community> on 6th March 2010.

Judicature at Allahabad from 11 March, 1919.[328]At present, there are only four women judges in the High Court.[329]

Andhra Pradesh High Court

The Andhra Pradesh High Court was set up on July 5, 1954 under the *Andhra State Act; 1953*.It has sanctioned judge strength of 39.[330]The court has two women judges.[331]

Bombay High Court

The Bombay High Court was inaugurated on 14 August 1862. The Bombay High Court has the sanctioned strength of 75 judges.[332] The Bombay High Court has seven women judges out of 62 male sitting judges.[333]

Calcutta High Court

The Calcutta High Court is the oldest High Court in India. It was established as the *High Court of Judicature at Fort William* on July 1, 1862 under the *High Courts Act, 1861*.[334] The court has sanctioned judge strength of 63 but has actually been carrying on with 39 judges, out of which two are women judges.[335]

---

328 "Allahabad High Court," *Wikipedia*. < http://en.wikipedia.org/wiki/Allahabad_High_Court> on 15th March 2010.

329 Shukla, Sourav; "Women less than 10 percent of India's higher judiciary," 7th March, New Delhi,<http://www.topnews.in/law/women-less-10-percent-indias-higer-judiciary-210886> on 12 March,2010.

330 "Andhra Pradesh High Court," *Wikipedia*. <http://en.wikipedia.org/wiki/Andhra_ Pradesh_High_Court> on 15th March 2010.

331 "Negligible presence of women judges in SC, HC," <http://www.expressindia.com/news/ fullstory> on 15th March 2010.

332 "Bombay High Court,' *Wikipedia*. < http://en.wikipedia.org/wiki/Bombay_High_Court> on 15th March 2010.

333 Shukla, Sourav; "Women less than 10 percent of India's higher judiciary," 7th March, New Delhi,<http://www.topnews.in/law/women-less-10-percent-indias-higer-judiciary-210886> on 12 March,2010.

334 "Calcutta High Court,' *Wikipedia*.< http://en.wikipedia.org/wiki/Calcutta_High_Court> on 15th March 2010

335 "Negligible presence of women judges in SC, HC,"<http://www.expressindia.com/ news/fullstory> on 15th March 2010.

Chhattisgarh High Court

The Chhattisgarh High Court is one of the newest High Courts in India. It was established on 11 January 2000 after the *Madhya Pradesh Reorganization Act, 2000* was passed.[336] The court has eighteen-sanctioned strength of judges. It has no woman judge.

Delhi High Court

It was established on October 31, 1966 after the *Delhi High Court Act* was passed. The sanctioned strength of judges at the Delhi High Court at present stands at 28 permanent judges and eight additional judges.[337] There are only eight women judges in Delhi High Court as on May11th, 2008.[338]

Gauhati High Court

The Gauhati High Court was established on March 1, 1948 after the *Government of India Act, 1935* was passed. It was originally known as the High Court of Assam and Nagaland, but renamed as Gauhati High Court in 1971 by the *North East Areas (Reorganisation) Act, 1971.*[339] The sanctioned strength of *Guwahati* High Court is 18 permanent /Additional Judges against the population of three crore thirteen lakh eighty six thousand nine hundred and eleven as per 1991 census. Accordingly, per judge population of the North East is seventeen lakh forty-three thousand seven hundred and seventeen as against the all India per judge population of fourteen lakh sixteen thousand six hundred and fifty one.[340] Smt. A. Hazarika was

---

336 "Chhattisgarh High Court," *Wikipedia.* <http://en.wikipedia.org/wiki/Chhattisgarh_High_Court> on 15th March 2010.

337 "Delhi High Court," *Wikipedia.* <http://en.wikipedia.org/wiki/Delhi_High_Court> on 15th March 2010.

338 Shukla, Sourav; "Women less than 10 percent of India's higher judiciary," 7th March, New Delhi. <http://www.topnews.in/law/women-less-10-percent-indias-higer-judiciary-210886> on 12 March, 2010.

339 "Gauhati High Court," *Wikipedia.* < http://en.wikipedia.org/wiki/Gauhati_High_Court> on 15th March 2010.

340 <http://pib.nic.in/archieve/lreleng/lyr2000/rnov2000/r28112000.html> on 15th March 2010.

sworn in as Additional Judge of the Gauhati High Court on 1st November 2004.She is the only women judge.[341]

The Gujarat High Court

The Gujarat High Court is the High Court of the state of Gujarat. It was established on May 1, 1960 under the *Bombay Re-organsisation Act, 1960* after the state split from Bombay State. The court has sanctioned judge strength of 42.[342] Smt. Justice Abhilasha Kumari has been appointed as a Judge of the Gujarat High Court.[343]

Himachal Pradesh High Court

The Himachal Pradesh High Court is the High Court of the state of Himachal Pradesh. It was established in 1971 under the *State of H.P. Act, 1970*. The court has sanctioned judge strength of 9 including the Chief Justice.[344]There is no woman judge in the High Court.

Jharkhand High Court

The Jharkhand High Court is one of the newest High Courts in India. It was established in 2000 under the *Bihar Reorganisation Act, 2000*, after the state of Jharkhand was carved out of the state of Bihar. The court has sanctioned judge strength of 20.[345] The first women Chief Justice of Jharkand High Court is Hon'ble Justice Gyan Sudha Mishra who was sworn in on 13[th]July, 2008.Another women judge, Hon'ble Jaya Roy was elevated as a Judge of Jharkhand High Court on 30.07.20 08.[346]

---

341 "Negligible presence of women judges in SC, HC,"<http://www.expressindia.com/news/fullstory> on 15th March 2010.

342 "Gujarat High Court,' *Wikipedia*. < http://en.wikipedia.org/wiki/Gujarat_High_Court> on 15th March 2010.

343 PIB Press Release, 11th September, 2006. <http://pib.nic.in/release/rel_print_page.asp?relid=20628> on 3rd March, 2009.

344 'Himachal Pradesh High Court," *Wikipedia*. <http://en.wikipedia.org/wiki/Himachal_Pradesh_High_Court> on 15th March 2010.

345 "Jharkhand High Court," *Wikipedia*. < http://en.wikipedia.org/wiki/Jharkhand_High_Court> on 15th March 2010.

346 Srivastave, Suman K; 'Judges, lawyers in title search', The Telegraph, Kolkata, India, 12th July 2008.

Jammu and Kashmir High Court

The Jammu and Kashmir High Court is the High Court of the state of Jammu and Kashmir. It was established on August 28, 1943 based on the *Letters Patent* issued by the Maharaja of Kashmir. The court has sanctioned judge strength of 14. J&K has a total of 10 High Court judges, two of them being posted in Rajasthan and Punjab & Haryana High Courts.[347] It has no woman judge.

The Karnataka High Court

The Karnataka High Court (locally called Attara Kacheri) is the High Court for the state of Karnataka. In 1884, it was established under the Mysore High Court Act, 1884 and was then known as the Mysore High Court until 1973, when the name of the state was altered. The headquarter of Karnataka High Court is in Bangalore which is the administrative capital of the state. The judge strength of Karnataka High Court is 40.There is only one woman judge.[348]

Kerala High Court

The High Court of Kerala was established on 1 November 1956 as the High Court designated for the State of Kerala. *The Kerala High Court Act,* 1958 defined the jurisdiction and various functions, and powers of the High Court of Kerala.[349] It has just one judge.

Madhya Pradesh High Court

The Madhya Pradesh High Court is the High Court of the state of Madhya Pradesh. It was established as the Nagpur High Court on January 2, 1936 under the *Government of India Act 1935; Letters Patent.* The Court was established in Nagpur,

---

347 "Jammu and Kashmir High Court," *Wikipedia,* <http://en.wikipedia.org/wiki/Jammu_and_Kashmir_High_Court> on 15th March 2010.

348 "Negligible presence of women judges in SC, HC," <http://www.expressindia.com/news/fullstory> on 15th March 2010.

349 "Kerala High Court," Wikepedia, < http://en.wikipedia.org/wiki/Kerala_High_Court> on 15th March 2010.

but after the reorganization of states on November 1, 1956, it was moved to Jabalpur. The court has sanctioned judge strength of 42.[350]

Madras High Court

The Madras High Court was established on June 26, 1862 as one of the three High Courts of India (others at Bombay and Calcutta) established at Presidency Towns by Letters Patent granted by Queen Victoria. The Madras High Court has 55 judges with a sanctioned strength of 60.The Madras High Court high court has four women judges.[351]

Orissa High Court

The Orissa High Court is the High Court of the state of Orissa. It was established on April 3, 1948 under the *Orissa High Court Order, 1948.*The court has sanctioned judge strength of 27.[352] It has a lone woman judge.[353]

The Patna High Court

The Patna High Court is the High Court of the state of Bihar. It was established on February 3, 1916 and later affiliated under the *Government of India Act, 1915.*[354] The sanctioned strength of Patna High Court is 43. It has four women judges.

Punjab and Haryana High Court

The Punjab and Haryana High Court is a common High Court for both the States of Punjab and Haryana and Union territory of Chandigarh. The sanctioned

---

350 "Madhya Pradesh High Court," *Wikepedia,*< http://en.wikipedia.org/wiki/Madhya_Pradesh_ High_Court> on 15th March 2010.

351 "Negligible presence of women judges in SC, HC," <http://www.expressindia.com/news/ fullstory> on 15th March 2010.

352 "Orissa High Court," *Wikipedia,*< http://en.wikipedia.org/wiki/Orissa_High_Court> on 15th March 2010.

353 "Negligible presence of women judges in SC, HC," < http://www.expressindia.com/ News/fullstory> on 15th March 2010.

354 "Patna High Court," *Wikipedia,*< http://en.wikipedia.org/wiki/Patna_High_Court>.> on 15th March 2010

strength of this High Court is 68 judges consisting of Chief Justice, 36 Permanent Judges and 21 Additional Judges. As on 22nd December 2009, there are 48 Judges.[355]

Rajasthan High Court

The Rajasthan High Court is the High Court of the state of Rajasthan. It was established on June 21, 1949 under the *Rajasthan High Court Ordinance, 1949*.The court has sanctioned judge strength of 40.[356]The High Court has only one woman judge.[357]

Sikkim High Court

The Sikkim High Court is the High Court of the state of Sikkim. The history of the court can be traced back to 1955, when the High Court of Judicature (Jurisdiction and Powers) Proclamation, 1955 was issued to establish a High Court in Sikkim. The court has sanctioned judge strength of 3. [358] It has no women judge.

Uttarakhand High Court

The Uttarakhand High Court is the High Court of the state of Uttarakhand. It was established on November 9, 2000 under the *U.P. Re-organsisation Act, 2000* after the state split from Uttar Pradesh. The sanctioned judge strength at the time of creation in 2000 was 7 which were later increased to 9 in 2003.[359]

6. 4. FAMILY COURTS IN INDIA

In 1975, the committee on the status of women recommended that all matters concerning the family should be dealt separately. It was therefore set up to promote

---

355 "Punjab and Haryana High Court," *Wikepedia*, <http://en.wikipedia.org/wiki/Punjab_and_Haryana_High_Court> on 15th March 2010.

356 "Rajasthan High Court," *Wikipedia*, < http://en.wikipedia.org/wiki/Rajasthan_High_Court> on 15th March 2010.

357 "Negligible presence of women judges in SC, HC,"<http://www.expressindia.com/news/fullstory> on 15th March 2010.

358 "Sikkim High Court," *Wikipedia*, < http://en.wikipedia.org/wiki/Sikkim_High_Court> on 15th March 2010.

359 "Uttarakhand High Court," *Wikipedia*,< http://en.wikipedia.org/wiki/Uttarakhand_High_Court> on 15th March 2010.

the welfare of the families as more and more cases of disputes within the family were arising. The Family *Courts Act* was passed in 1984 to set up Family courts in India. The purpose and aim of establishing Family Courts is to protect and preserve the institution of marriage and to promote the welfare of children and provide for settlement of disputes by conciliation. After the enactment of the *Family Courts Act, 1984*, 61 Family Courts were set up which are as follows:[360]

- Uttar Pradesh-16,
- Rajasthan-5,
- Maharashtra -13,
- Orissa-2,
- Karnataka-4,
- Tamil Nadu-5,
- Kerala-5,
- Bihar-2,
- Assam-1,
- Manipur-1,
- Andhra Pradesh-6,
- And Pondicherry-1.

But after so many years, the current Family court system has a thoroughly dissatisfying record. Even after 25 years of its enactment where do we stand? There is non-existence of Family court in most of the districts of the states. *The Family Court Act* was enacted with the idea of removing gender bias in statutory legislation. But 25 years after the legislation - which was passed in response to the demands of women's organizations then - millions of women still continue to be deprived of the benefits which would have otherwise accrued to them by way of quick and fair disposal of matrimonial disputes.

---

360 Ministry of Law and Justice, Department of Justice <http://lawmin.nic.in/Just.htm >6th March 2008.

Of the 84 family courts established so far until 2001, a majority of them are in metropolitan cities and are not in eligible towns and cities forcing women to either travel long distances for seeking justice or abandoning the idea. The Government has created 153 Family Courts in various States and Union Territories (UTs) in India.

There are around 159 Family courts functioning in our country as on 22nd May, 2006.[361] There is no family court yet established in the States of Haryana, Arunachal Pradesh, Mizoram and Meghalaya and in the UTs Chandigarh and Andman & Nicobar.[362] As per the Act, it is required to be set up in almost all cities where the population is one million. There are shortages of judges and supporting staffs and very few women judges have been appointed so far. In the course of the workshop organised in March 2002 by the NCW, it was noted that there were only 18 women judges till then in the Family Courts in India out of 84 judges in all the 84 courts that existed at that time. Thus, till 2001, there were only 18 women judges in the Family courts in India.[363]

As the incidence of crimes against women is increasing, there is a growing need to strengthen the judicial system by appointing more women judges to deal with issues relating to women and family. For e.g., the State Women's Commission registered 268 cases of atrocities against women in 2006-07. Most of them were on dowry harassment, property disputes, lack of maintenance etc in the state of Karnataka. But, there are only three family courts in Bangalore, and one each in Mysore, Gulbarga, Bijapur, Belgaum, Mangalore, and Davangere districts. Similarly in Uttar Pradesh the Family courts are struggling under the deluge of divorce cases. Lucknow has 13,000 cases while two family Courts of Allahabad has more than 7000cases while the Family court in Gorakhpur gets five to six cases everyday. The Lucknow court lists about 250 cases but gets to hear only 20 cases. Only recently two women judges were appointed in Family Courts of Allahabad. There are six Family

---

361 "Demand for grants (2006-07) of the ministry of Law and Justice," (Presented to the Rajya Sabha on 22nd May, 2006) ,<164.100.24.167/book2/reports/personnel/15threport.htm> 12th March 2008.

362 "153 Family Courts In India: Call to amend Family Courts Act," 2nd December, 2005, Online edition , <http://news.indlaw.com/> 9th March 2008.

363 "Family Courts in India-An Overview," < http://www.legalserviceindia.com/article/l356-Family-Courts-in-India.html> on 14th Dec, 2008.

Courts, three at Chennai, and one each at Madurai, Coimbatore and Salem. At present, two Family Courts have been established in Kolkata. While there are only two women judges.[364] . Only recently, the Governments of Delhi and Chhattisgarh have decided to establish two family courts each. While there are 32 family courts in Bihar. Stiff resistance from the lawyers' lobby is the primary reason in most of the States for not establishing any Family Courts. The data is shown in Table - 6.6

364 "Family Courts in West Bengal," *West Bengal Commission for Women*, <http://www.wbcw.org/index.php/family-court/family-courts-in-west-bengal> 8th March 2008.

TABLE 6.6

159 FAMILY COURTS FUNCTIONING AS ON 22ND MAY 2006

State	City	No. of Family Courts	Women Judges
	Delhi	2	
Karnataka	Bangalore	3	
	Mysore	1	
	Gulbarga	1	
	Bijapur	1	
	Belgaum	1	
	Mangalore	1	
	Davangere	1	
Uttar Pradesh	Allahabad	2	Had Women Judges
	Lucknow	1	
	Gorakhpur	1	
West Bengal	Kolkata	2	Has Women Judges
Bihar	Patna	1	Had Women Judge
	Muzzaffarpur	1	
Tamil Nadu	Chennai	3	
	Madurai	1	
	Coimbatore	1	
	Salem	1	
Chattishgarh	Bilaspur	1	
	Raipur	1	

Source: Ministry of Law and Justice (presented to the Rajya Sabha on 22nd May, 2006 and was also laid on the table of the Lok Sabha on 22nd May, 2006).

6.4.1. AN ANALYSIS OF FAMILY COURTS

Though the Family Court was aimed at removing the gender bias in statutory legislation, the goal is yet to be achieved. The Act provides that persons who are appointed to the Family Courts should be committed to the need to protect and preserve the institution of marriage and to promote the settlement of disputes by conciliation and counseling. It was laid down that preference should also be given to the appointment of women as Family Court judges. The criteria for appointment of Family Court judges are the same as those for appointment of District Judges requiring seven years experience in judicial office or seven years practice as an advocate. Yet little importance is given to appoint women judges in Family court.

A. *LAUNCHED WITHOUT PROPER PLANNING*

The Family Courts were launched almost overnight, without proper and adequate planning and preparation. The lack of infrastructure and basic facilities make the fight for justice a Herculean task. While both men and women are affected, in any given situation women, who generally lack exposure to and experience in dealing with public institutions, are the worst sufferers. Infrastructure has another angle: the infrastructure that is necessary for a FC should be studied at the time of establishing it; otherwise it adds to the backlog of cases.

The record of the current family court system is a mixed bag—in any case, not a commendable record. Over the last nearly quarter of a century, the system has given rise to anger, frustration and resentment over its functioning. The system lacks the trust of the majority of justice seeking population regarding its capability to provide a fair and just forum for handling family disputes. Unless the present situation of the family courts is remedied, the women will be forced to remain unsecured within their families and society. The overall situation is the same everywhere with minor differences. It has still to go a long way to accomplish the objectives implied in the *Family Courts Act, 1984.*

B. *LACK OF EXPERIENCE*

The judges appointed to the family court do not have any special experience/expertise in dealing with family matters, nor have they any special expertise in settling disputes through conciliation, a requirement prescribed in the Act.

C. *LESS NUMBER OF WOMEN JUDGES*

The provision of the *Family Courts Act* specially mentions that women judges should be appointed and that the judges should have expertise and experience in settling family disputes, more or less, has remained only on paper. In many states the Family Courts s does not have a single woman judge. The emphasis of the legislation is on 'family', 'counsellors' and simplification of procedures. But many of the judges who are posted as judges of Family Court feel it as a punishment postings. Thereby do not perform effectively.

D. *LACK OF UNIFORM RULES*

Though the Code of Civil Procedure was amended to do away with the rigid rules of procedure, the Family Courts, however, continue to deal with the family disputes in the same manner as other civil matters and, by and large, the same adversary approach prevails. The need for a set of uniform rules, therefore, has been felt imperative. While the Act laid down the broad guidelines, it was left to the State governments to frame the rules of procedure. Over and above this, there are still several States, which have either not set up family courts, or if they have, they have not bothered to frame the rules of procedure. In order to give effect to the paradigm shift from adversarial model to a conciliatory (or even inquisitorial) model envisaged under the Act, the description of the subject as A versus B, which indicates hostility, should rather be addressed as in the matter of A and B. Once the matter reaches the trial/contest stage, the same adversarial approach, unfortunately, gets to the fore.

An example where the objective of the Family Court is diminished due to procedural inertia or lapses may be cited. Rules formulated are yet to provide a specific format for the interim applications, summons etc. Many lawyers still use the format which is provided in the Civil Procedure Code which uses words like 'Counsel can be heard by'; 'Counsel for the Petitioner', although the lawyers were earlier not allowed representing clients.

The Rules provide for tape recorders for recording evidence at trial proceedings, which could be used at the appeal stage, but this proposal seems too far-fetched for the family courts, which do not even have adequate provisions for paper and stationery to begin with. Different High Courts have laid down different rules of procedure. Unless these lacunae are removed the family courts cannot render an effective aid to women's fight for justice.

E. *NON ENFORCEMENT OF RIGHTS*

The legislative framework provided in the Constitution provides for equality in society between men and women. In order to fulfill this constitutional mandate the Parliament

and the Judiciary have from time to time made laws and interpreted the existing ones that would guarantee gender justice. However since law, the legal system and society are closely interlinked it is not possible to enforce the rights provided in law without changes in social institutions, values and attitudes. Social change cannot be brought about through law. It is only through the process of sensitizing various branches of the government and more importantly the members of society to the rights and concerns of women can gender justice become a reality. Law is not the only one method by which the various problems of women can be resolved. Law can empower women at one level. It is not possible to completely eradicate the subordination of women or the discriminatory practices merely through the legal system. However; the regular courts are brim with civil disputes and could not be expected to provide expeditious relief to these harassed victims. With the heavy work load the judges could not be expected to display the sensitivity required in dealing with broken marriages.

F. *UNSATISFACTORY WORKING CONDITIONS*

The Family Courts generally suffer from unsatisfactory conditions. There is no proper place for the judges to be seated and working conditions, by and large, are unhygienic and poor. There is no proper space allotted for the children to meet their separated parents. An empirical in-depth extensive study in Delhi and Jaipur done reveal that as many as 36 percent felt that the Family Courts lacked essential public conveniences like drinking water, waiting room, etc and facilities like photocopying, paid public telephone, availability of stamps, stationery etc. In the absence of basic infrastructure like a stamp office, typist and stationery, services of a notary or even adequate sitting arrangements, canteen and drinking water, the litigants are subjected to endless hardships.

The study found that many advocates and litigants expressed their dissatisfaction regarding their experience with Family Courts and stated that their expectations had not been met. The reasons for dissatisfaction found were: procrastination and dilatory decisions, overworked counsellors, and undue pressure exercised on women litigants for reconciliation, etc. On average, a litigant had to visit the Family Court as many as 21 times before the case was decided. Only 14 percent of the cases were decided within the statutorily laid down time-frame of six months, while the remaining large number of cases were decided within a time frame ranging between more than six months and as long as nine years.

G. *THE FAMILY COURTS ARE NOT EASILY ACCESSIBLE*

The Family Courts should be located in easily accessible residential colonies where aggrieved women, for whose benefit the courts have been created, may go without hesitation. Women and children of rural area are deprived of its benefits because of the financial constraints and their inability to reach the courts, which are situated at the district levels. Also the Family Courts practically is no help to the rural areas where women because of their ignorance are not in a position to know the income of their husbands. It is difficult for battered women to collect medical certificates and other documents to prove the truth of her statement. The intimidating atmosphere of normal law courts generally overawes women in social distress seeking judicial relief. The main objective in seeking the establishment of Family Courts was to take family and marital disputes away from the overcrowded, intimidating and congested environs of traditional courts of law and bring these to congenial, sympathetic and supportive surroundings. Efforts made over the past more than two decades to provide prompt and easily accessible justice to women in social distress should not be nullified by the insistence of lawyers not to shift the Family Courts to various places. The primary objective of any law is to provide justice to the needy and not be merely a source of income for any profession, as was noted by a former Chairperson of the Delhi Women's Commission. Convenience of the practitioners of law is secondary to prompt dispensation of justice and alleviation of the suffering of those seeking justice.

H. *COMPLEX PROCEDURES*

The measures like simplification of procedures, speedy settlement of disputes, a permanent cadre of competent counsellors who are capable of providing scientific and professional services, informal atmosphere in courts, qualified social workers, appointment of gender sensitized judges, uniformity of rules, extension of the FC services to all districts of India, strengthening of the system of probation officers, provision/creation of necessary infrastructure, model rules for appointment of judges, allowing the woman to file a case in the district or state where she resides rather than at the place where the marriage took place or where the husband resides or where they both last resided should be undertaken. Gender justice should be a component for recruitment and it should be made essential for a judge to have undergone a gender sensitization course/training before taking the position as a judge. The FC needs to be empowered in the true sense of the term and the enforcement mechanism needs to be strengthened.

Maharashtra is the one of the few States that have detailed and elaborate rules regarding the functioning of the Family Curt as well as regarding the service conditions, recruitment, remuneration of the counsellors etc. Maharashtra also has the unique distinction of having a children complex within the premises of the Family Court.

So far 159 Family Courts in various States and Union Territories (UTs) in India have been established. However, there are no family courts yet in the States of Haryana, Arunachal Pradesh, Mizoram and Meghalaya and in the Union Territories of Chandigarh, and Andaman and Nicobar Islands. Though the Family Court Act envisaged the establishment of Family Courts in all cities with a population exceeding one million, there is a need to establish such courts in each district of India in view of the prevailing conditions of increasing incidence of marital discord and divorce

6. 5. THE JUVENILE JUSTICE BOARD

The *Juvenile Justice (Care and Protection) Act 2000* that was passed eight years ago is meant to safeguard the rights of children. The Act is applicable to all states except Jammu and Kashmir, and is in keeping with the guidelines set down in the UN Convention on the Rights of the Child (UNCRC). The *Juvenile Justice Act* has established two bodies -- the Child Welfare Committee (CWC) to specifically address the needs of 'children in need of care and protection' and the Juvenile Justice Board to look into matters concerning 'children in conflict with the law'. Both committees are constituted either for every district or a group of districts in the state. The CWC consists of a chairperson and four other members, at least one of them a woman. While all members are non-judicial persons, they exercise the powers of a magistrate. The committee meets thrice a week and is the final authority on the disposal of cases and rehabilitation of children.

In the case of 'children in conflict with the law', the Act mandates that after being apprehended the child must be brought before the Juvenile Justice Board (JJB) within 24 hours, or a metropolitan court that may be holding charge of the JJB. The Juvenile Justice Board has three members, the judge and two people outside the judiciary system who are nevertheless engaged in work related to child rights. The board meets twice a week.

Each Juvenile board consists of a Metropolitan Magistrate, trained in Child Psychology and two social workers, at least one of them a woman. Every such Board shall have the powers conferred by the Code of Criminal Procedure, 1973, on a Metropolitan Working under considerable handicaps such as inadequate funds, budgetary allocations for law and justice not being part of plan expenditure, lack of resources, shortage of staff and infrastructure, the Indian judiciary is facing today. More women probation officers as well as employees in observation homes should be recruited.

6. 6. GLANCES INTO OTHER SERVICES

Women are already serving in the three services in education, legal, logistics, administration, finance and technical support areas. In the air force, they fly transport aircraft and helicopters. Hence to think now that woman as the weaker sex is a misnomer. The memory levels of women are far better than that of men. It has also been found that women are more sincere, articulate, meticulous and transparent in their dealings, both administratively and financially. In fact, in managerial roles, the females proved more mature in their dealings with subordinate staff.[365]

The prestige of the civil service is still very high, and its members enjoy a status and influence in society that compensate for their comparatively low salaries. After independence, there were hardly any women in the higher civil service. Now female recruits represent approximately one fourth of each IAS batch, and their profile is more elitist than the average. They are often top rankers in the civil service competitive examination and come mostly from the well-off urban classes and upper castes. Among the women recruited in the IAS between 2001 and 2005, less than 15 percent had a rural background, as against 43percent among the men. While the data in Table -22 shows that in 2002, 10.42 percent of women were in the Indian Administrative service compared to 4 percent of women in judiciary. It reveals that women opt more for civil services rather than for judicial services.

Rajasthan, Uttar Pradesh and Bihar are relatively poor states but are well represented in the IAS, because in these states the prestige of the civil service is very high and many candidates try their luck every year by sitting for the examination. An officer explains: 'After my graduation from Patna University, I left Bihar for Delhi where I did a Master degree at the Jawaharlal Nehru University while preparing for the civil service examination. Many of my classmates in Patna did the same because there are very few jobs in the private sector in Bihar, and there the civil service commands a lot of respect'. By contrast, states like Gujarat, Maharashtra and Andhra Pradesh are more developed, their educational structures are better, and thus their success ratio in the civil service exam might be higher, but there are fewer candidates since these states offer many other avenues for employment to their best students, who can take up private jobs.[366]

---

365 "A Few Good Women,"(The study, incidentally, is based on the conduct, behaviour and fitness levels of officers and subordinate staff—both men and women—in the AFMS itself. For mental, physiological and psychological fitness at the entry level, MBBS and MD students of the Armed Forces Medical College, Pune, were taken as samples),*Outlook*,24th April,2006,< http://www.outlookindia.com/article.aspx?231005> on 9th May2009.

366 "Questioning the Role of the Indian Administrative Service in National Integration," *South Asia Multidisciplinary Academic Journal*, < http://samaj.revues.org/index633.html#bibliography> on 14th Dec, 2008.

In 1997, women as I.A.S officers were 7.4 percent. In 1997, women comprised10.2 percent. While in 2000 women comprised 10.4 percent as I.A.S officers. In 1997, women as Police officers comprised 2.2 percent .In 2000, the percentage increased to 3.3 percent which apparently shows that more and more Indian women are inclined to join these services. The data is shown in Table 6.7.

TABLE 6.7

WOMEN IN PREMIER SERVICES (1987-2000)

Service	1987			1997			2000		
	Women	Total	(%)	Women	Total	(%)	Women	Total	(%)
IAS	339	4,204	7.5	512	4,991	10.2	535	5,159	10.4
IPS	21	2,418	0.9	67	3,045	2.2	110	3,301	3.3
TOTAL	360	6,622	5.4	579	8,036	7.2	645	8,460	7.6

Source: Planning Commission, (2000); Development Indicators: A Comparative Picture of the Status of Women and Men in India: Data Sheet. New Delhi. India, P. 1, *Centre for Women Studies.*

Note: 1. Department of Personnel and Training, Government of India, New Delhi. 2. Ministry of Home Affairs, Government of India, New Delhi.

In Central Services, for e.g. the Indian Audit and Accounts service, women comprised 19.94 percent. It increased to 22.31 percent in 2002. In the year 2003, women comprised 21.56 percent in the Indian Economic Service. The Indian Statistical Service had 12.94 percent in the year 2002.In comparison to All India and Central Services, women as jüdges were far less comprising 4 percent in Supreme Court and 3.31 percent in High Court in 2003.The data is shown in Table 6.8.

TABLE 6.8

PERSONNEL BY GENDER—WISE IN ALL INDIA AND CENTRAL SERVICE

Sl. No.		Female	Male	Total	Female Percentage to Total
1	Supreme Court Judges 2003	1	24	25	4
2	High Court Judges 2003	17	497	514	3.31
3	Indian Administrative Service 1997	512	4479	5011	10.22
	2002	535	4624	5159	10.42
4	Indian Audit and Account Service 1997	129	519	647	19.94
	2002	143	498	641	22.31
5	Indian Customs and Central Excise Service 1995	117	1520	1637	7.5
	1996	130	1531	1661	7.83
6	Indian Economic Service 1996	64	330	394	16.24
	2003	91	331	422	21.56
7	Indian Foreign Service 1997	67	519	586	11.43
	2002	78	505	583	13.38
8	Indian Forest Service 1995	73	2390	2463	2.96
	1996	78	2387	2465	3.16
9	Indian Information Service 1995	76	417	493	5.42
	1996	74	400	474	5.61

Sl. No.		Female	Male	Total	Female Percentage to Total
10	Indian Police Service 1997	96	2868	2964	3.24
	2002	124	3112	3236	3.83
11	Indian Postal Service 1995	70	256	326	21.47
	1996	77	282	259	21.45
12	Indian Revenue Service 1994	246	2022	2268	10.85
	1995	276	1980	2256	12.23
13	Indian Statistical Service 1997	38	492	530	7.17
	2002	73	491	564	12.94
14	Central Secretariat Service				
	1995	NA	NA	678	-
	1996	51	657	708	7.2
15	Central Cabinet Minister 1997	0	20	20	0
	2002	2	30	32	6.25
16	Minister of State 1997	5	19	24	20.83
	2002	6	35	41	14.63

Source: India, Ministry of Human Resource Development, Department of Women and Child Development. (2004). Government of India, II & IIIrd Periodic Report on the Convention on the Elimination of All Forms of Discrimination against Women.

The ratio of women in Indian Foreign was found to be more than higher judiciary. In the year 2003, there were 78 women in the Indian Foreign Service in sharp contrast to 17 women judges in higher judiciary. Thus it is found women are more inclined to join central services in India.[367] The data is given in Table-6.19.

[367] Ministry of Statistics and Programme Implementation, Central Statisticalsation. (2003). Women and Men in India 2002. New Delhi. p.98.

TABLE 6.9

CENTRAL SERVICES

Sl. No.	Services	Year	Total			Scheduled Castes		Scheduled Tribes	
			Female	Male	Total	Female	Male	Female	Male
1.	Indian Administrative Service	**1998**	522	4489	**5011**	-	-	-	-
2.	Indian Foreign Service	**2002**	78	505	**583**	5	87	4	38
3.	Indian Police Service	**2003**	124	3112	**3236**	-	-	-	-

Source: Ministry of Statistics and Programme Implementation, Central Statisticalsation. (2003). Women and Men in India 2002. New Delhi, p.98.

Note: Ministry of Home Affairs Ministry of External Affairs as on 31.12.98 (includes1999 Batch). 2001 batch as on 31.12.2003 and 2002 batch as on 01.01.2001

We have now got a network of over 14 thousand courts all over India and these courts are dealing with 4 crores of cases. India has the lowest ratio of Judicial officers being 10 for one million, whereas United States of America has 117 Judicial Officers per million. The Supreme Court in a recent judgment has directed the State Governments to increase the Judge strength five times, so as to have a ratio of 50 per million. Even in several States, the existing Judge strength is not filled up always and vacancies remain unfilled for a considerable period. Lack of infrastructural facilities is yet another cause, which causes hindrance in quick disposal of cases by a Judicial Officer, but notwithstanding these difficulties, one will have to strive hard and put in all your efforts to dispose of the matters early, so that the litigant public is not harassed by protraction of litigation for years together.

6.7. JUDICIAL REFORMS: NEW INTIATIVE BY THE GOVERNMENT

In spite of all the feathers in its cap, the Indian judiciary is often criticized for three reasons:

(i) The ever-mounting backlog of arrears accusing the judiciary of its inability to clear the same;

(ii) Occasional reports of such conduct on the part of the individual judges which is unbecoming of them; and

(iii) Some complaints of corruption.

The question as to how our courts are crowded and to what extent this situation could be remedied needs to be addressed. There could be so many administrative reforms that can prevent the number of litigation coming to courts. In a large number of cases pending in Courts, especially in higher Courts, Government is one of the parties either as defendant or as appellant. These litigations are on account of lack of proper governmental administration. If the decision making authorities take firm, independent and impartial decisions, the citizens would not normally be driven to litigations. Lack of proper and good governance largely contributes to the number of cases in subordinate courts.

National Minimum Court Performance Standards that will set the minimum that the people of India can expect from the subordinate courts. We propose to have the following elements: -

i. Disposal level of the national system should be raised from 60percent of total case load (as of now) to 95percent-100percent of total case load in five years. This will require this target to be established at the court, district, and State levels as well.

ii. Each court to ensure that not more than 5percent of the cases in that court should be more than 5 years old (5x5 rule) within the next three years; and in 5 years to ensure that not more than 1percentof the cases should be more than 1 years old (1x1 rule).

iii. Timetables to be established for every contested case and monitored through a computerized signaling system

The Government has taken several milestone steps to improve the lot of people during the first three years since October, 1999 through adjustment of laws, enactment of new laws intended to simplify laws relating to justice delivery system under a time bound programme, making the institution of Lok Adalats permanent to bring in it public utilities so as to provide time bound and cost effective justice to the people at the pre-litigative and otherwise stage of disputes resolution at the cutting edge of public administration, effecting personal law reforms through amendments in various marriage and other laws by making it mandatory for the courts to provide interim judgments within 60 days in the matter of alimony, maintenance and compensation to women in distress in divorce suits, maintenance of children and old parents, bringing the junior lawyers and advocates in general within the net of social security through Advocates Welfare Fund, adjusting registration, transfer of property and stamp laws to prevent malpractices in registration of properties, evolving transparency through amendments in election laws and various amendments effected in the Companies Act to evolve a productive, efficient and competitive corporate sector in tune with the emerging globalization of Indian economy and the best global practices, to protect interest of investors by increasing accountability of corporate sector and introducing the system of corporate and E - governance.

Initiative for the introduction of Information Technology in courts was taken by earmarking a portion of Centrally Sponsored Scheme (CSS) funds exclusively for the use of Information Technology. Plans were prepared for the Pilot Project of Computerization of courts in the four major metros—Delhi, Mumbai, Kolkata and Chennai to serve as a model for the use of Information Technology in courts.

A. *COMPUTERIZATION OF COURTS*

Execution of pilot project of computerization and networking of courts in four metropolitan cities of Delhi, Kolkata, Chennai and Mumbai has started. The project further envisages computerization of subordinate courts in State Capitals in the second phase.

B. *FAST TRACK COURTS*

The scheme of setting up Fast Track Courts was started on the initiatives of the Department of Justice from funds allocated by the Eleventh Finance Commission. The Fast Track Courts have been set up to clear the backlog of pending cases in various session courts of the country. While keeping in view about 2.39 crore cases as of 2001 pending in various courts of the country and also the 204480 under-trials languishing in various prisons the Government has come out with the innovative idea of setting-up "Fast-Track Courts" throughout the country to dispose criminal cases. The actions initiated so far include:

- A total of 1,734 Fast Track Courts fully funded by the Centre at Sessions Court level throughout the country to be set up.
- All the Fast Track Courts to be functional.
- So far 1,150 Fast Track Courts have been set up.
- These courts have disposed of many cases while many have been transferred. All the under-trial cases have been given priority for disposal.
- All Sessions cases pending for two years or more have been given priority for disposal.

The Supreme Court has approved the Constitutional validity of Fast Track Courts and directed the Chief Justices of High Courts and the Chief Ministers of States to fill all the vacancies of presiding judges of Fast Track Courts.

C. *MAHILA COURTS*

Besides, keeping in view the specific needs of women various States including Delhi have set up Mahila courts. The main idea behind setting up of these courts was that it was felt by many that a woman judge only could understand her counterparts and weigh the damage caused to her. The Mahila Court is headed by Additional Chief Metropolitan Magistrate cum Assistant Sessions Judge. The Mahila court is presided by a woman judge. This is called Mahila court as it exclusively deals with cases of crimes committed against women.

The National Commission for Women while keeping in view the number of cases pending before the courts launched the innovative 'parivarik mahila lok adalats programme' with support from judiciary in 1996. Through this programme cases concerning family disputes will be taken up by the lok adalats (public courts presided by judges) and settled amicably through counselling. These adalats are organized under the Legal Services Authorities Act, 1987 and the decision of the adalat is binding on both the parties. The Courts must show more responsibility and sensitivity while dealing with sexual assault cases. The female judges will also deal with cases of sexual harassment and dowry-related offences in India.[368]

D. *NEWLY CREATED HIGH COURTS / HIGH COURT BENCHES*

- After the reorganization of Madhya Pradesh, Uttar Pradesh and Bihar, three High Courts were established in the newly created States of Chattisgarh, Uttaranchal and Jharkhand and they have started functioning from November 1, 9 and 15, 2000, respectively. A plan has also been drawn for building/extension in these newly created High Courts and other High Courts.

- A Bench of Guwahati High Court has been set up at Itanagar in Arunachal Pradesh on August 12, 2000. A Bench of Madras High Court at Madurai is

---

368 National resource centre for women, Department for women and child Development, Government of India <http://nrcw.nic.in/index2.asp?sublinkid=478> on 19th Dec, 2008.

proposed to be set up as soon as the infrastructural facilities are developed to the satisfaction of the Chief Justice of the Madras High Court. This would involve a Parliamentary legislation. A Bench of the Calcutta High Court at Jalpaiguri is also contemplated subject to development of infrastructural facilities.

E. *FILLING UP VACANCIES OF JUDGES*

Action plan for filling up all the 2,216 vacant posts of judges and magistrates in district/subordinate courts has been drawn up for the year 2002-2003 as per the directions of the Supreme Court in Judges Case in March, 2002.

- With filling of all the 2,216 vacancies of judges in the subordinate courts and all the 1,734 Fast Track Courts becoming fully functional during 2002-2003, a total of 3,950 additional courts will get added to the present number of 12,737 courts to make 32 percentmore additional courts.

- There are 21 High Courts in the country with the approved strength of 647 judges. As on date, there are 141 vacancies in the High Courts. In view of the Prime Minister's direction to fill up vacancies in the High Courts expeditiously, the Chief Justices of the High Courts were advised to speed up their recommendations for filling up the vacant posts. The apex court alone has some 50,000 cases pending and about 73,000 new lawsuits as of September this year.[369]

- The Government has been urging upon the Chief Justices of the High Courts to make recommendations for filling up vacancies in the High Courts. The Ministry has received proposals for filling up 65 vacancies in the High Courts which are under examination.

- Action plan has been worked out for 34 new Family Courts and allocation of funds for setting up of more Family Courts on 50:50 cost sharing basis as and

---

[369] Nayak, Malaithi.; "Divided views on women's quota in India's higher judiciary," *One World South Asia.*< http://southasia.oneworld.net/todaysheadlines/divided-views-on-womens-quota-in-higher-judiciary> on 29th Dec,2008,

when demanded by States. Already 97 such Family Courts are functioning in different States.

- The Centre has urged the State governments to set up Family Courts in each district on cost sharing basis to resolve family and matrimonial disputes.[370]

- Supreme Court has set up special courts to deal with rape cases that will be judged by female judges.

- The Supreme Court has asked that all courts show more responsibility and sensitivity while sexual assault cases.

- The female judges will also deal with cases of sexual harassment and dowry-related offences in India.

- It appears that it is now time for some rethinking about the desirability of having an Indian Judicial Service on the pattern of the Indian Administrative Service. There is no denying the fact that very few good students take up the study of law by choice and quite often the source is from the residue left after most of them have chosen medicine or any other technical branch of a prestigious service.

- Easy graduation in law makes things worse. Bulk of the Bar being so constituted, its quality suffers. If there be an Indian Judicial Service constituted on the pattern of the Indian Administrative Service, many bright young men may be inclined to opt for it and even those unsuccessful who join the Bar would be of superior quality.

- Level of legal education of those candidates would automatically improve because of greater seriousness of their study. Constitution of the Indian Judicial Service would improve the quality of the judiciary at the subordinate

---

370 Press Releases, October, 2002, Milestones 2002, Law & Justice; <http://pib.nic.in/archieve/ppinti/ milestones2002/milestones_02_law_justice.html> on 18th Dec, 2008.

level and in turn provide for better quality of Judges from that source for the higher judiciary.

- The recent trend of disinclination of successful members of the Bar to accept a Judgeship because for them the profession is more lucrative is creating a problem which, to some extent at least, can be solved by this method.

- The bright young men who join the Indian Judicial Service would in due course constitute a section of the higher judiciary. Improvement of the stock has to be made keeping in view the future need

We need more women in our judiciary, women who can make a difference to and in the system. That part of your mentoring scheme extends to judicial appointments. Closing the gender pay gap can help to create a more equal and cohesive society. Valuing women's work and skills will motivate their performance and improve their economic independence. By increasing women's earnings throughout the lifecycle, the risk of falling into poverty will be reduced.

The importance of women on the Bench is necessary to the public confidence of our judicial systems. From the view point of public perception, the presence of women on the Bench makes the legal system less alien and more relevant to the female half of our population. The courts of our country should no longer be viewed as all male preserves. For women, the path to equality is linked to developing better judiciaries, where de jure rights can be transformed to de facto ones. Pressing developing countries to empower the judiciary is thus essential for the global campaign. However, we have little evidence as to whether elites, who are often prime movers of policy, see the judiciary as essential to their country, a democratic progress and implicitly to the advancement of women's rights. This question is important because if elites fail to see courts as an important venue on which democratic progress is predicated then the strategies advocated by the campaign have dim prospects for success.

The most important reason why we need women on our Benches is because we need the perspectives that women can bring to judging. For cultural, biological, social and historic reasons, women do have different experiences than men. Women as judges can therefore make a unique contribution to the deliberations in our courts. The presence of women on the Bench can will make a substantive difference. Insofar as women are possessed of special experiences, concerns and interests, these must inevitably affect the way they address the problems that confront them. This is not to say that men may not share, or indeed lead, in the enunciation of these perspectives; it is to say, however, that the presence of women on the Bench helps ensure that they are brought to the fore. The wide gap between the goals enunciated in the constitution and related mechanisms looking into the situational reality therefore need to be bridged into.

6.8 CRITICAL ANALYSIS:

An analysis of the above makes it is clear that the Judiciary has not come close to anything resembling gender equality. *Therefore the question arises is there any justification for the lack of more women judges in India?*

The case for gender equality on the Bench would seem too uncontroversial to require justification. Yet the practical reality of the slow progress of women towards equality of participation, both quantitative and qualitative, in the Judiciary testifies to the continuing need to argue the case for change.

In terms of employment as well as promotion in work and occupation, women often face greater handicap than men. The Supreme Court doesn't have a single woman judge? The Indian judiciary continues to turn a Nelson's eye to gender parity despite the Government making a concerted bid to raise women's representation in parliament and state legislatures to 33 percent. Despite several women making a name for themselves as lawyers practising in the apex court and various high courts, the participation of women as judges in India's higher judiciary is less than 10 percent. Nearly 90 years later, women are no longer prohibited from entering any profession. Still, a stark gender divides remains.

Does it not unwittingly convey the impression that there are not many good lawyers and judges in the high courts to be elevated as apex court judges?

Today, women represent a paltry 8.5 percent of judges presiding over India's higher courts which is apparent from the avalable data's given in Table - 6.1, Table - 6.4 and Table - 6.5. This gender gap becomes particularly relevant with respect to judgements and jurisprudence affecting women.Fight for gender justice is not to be considered a fight against men but a fight against traditions that have chained-a fight against attitude that are grained in the society.Men must rise to the occasion.

A recent Supreme Court judgement excluding "mistresses" and "keeps" from alimony (maintenance) from a live-in relationship is just one example. Written by an all-male bench, the controversial portions of the judgement were deleted only after Indira Jaising—the first woman to be appointed senior law officer to the government and one of the primary architects of the domestic violence law—denounced it in open court.Law goes against traditional norms of what it means to be a woman, because it's about standing up and being vocal, and requires long hours.Unless you have a very supportive husband and family, it's very difficult to maintain.[371]

Thus, one of the important tasks a judge is expected to perform is to be responsive and responsible.He must be creatice and create precendent, where no law exists for women but were it is actually needed.Judicial decisions can influence and undwer certain circumstances even compel the government to enact provisions to cover up the deficiency in the existing law.[372]

For women, these hurdles are much tougher to scale.Although family connections generally benefit litigators of both genders, some legal families actively discourage their women from pursuing litigation, pushing them instead towards jobs in law firms or in-house counsel that have more family-friendly hours and better starting salaries, she said. Of those who pursue litigation, many drop out once they start families. Along with gender discrimination, factors such as women's high rates of illiteracy and poverty, lack of awareness of their rights, and absence from public life and the workforce, may serve to restrict women's access to justice. Furthermore, a socially short-sighted view of women, combined with financial and administrative

---

371 Gender gap in the judiciary.< www.livemint.com/2011/03/07232118/Gen> on 22nd March 2011.

372 Anand,Justice A.S;Relevance for equality—Equality for judges,Universal Law Publishing Co,New Delhi,2008,p89.

corruption at almost all levels of the state and judiciary, pose obstacles to women's justice. Access to justice is particularly difficult for poor and rural women without a male guardian and for members of marginalized communities.[373]

Regardless of gender, litigation is a tough field to break into. In order to build credibility and clientele, new law graduates must apprentice under senior advocates as juniors, which means working long hours for little or no pay before they can start on their own. Practising litigators report stereotypes that women are gentler and less corruptible than men often determines the type of cases they get. "There are very few women in criminal law.The perception of women as soft still dominates this practice area.This might explain why women tend to gravitate towards family and divorce law. A 2009 study by Research Foundation for Governance in India (RFGI) found more than 70 percent of the country's top law graduates are choosing jobs at law firms or as in-house counsels in companies. Lack of family connections and poor pay were cited as major reasons for pursuing other tracks. Litigation has become like the caste system. Only the person having a father (in litigation) can enter it is the general notion among the public.

The situation is perhaps worst for women practising in smaller jurisdictions. In the lower courts of Aurangabad in Bihar, it was so unusual for women to practice. Delhi-based senior advocate Pinky Anand remembers a time when 300-400 male lawyers followed her around the corridors and the judge "actually took time" before coming in to hear her case. In an effort to address the gender gap and to network women across the legal profession, a group of lawyers have started now the Society of Women Lawyers (SOWL) very recently in 2011. SOWL aims to promote women to leadership positions in the legal profession, judiciary, and workplace, and review legislation relevant to women.

To date, the primary argument for promoting gender equality has been that women will bring a unique contribution to the Bench as a result of their different life experiences, values and attitudes. Such arguments may have a strong appeal since they appear to give legitimacy to the undervalued attributes traditionally associated as

---

373 Freedom House, ***Women's Rights in the Middle East and North Africa - Yemen***, 14 October 2005, < http://www.unhcr.org/refworld/docid/47387b712f.html> on 21stmarch2011.

feminine while also promoting the merit by claiming to improve the quality of justice. Instead, it the adoption of a rationale for gender equalitybased on equity and legitimacy; that equalparticipation of men and women in the justicesystem is an inherent and essential feature ofa democracy without which the judiciary willlose public confidence. This approach, thoughless immediately appealing, is ultimately moresound.

Women judges have come to the bench via work as advocates in private practice, having already attained the status of partners. While the Law Schools coming up in every state, students have been graduating in equal numbers of men and women, and firms are absorbing new associates in numbers that largely reflect that balance.But, something unusual happens to most women after they begin to climb into the upper tiers of law firms — they disappear. Why?

As it stands, society has historically favoured men over women. While individual women may have broken the glass ceiling, potentially women have yet to feel secure in their respective power positions to pull other women along. The public today, more than at any other point in our nation's history, has accepted the notion that women are just as qualified, just as smart and just as hardworking as men. The question that needs to be addressed now is: How will gender equality in the Judiciary be furthered in the future?

It is now so widely accepted that the goal of gender equality in public life generally, and the Judiciary specifically, is an unqualified good. Therefore, to ask the question why this is necessary seems redundant, if not perverse. Nevertheless, the question is important for three reasons.

First, the rationale for equality needs to be theoretically sound and empirically grounded if it is to provide the basis for a successful strategy for change. This is particularly so if change can only be achieved through proactive reform. Second, the answer determines what form of actions may legitimately be pursued to achieve the goal of gender equality — whether, for example, it would ever be acceptable to appoint a less qualified woman over a more qualified man. Third, it determines what level of participation by women is necessary; whether proportionate representation is required or if some lesser (or indeed greater) participation is needed.[374]

To date, two main rationales have been put forward as the justification for equality in the Judiciary. The first is that changing the gender balance on the Bench will improve the quality of justice dispensed because women bring something different to the adjudication process. The second is that the principle of equity requires that women have an equal opportunity to participate in public decision-making institutions and that their absence undermines the democratic legitimacy of those bodies.

To date, difference-based arguments have dominated the debate and equity and merit arguments have played a limited supporting role. It highlights the theoretical and empirical weaknesses of gender difference in judicial decision-making and argues that it must be used with great caution as a rationale for gender equality on the Bench. Some of the problems it generates are common to gender theory and practice generally, but others arise as a result of the particular institutional conditions of the judiciary. In contrast, equity- and legitimacy-based arguments, although less superficially attractive, provide a more theoretically, empirically and strategically sound rationale for gender equality.

The argument that gender equality in the Judiciary is a requirement of equity is based on the principle that it is inherently unfair that men enjoy a near monopoly of judicial power. This claim is founded on certain assumptions.

First, that there are no qualities or characteristics, whether genetic or learnt, which make men better suited to public life and justify their domination of decision-making bodies. Second, that since this is the case, the disproportionate levels of participation of men in the law generally and in the Judiciary specifically is the result of unfair arrangements, both past and present, which disadvantage women. These may be inherent to the institutions such as the courts and legal profession or the result of

---

[374] Politzer, Malia & Kanekal, Nikhil: Gender *gap in judiciary* published on March 7th2011 <http://www.livemint.com/2011/03/07232118/Gender-gap-in-judiciary.html> on 21st march2011.

external conditions such as cultural values or the traditional division of labour between the sexes.

These assumptions may still be contested in certain circles, but they are sufficiently entrenched in mainstream political discourse to provide a sound theoretical basis for most equality claims. Beyond this, however, the limitations, in practice, of equity-based approaches for delivering equality are very familiar. The history of own goals and setbacks of equity-based equal opportunities policies demonstrate the problems of translating a straightforward and relatively uncontentious principle into a practical basis for change. The struggles to move beyond formal equality to substantive equality and from direct discrimination to indirect, which marked the early years of the equal opportunities are evidence of these difficulties. Nevertheless, those barriers have not proved insurmountable and the language of equity has been sufficiently flexible to adapt in order to overcome them.

Equity-based arguments need to be supplemented with a rationale, which demonstrates that equal participation is a prerequisite for the proper functioning of that institution yet which do not rely on difference-based quality of justice arguments. This can be found in the concept of legitimacy.

The merit-based judicial appointments system is rigidly interpreted as 'gender blind' rather than actively promoting gender equality. The notion that the definition of merit and the priorities of the judicial appointments process might need to be reconstructed if gender equality is to be achieved has not, to date, been a popular one.

The patience that has been shown by supporters of gender equality over the last century since the legal barriers to the participation of women in the Judiciary were removed is unlikely to last indefinitely. As the number of women who are appointed to the senior ranks remains at a token level, the fallacy of the 'trickle-up' approach, which assumes a natural and automatic progress to equality, will be increasingly recognised.

A willingness to 'think the unthinkable' and explore options for more radical action are likely to grow, as they have done in other countries and other areas of public life. If and when that occurs, the development of sound arguments which can justify and support the application of proactive policies for promoting gender equality in Kenya, need to be put in place.

The argument advanced here does not reject the claim that women judges might do their jobs differently from their male counterparts in some respects. Indeed, given the differences in life experiences, it is quite probable that many sometimes do so. Moreover, there are clearly sound arguments for saying that there are likely to be benefits to the culture of the Judiciary in general terms, if not specific decision-making, by the inclusion of women.

The increase of women on the Bench may indeed counter gender bias in some areas and allow the voices of some women to be heard more than they have in the past. In addition, while there may be little or no difference in decision-making, there may be a difference in approach and style. The presence of more women on the Bench may contribute to the developing debates around gender issues.

Without rejecting completely the presence of gender difference, I am arguing that the empirical, theoretical and strategic problems identified above are such that difference-based arguments are too weak to stand as the principal foundation of gender equality on the Bench. One answer to this might be to suggest that difference should be employed strategically. Whatever its shortcomings, if it has a widespread appeal which will promote the goal of equality it can and should be utilised until it is no longer needed, when it can be discarded.

The problem with this argument is that it is a double-edged sword. If the rationale for seeking gender equality on the Bench is based on the value of incorporating the feminine perspective and if it emerges that the decision-making of women judges is much the same as their male counterparts and that women do not appear to bring with them a different voice to the adjudication process, or if early differences disappear as numbers grow, the basis for seeking equal numbers of women judges is undermined. Arguments based on equity and merit provide a sounder foundation for equality. Each alone does not provide a complete basis for requiring full equality of participation and for legitimising the necessary positive action to achieve this, but taken together they do so.

The key advantage of these rationales is that they presume a requirement of numerical and functional parity and are based on the claim that gender equality is necessary in its own right and is not dependent on improved outcomes. This means that they are not undermined if the decision-making and attitudes of women judges are indistinguishable from those of men, now or in the future. In addition, and crucially, it flows from this that it may be acceptable to risk trading-off in the short-term a degree of quality of justice to achieve long term equal participation through the appointment of women judges who come to the bench with less or different experiences from male candidates.[375]

6. 9. A SUM UP

The chapter reveals the following facts:

(i) Patriarchy in character is standing on the way of women.

(ii) Indian women are getting much more less than what they deserve and less than their counter part men in terms of remuneration and benefits for the same work.

(iii) This issue is almost ignored by everybody, including governments, academic research and civil society sectors in India.

(iv) Since representation of women is so low, priority must be given of having more women as judges as the backlog of cases in high court is huge. The country's judiciary has an enormous number of lawsuits pending and the higher courts are no exception.

(v) The high courts should be on the look-out for brilliant women lawyers who have the potential for delivering good justice, though they may not have enough experience.

375 Maleson, Kate; *Justyfing Gender inequality on the Bench: Why differences wint be*, Feminist legal studies, Vol. II, Kuwer Academic publishers, Netherlands, pp.1-24 < http://www.springerlink.com.> 8 on 21stMarch2011.

(vi) Women should be encouraged to join women into the judiciary and promoting them as judges was necessary.

(vii) The female members of the Bar may be encouraged in the profession, may be given assignments as Court Commissioners for inspections and recording statements of witnesses.

(viii) Preference may be given to female lawyers in the matter of assigning legal aid work or amicus curiae briefs so that they have more and more effective appearances in courts and to treat women with courtesy.

(ix) Any gender bias had to be carefully guarded against in the court room and this protection should be extended to any women present or appearing in the court either as a member of the staff, party, witness of member of legal profession.

(x) The government to make efforts to render a woman victim quick, speedy, cheaper and effective justice.

(xi) Landmark decisions delivered by the Indian judiciary in the past two decades bore testimony to the fact that judges could not be accused of gender injustice but such sensitivity of individual needs to be institutionalized.

(xii) Despite international conventions, gender equality enshrined in the Constitution and a plethora of laws, widespread violations of women's rights continued to persist.

(xiii) The forces of globalization and extremism and the unwillingness of other segments of humanity continue to pose a threat to women's human rights.

(xiv) Structural inequalities and power imbalances facilitate such violations as do the urge for easy money which makes women more susceptible to exploitation and violence.

(xv) A judge can make a correct and realistic evaluation of the laws and find out authoritatively the difficulties in implementation of or lacuna in legislation or while administering the laws. But, if deprived of requisite sensitivity, it may frustrate the objectives sought to be achieved by the best of the laws.

(xvi) The government is now thinking for induction of more women judges. Centre is willing to increase the present strength of the judges in the Supreme Court and various High Courts to ensure fast disposal of backlog of cases.

(xvii) However, women comparatively seem to be better represented in top positions in politics (20-30 percent), the civil service (19 percent) and the legal profession (approx 20 percent) than in business (3.6 percent and academia (12 percent), sciences (10 percent).

(xviii) The first hitch in implementing such a recommendations is that there are not enough number women judges to cope up with the abysmally large number of number of pending cases pertaining to violence. The government should first work towards addressing this anomaly so that these recommendations can be implemented.

(xix) The need for appointing more women judges to High Courts is to ensure speedy delivery of justice to women. The High Courts must be on the look-out for brilliant women lawyers who have the potential for delivering good justice, though they may not have enough experience.

(xx) Judges and lawyers must treat women with courtesy and dignity while appearing in the court.

(xxi) Any gender bias has to be carefully guarded against in the court room and this protection should be extended to any women present or appearing in the court either as a member of the staff, party, witness of member of legal profession.

(xxii) Women in judiciary can play an important role in sensitizing the judicial system towards gender issues. As the incidence of crimes against women is increasing, there is need to strengthen the judicial system by appointing more women judges to deal with issues relating to women and the family.

(xxiii) The Supreme Court of India has set up special courts to deal with rape cases that will be judged by female judges.

(xxiv) Women judicial officers should be given necessary training to sensitize them that while dealing with cases of violence, harassment or discrimination against women they should ensure speedy justice.

(xxv) The importance of simple procedures that can easily be understood must not be over-emphasized with regard to access to justice to women. The procedures must be made and the delivery mechanisms brought nearer so that people gain better access to it.

(xxvi) The general impression of the people is that a large number of cases are being delayed and, if any case is filed, it would take years to get a relief. This impression about the performance of Indian Judiciary is not fully correct. Out of total pendency of these cases, only 40percent cases are less than one year old. 90percent of delayed cases are pending in the subordinate courts.

(xxvii) We should have a national planning and management system for the administration of justice. What the Indian judicial system lacks is a systematic plan at the State and National levels to overcome the delay and arrears of cases.

(xxviii) Gender justice is being recognized in modern times. It is most appropriate that it should meaningfully address the woman question and respond to the challenges by stimulating the whole legal profession towards a greater concern for, and protection of women.

CHAPTER– VII

FEMINIZATION OF THE LEGAL PROFESSION – ITS IMPACT

"There are more women lawyers now than ever before and there will be even more in the coming years. What makes this an interesting social process to watch is the question of whether the women will have a unique perspective to offer the practice of law or the development of substantive doctrine?"

- Carrie Menkel Meadow

'Women at work', 1987

7.1. AN OVERVIEW

In the previous chapter we have noted the trends of feminization of the legal profession through the gradual increase of women lawyers and the efficient contribution of women in legal profession. In this chapter we will directly focus on the feminization of legal profession and its impact today. The chapter includes the study as to what are implications on the rapid influx of women lawyers into different segments of the legal profession.

Women's entry to law raises several questions. Since gaining admission to the profession, have women successfully entered all legal specialties, practice settings, and higher echelons of status and influence? What barriers to gender equality persist within the profession? How have women lawyers responded to the organizations in which they work, particularly when these organizations have been reticent to change or resisted to change altogether?[376]

We have seen earlier that the journey of women in the legal profession has been one of a long and hard struggle. Mary Wollstonecraft's classic work 'A Vindication of the Rights of Woman' published in 1792 spoke about not only the

---

376 Kay, Fiona and Gorman, Elizabeth; "Women in the Legal Profession", *Annual Review of Law and Social Science*, Vol. 4: pp.299-332

well-being of women but also rights that were aimed at the free agency of women. Not long ago, the task was to achieve better treatment for women — a squarer deal. The concentration was mainly on the well-being of women. Those objectives have gradually evolved or broadened to include the active role of women's agency. Women are no longer the passive recipients of welfare-enhancing help, but are increasingly seen as active agents of change: the dynamic promoters of social transformation that can alter the lives of both women and men.

The amount of women taking admission at top law schools have undoubtedly increased tremendously over the past few years. Unfortunately, this level of achievement for women has not carried over to the workplace once these students begin practicing law. The progress women have made in the legal profession in the last three decades is creditable, yet there is still a long way to go. So, beyond the careers of individual women lawyers, what impact will the advent of a significant number of women in the legal profession have on the practice of law?

One of the most dramatic changes in the legal profession in recent years has been the influx of women. In many countries women now constitute close to half of all law students, although it will be the turn of the century before this representation is fully mirrored among practitioners. This chapter explores the meaning of these changes for the profession and women, various theoretical frameworks through which we can interpret these data. The influx of women into the legal profession has prompted speculations among both academics, political and social activists that women would bring about change in the nature of substantive law and how law is practiced. The question of whether the profession 'feminized' have changed or influenced by the influx of women in the profession or what difference does it makes which includes increasing number of women? Or, beyond the careers of individual women lawyers, what impact had been made on legal rules and concepts, and on the role lawyers play in the society? Most importantly will women, who become lawyers, be just like men who are lawyers or will they bring a new dimension to legal profession?

Finally, does the nature of law itself tell us anything about the contributions women might make? Do legal ideals of equality shape women lawyers' conceptions of their roles in ways that diverge from the service ideal prevalent in medicine and other professions? Will the contribution of women differ in common law and civil law countries? Do highly bureaucratic legal systems permit less innovation than individualistic, litigation-oriented systems? Do political regimes (socialist versus capitalist) or religious beliefs (such as Islam or Confucianism) affect the influence of women? These questions are as pertinent today.

Because these developments are still relatively new and the theoretical terrain is shifting, it has been discussed in detail under the following heads:

- **Substantive Law Reform**
- **Social Structure of the Professions**
- **Impact of women judges,**
- **Feminist consciousness in Decision making**
- **Feminist views**
- **A Sum up**

The proportions of female and male law students are pretty equal especially in law schools. Both here and abroad female judges have been appointed to high office but women are granted fewer advancement opportunities in major law firms, specifically to the level of partner in compare to their male counterparts. There are few women who have become deans and professors at universities. They are just a handful of successful women and it is still the case that women, although they work hard they do not seem to reap the same rewards and advancements. The study shows that the issues of gender equality in law and legal professions still continue to present a challenge today all over the world.

7.1. SUBSTANTIVE LAW REFORM

At the simplest level, we can consider the profession feminized simply because it contains more women. However, whether the profession will be changed by the presence of women is a different question. For those who attribute 'feminine' qualities to women (or men), the legal profession becomes feminized when traits such as empathy, relatedness, nurturance, and collectiveness are recognized, valued, and expressed in the performance of legal tasks and functions. For others, the profession becomes 'feminized' not by stereotypic attributions of gender qualities but by a 'feminist' influence on the profession, which includes changes in both the practice of law (e.g., adaptations of work to family) and substantive rules (in areas ranging from employment discrimination to family law and criminal law). In this sense, feminism is the political and intellectual program of analyzing law from the point of view of women and working toward legal changes that will improve their material and cultural conditions. Indeed, it has been argued that the determination of some women reformers to change oppressive laws compelled them to seek admission to the bar in order to counteract the self-interest of male lawyers.

In many nations the entry of women into the profession coincided with law reform on issues affecting women, such as civil rights, discrimination, abortion, divorce, pregnancy benefits, and marital property (Marcus, 1987; Fineman, 1983, 1987). Yet, women do not always seek liberal social reforms. In Germany, for example, recent women entrants to the legal profession seem to be politically more conservative than their male counterparts (Blankenburg & Schultz, 1988). American data also reveal that male and female prelaw college students are preoccupied with individual success and financial security, resembling each other more than those of their sex who are attracted to other fields of study (A. Astin, 1984; Komarovsky, 1985). However, the increasing number of women in the profession seems to have changed some of our juridical concepts: equality has been replaced by equity in some contexts (comparable worth in North America, equal value in Europe) and individualistic rights by more collective or group-based rights (in health care and reproductive freedom).[377]

With respect to women's impact on substantive law, empirical research provides some support for the feminist consciousness view. It seems clear that women and men lawyers and judges draw on different background experiences in thinking about their legal roles. Women judges were more likely than their male counterparts

---

377 "Feminization of the Legal Profession: "The Comparative Sociology of Women Lawyers," *Lawyers in Society*, University of California press,1996, Los Angeles,pp.221-224.

to have experienced sex discrimination and conflict between their work and family roles.[378]

7.2. SOCIAL STRUCTURE OF THE PROFESSION

Whether women will structure and practice law differently remains unanswerable. As a result of widespread occupational segregation, women still occupy lower positions in the power hierarchy and particular fields and jobs on the horizontal axis. The evidence from other professions suggests that women will assimilate to male modes of practice. Chamber's study (1987) demonstrates that the gap may be narrowing between women and men in private practice. But studies of women in large firms (Fenning, 1954, *Law Letters,* 1984) and in management (Harlan & Weiss, 1981) suggest that, although they occupy entry-level positions, they have not made much progress vertically, even if we control for experience. It has been observed that there has not been much attitudinal change among senior male professionals with increased numbers of women professionals (Harlan & Weiss, 1981; *Hishon v. King & Spaulding,* 1984; *Hopkins v. Price Waterhouse,* 1985). Perhaps the degree of innovation varies with the structure of the profession. To the extent that law and business are characterized by competitive cultures. In hierarchical organizations, it may be more difficult for women to alter the basic structures and cultural norms. In medicine, by contrast, where the cultural norm is to heal rather than win, there may be better opportunity for change. Yet, there, too, the delivery of care is increasingly bureaucratized, and women are more likely to be salaried employees than independent practitioners. The unit of work may also be significant. In architecture and law, small work groups can develop egalitarian norms and engage in oppositional practices.

If feminism's purpose is to advance humanism, then the feminization of the legal profession should help to redeem it from the flaws of domination (both by and of clients) If it does not, then women will find themselves transformed by the male professional world—working long hours, estranged from their families, and perhaps

---

378 Martin E; "Men and women on the bench: what is the difference?," *Judicature* 73, 1990, pp. 204–208.

exploiting another class of women to perform traditional female roles (housework and childrearing).[379]

7.3 IMPACT IN LEGAL MATTERS

There has been [a] gradual erosion of the legal profession's external closure regime, which seems to be associated with the gradual feminization of the legal profession. The success rate of women in private practice has broad implications for all women lawyers. Women continue to enter the legal profession and, in many cases, are able to creatively forge new and rewarding paths that combine career and personal fulfillment. Expectations that women's legal thinking and behavior would differ from men which have grounded some new theories: that women lawyers and judges have a stronger feminist consciousness or that they think about legal issues using a different moral voice. But, the robes of lawyers remain 'ill-fitting and inadequate' for most women employed 'in a culture bound by men's rules.' Unwritten and heavily 'guarded' 'codes' of conduct pertaining to the need for a lawyer's open-ended availability has proven resistant to change.

Feminist scholars wonder if the presence of women and a female voice would alter the way the law made decisions about women, and whether the profession would change to incorporate and accommodate women's life cycles, or simply force women to assimilate and adopt the typical male work pattern. Workplace supports and flexibility remain inadequate. The research raises questions about the impact of workplace norms on women and the impact of women on workplace norms. While it can be concluded that workplace norms have not improved and may have even worsen in some cases.

The feminist consciousness view contends that women lawyers and judges are most likely to make an impact on legal matters affecting women's interests or involving female clients or litigants. According to one version of this view, women lawyers and judges view themselves as representatives of women in general and thus as having a special responsibility to act to mitigate the disadvantages that women

379 "Feminization of the Legal Profession: The Comparative Sociology of Women Lawyers," *Lawyers in Society*, University of California press,1996, Los Angeles,pp.261-262.

face. According to a somewhat different version, women's experiences in a subordinate and less powerful status in the broader societal system of gender relations should lead them to be more aware of the unequal treatment of women and more willing to reject cultural ideas and legal rules that favour men over women.[380]

Women judges are probably more sensitive to claimants raising issues of sexual discrimination than are men. Women judges are more likely than their male colleagues to reach legal conclusions that favor the interests of women. Female justices are more likely to support the woman's position in cases involving child support, sexual assault, and property settlement on divorce. Thus, the presence of a female judge on a decision-making panel increases the probability of changing the mindset and attitude in the society. As women are more sensitive to gender related issues.

In some cases it has been found that women lawyers experienced both gender disparagement and sexual harassment more frequently than men. Women lawyers and judges also rejected traditional stereotypical descriptions of women. It has also been observed that many a time's women judges gave judgment favouring men in cases of domestic violence and the allocation of property in divorce proceedings. Finally, the association between observations of gender disparagement and sexual harassment, on the one hand, and judges' role, on the other, suggested that their personal experiences may affect their opinions.[381]

There is also considerable evidences that female judges are more likely than their male colleagues to reach legal conclusions that favour the interests of women. For e.g. in the United States, female justices were more likely to support the woman's position in cases involving child support, sexual assault, birth control, and property settlement on divorce.[382] Several analyses of United States Court of Appeals decisions in employment discrimination cases found that female judges supported female

380 Marks L; "Alternative work schedules in law: It's about time!," *N. Y. Law Sch. Law Rev.* 35, 1990, pp.361–67

381 Martin,E; "The representative role of women judges," <http://heinonline.org/HOL/LandingPage?collection>

382 Allen D, Wall D; "Role orientations and women state Supreme Court justices," ***Judicature*** 77, 1993, pp.156–165

plaintiffs more often than did male judges. In another instance, the Court of Appeal for Ontario, Canada, it was found that women judges are more likely to rule against defendants in criminal sexual assault cases and against male litigants in family law cases. In contrast, two studies of federal district court judges appointed by Democratic presidents found that female judges were not more likely to rule for the female party in cases involving sex discrimination, sexual harassment, maternity rights, or reproductive freedom (Walker & Barrow 1985, Segal 2000). Thus, it may be that the effect of judge's gender in cases involving women's issues is less noticeable among judges who generally hold liberal-leaning views. Interestingly, women judges appear to influence their male colleagues. The presence of a female judge on a decision-making panel increases the probability that may favour the women litigants in cases of matrimonial disputes and those in employment matters. Expectations are that women's legal thinking and behavior would differ from men. It has usually been grounded into experience that women lawyers and judges have a stronger feminist consciousness or that they think about legal issues using a different moral voice.

7.4. FEMINIST CONSCIOUSNESS IN DECISION MAKING

Although there is of course tremendous overlap in personal characteristics between the genders, on average the women report that they are more desirous of social change, compassionate, honest and liberal than the men. The entry of women into the legal profession has changed both lawyers and the legal profession. Women have brought to the profession a different set of assets and problems than men. On the other hand, men have a greater desire for money and are more confident, better dealmakers and more aggressive than the women. Also, because of their different roles in courtship and in the family, men and women lawyers tend to have different family characteristics and tend to address the problem of accommodating work and family in different ways. Men are more likely to be married, have a spouse who focuses on childcare while women are more likely to have a spouse with an intense job and enjoy much higher spousal income. In balancing productivity in the workplace and the home, men work more hours outside the home than women. While women have to take their time off from paid work to do childcare.

Perhaps most related to the women's roles is the obvious connection between personal lives to professional lives. While women continue to bear the children, there is a biological necessity for reconciling the complicated relationship between personal life and professional work. While some countries have provided solutions, in India it is still to achieve. Some have urged that women connection work and family may change the work style and commitments of all legal professionals offering a healthier balance between the institution of work and life.

These differences in personal and family characteristics can have an enormous impact on a person's career. Reflecting their different levels of desire for money and social change, and their different commitments to childcare, men are more likely to go into private practice and business, while women are more likely to go into corporate counsel positions, government work, public interest work and legal education. Within practice, men are disproportionately drawn to specialties and activities that yield high income while women are drawn to specialties and activities that yield predictable and lower hours.

Men are more likely to enter and stay in private practice and be a partner, in compare to women who have missed paid work to do childcare. This shows an insignificantly negative effect for being a woman. This effect is disproportionately borne by women who do childcare who suffer a disadvantage similar to that of men who do childcare.

The thrust of the 19th century is to construe Indian womanhood in terms of an amalgam of educational modernization and retention of femininity. Such a synthesis did not change ideas of female modesty and economic dependence of the women on men. The nationalist movement and post-independent Indian State continued to emphasize this tendency towards defining a primary role for women as homemakers. The changes in law created a framework for equalization of gender roles without providing the catalytical element of radical overhaul of gender relations. The result is that the supposed progress in status and opportunity for Indian women is only cosmetic without any qualitative attitudinal change. In spite of availing employment opportunities the acceptable female behaviour is seen in terms of nurturing maternal and homemaking role. Most women's magazines contain lifestyle choices, fashion, decor and child-care advice. There is great stress on the cult of beauty and craze for fitness, grooming to be more attractive and feminine. The career of Indian woman is sought as a supplement to the traditional role of a successful homemaker. Women themselves acquiesce to this value system, for it affords them the security of psychological dependence, social prestige and adherence to the superficial westernisation. In the west, to be 'unfeminine' is no longer a slur, but in India, to deviate from mother-wife role is not socially acceptable.

In the Indian situation, such a woman has to face social barbs, suspicion or accept sympathy. This is a vicious circle leading to compromises and quest for security which results in female acquiescence to the continued validity of accepted social mores. If we indulge in serious thinking as to model gender relation in the next century, there is need to play a far more activist's role — being prepared to sacrifice the desires for security and the craving for conformity to sanctioned role expectations. Otherwise, superficial changes in fashion, enforced mobility of education or even employment could hardly be described as emancipation.

Exercise of democratic rights, education, employment, with stress on the cult of beauty as a supplement to the traditional role of wife-mother will only have cosmetic effect unless women come out of the shell of femininity. A more activist role is required to model gender relations by developing appropriate attitudinal transformation in the social system. Else, she becomes a mute symbol in the unfinished agenda of emancipation.

The claims of equality in social arrangements lead us to the question of what its content is. A common characteristic of all contemporary approaches could be identified. They all demand something central to that particular theory. If libertarians demand equal rights, the income egalitarians argue for equal incomes. The basic issue that divides the different approaches is not 'whether equality' or 'why equality' but 'equality of what'.

7.5 FEMINIST VIEWS

The more interesting question, however, is whether women will have a different perspective to offer the practice of law or the development of substantive doctrine. Such questions implicate important issues in feminist theory. If women demand equality with men on the basis that they are the same, then more women in the profession should have no greater significance than more blue-eyed lawyers. However, some feminists believe that equal participation does not necessarily require 'sameness,' particularly conformity to a male model. Although the male-dominated profession presently appears to be 'winning'—requiring women to adapt to its norms (C. Epstein, 1981)—it is imperative to explore the possibilities of reversing that trend.

The observation of how women's entry into male dominated field has changed both the knowledge base of the field and the methodology by which knowledge is acquired. The studies have earlier shown that the function of the legal profession was based exclusively on male norms. With more women lawyers entering into the legal performance and performing lawyering task different from men has oriented the legal profession and has brought the increased presence of women on broad institutional effects. The realization is that women can transform a profession, give expression to values and behaviours with the belief that this will produce a better legal system for lawyers, clients and others who are affected by our legal institutions.

A second perspective draws on the theory of psychologist Carol Gilligan, who argues that girls and women tend to view the resolution of conflicts as a problem of care and responsibility in relationships, whereas boys and men tend to view it as a problem of rights and rules. A rights-based approach to resolving a conflict involves identifying the interests of the parties in abstract terms and deciding which party's interest is more important; this reasoning process leads to an outcome in which one party wins and the other loses. A care-based approach, in contrast, involves considering the contextual details of the situation in an attempt to construct a compromise that takes into account the interests of both parties.[383] Tracing the implications of Gilligan's framework for substantive law, legal scholars have argued that a care-based feminine jurisprudence would demonstrate an emphasis on protecting the interests of communities and individuals' memberships in communities; on contextual circumstances as opposed to bright-line rules; and on the affirmative responsibilities of courts and governmental actors has applied Gilligan's ideas to legal practice, suggesting that women lawyers might organize their practices

383 Gilligan C. 1982. *In a Different Voice: Psychological Theory and Women's Development.* Harvard Univ. Press, Cambridge, MA:

on a more collaborative basis; might maintain more cooperative, empathetic relationships with clients; and might make greater efforts to pursue negotiated settlements of litigation or non adversarial modes of dispute resolution.[384]

Karst's analysis suggests that a women's voice of care and connection might lead to doctrinal changes in the areas of state action in discrimination law and in the state's affirmative duty to assist all its members to be able to fully participate in the community. Thus, our conception of state responsibility under the Constitution might be enlarged, and a conception of responsibility might supplement or replace altogether our notion of individualistic constitutional "rights".[385]

Although research examining the 'different voice' perspective is scarce, the few existing studies provide no evidence that women draw on a different ethic of care in formulating legal arguments and conclusions. Moving beyond a limited focus on judges' votes to analyze their reasoning, Davis (1993) examined opinions of the U.S. Court of Appeals for the Ninth Circuit in cases involving sex discrimination, race discrimination, or deprivation of constitutional rights, but found no noticeable differences in moral reasoning between the opinions of male and female judges.

There has been less attention to the question of gender differences in style of legal practice. Studies in this area have generally framed their inquiry in terms of Gilligan's 'different voice' theory and related feminist theories, asking whether women approach the practice of law in a more cooperative, caring fashion and take into account more of the contextual details of their clients' lives. Findings provide only very limited support for this view. Based on interviews with 36 lawyers in Washington state, Jack & Jack (1989) concluded that some women lawyers do adopt an attitude of personal concern toward their clients and take a holistic interest in the context surrounding the client's legal problem, but others either adapted easily to the prevailing 'masculine' mode of legal practice or attempted to compartmentalize their lives, interacting with others in a "masculine" mode at work and a "feminine" mode

[384] Kay, Fiona and Gorman Elizabeth; "Women in the Legal Profession," *Annual Review of Law and Social Science,* Vol. 4: pp.299-332

[385] Menkel-Meadow C; "The comparative sociology of women lawyers: the feminization of the legal profession," 24 Osgoode *Hall Law J.*, 1986, pp.897–910.

in their personal relationships. Moreover, women who attempted to practice in a care mode found themselves facing emotional exhaustion and burnout.[386]

Analyzing transcripts of interactions between legal aid lawyers and their clients in a city in Israel, Bogoch (1997) observed numerous differences in the way clients spoke to male and female lawyers but few gender differences in the interactional styles of lawyers themselves. Women and men lawyers interrupted clients equally frequently, were equally likely to initiate topic changes, gave cooperative responses to clients equally frequently, and were equally likely to use indirection or politeness markers when speaking to clients. A survey of lawyers in Phoenix, Arizona, concerning the negotiation style of the opposing counsel in a recent settlement or transaction yielded no gender difference in the ratings of lawyers on care dimensions (e.g., adaptable, communicative, helpful) or rights dimensions (e.g., analytical, objective, rational) . Interestingly, ratings on both types of items were positively associated with assessments of negotiating effectiveness (see also Craver 1990).An ethic of care could arguably lead women lawyers to avoid overly aggressive or dishonest lawyering behavior that risks running afoul of professional ethical rules. Analyzing data on state lawyer disciplinary proceedings in 2000, Hatamyar & Simmons (2004) found that relative to the state lawyer population, women were disciplined less often than men. Moreover, this gender gap held across all types of disciplinary violations (e.g., incompetence, conflict of interest, misappropriation of client property, improper litigation conduct, etc.).[387]

The constraints that women face in and outside the home also affect in their professional career. For example women in the villages of West Bengal are commonly portrayed as among the most oppressed and majority of them are grounded in both poverty and patriarchy. Patriarchy limits women's ownership and control over property and other economic resources including the products of their own labour. Women's mobility in West Bengal is constrained and their access to education and information hindered. The clearest examples of gender inequality are the various forms of violence systematically meted out against women. They are practically

386 Ibid pp.943-967

387 Kay, Fiona and Gorman Elizabeth; "Women in the Legal Profession," *Annual Review of Law and Social Science*, Vol. 4: pp.299-332

excluded from decision making though education for women have reached earlier in comparison to other states.

Oppression on women, system, still exists in the society. Early motherhood, ill health due to malnutrition, concept of male and female child in obtaining higher education has worried the government, administration and social scientists. According to census, 2001 the gender development index in West Bengal is 0.549. Districts like Howrah, North 24 Parganas, Burdwan and Cooch Behar obtain gender inequality as an alarming situation. The reservation for women has already been put in place in Panchayats and local bodies and experience of its working can only be described as encouraging. The proportion of women entering the male dominated profession did increase but made very little headway.[388] The study thus has disclosed major issues relating to gender within the different branches of the legal profession in India. These centre on levels of remuneration, the high incidence of gender perception gaps and the continuing under-representation of women at equity partner level. The overall picture of earnings of lawyer discloses a disturbing gender pay gap. Even when those working part-time are excluded, a pay gap remains at most levels and especially within private practice. In terms of attitudes within the profession, on gender neutral issues to which all respond primarily as lawyers there is general unanimity. However, when a question relates to gender and equality, either directly or indirectly, distinct perception gaps emerge which are based on gender and which in many instances are very significant.

To allow women to take up employment or hold elective offices and inherit property is not yet socially accepted wholeheartedly. We have the duty, therefore, to educate our society, to bring awareness as to the need for such laws or the necessity for women to take up employment which in fact results in empowerment of women. Unless there is social acceptability of a law the effectiveness thereof would be in serious doubt as, for example, in the last century the *Child Marriage Restraint Act* was passed and still in certain areas in this country, even today child marriages take place. These instances clearly point out that law alone cannot tackle social problems

---

388 Mukhopadhyay, Pallav; "Problem of Gender Inequality and Expansion of Education of Women in West Bengal,"<http:// www.isical.ac.in/~wemp/Papers/PaperPallavMukhopadhyay.doc>on 6th March 2010.

and a lot of awareness is required among the public before such laws are accepted or such laws are promoted. Therefore there is a great need for us to go to the villages and educate people at different levels of the need and efficacy of such laws so that there may be social acceptability and success of the same. As long as there is no empowerment to women, no society can progress.

The claims of equality in social arrangements lead us to the question of what its content is. A common characteristic of all contemporary approaches could be identified. They all demand something central to that particular theory. If libertarians demand equal rights, the income egalitarians argue for equal incomes. The basic issue that divides the different approaches is not "whether equality" or "why equality" but "equality of what". The latter question derives importance from the actual diversity of human beings so that demanding equality in terms of one variable tends to clash with that wanting equality in terms of another. We are deeply diverse in internal characteristics such as inherited fortunes, age, gender, general disabilities, particular talents, and proneness to illness and so on, as well as in external circumstances such as ownership of assets, social background, and environmental predicaments and so on. It is precisely because of such diversity that insistence on egalitarianism in one field requires rejection of egalitarianism in another.

There is a well-known presumption that all men are born equal. Despite such presumption the substantive importance of the question posed relates to the empirical fact of pervasive human diversity. Investigation of equality that proceeds with the assumption of antecedent uniformity thus misses out all major aspects of the problem. Human diversity is a fundamental aspect of our interest in equality.

Not long ago, the task was to achieve better treatment for women — a squarer deal. The concentration was mainly on the well-being of women. No longer the passive recipients of welfare-enhancing help, women are increasingly seen, by men as well as women as active agents of change: the dynamic promoters of social transformation that can alter the lives of both women and men.

In spite of long decade of post-independent democratization, preferential rights in the Constitution and legislative enactments and a superficial modernization, social changes are still stuck in the century-old mould. The major reason for this status quo is the entrenchment of patriarchal mores with which women themselves collaborate. The thrust of the 19th century is to construe Indian womanhood in terms of an amalgam of educational modernization and retention of femininity. Such a synthesis did not change ideas of female modesty and economic dependence of the women on men. The nationalist movement and post-independent Indian State continued to emphasize this tendency towards defining a primary role for women as homemakers. The changes in law created a framework for equalization of gender roles without providing the catalytically element of radical overhaul of gender relations. The result is that the supposed progress in status and opportunity for Indian women is only cosmetic without any qualitative attitudinal change. In spite of availing employment opportunities the acceptable female behaviors is seen in terms of nurturing maternal and homemaking role. Most women's magazines contain lifestyle choices, fashion, decor and child-care advice. There is great stress on the cult of beauty and craze for fitness, grooming to be more attractive and feminine. The career of Indian woman is sought as a supplement to the traditional role of a successful homemaker. Women themselves acquiesce to this value system, for it affords them the security of psychological dependence, social prestige and adherence to the superficial westernization. In the west, to be 'unfeminine' is no longer a slur, or to deviate from mother-wife role is not socially unacceptable. In the Indian situation, such a woman has to face social barbs, suspicion or accept sympathy. This is a vicious circle leading to compromises and quest for security which results in female acquiescence to the continued validity of accepted social mores. If we indulge in serious thinking as to model gender relation in the next century, there is need to play a far more activist's role — being prepared to sacrifice the desires for security and the craving for conformity to sanctioned role expectations. Otherwise, superficial changes in fashion, enforced mobility of education or even employment could hardly be described as emancipation.

Exercise of democratic rights, education, employment, with stress on the cult of beauty as a supplement to the traditional role of wife-mother will only have cosmetic effect unless women come out of the shell of femininity. A more activist role is required to model gender relations by developing appropriate attitudinal transformation in the social system. Else, she becomes a mute symbol in the unfinished agenda of emancipation.

The claims of equality in social arrangements lead us to the question of what its content is. A common characteristic of all contemporary approaches could be identified. They all demand something central to that particular theory. If libertarians demand equal rights, the income egalitarians argue for equal incomes. The basic issue that divides the different approaches is not 'whether equality' or 'why equality' but 'equality of what'. The latter question derives importance from the actual diversity of human beings so that demanding equality in terms of one variable tends to clash with that wanting equality in terms of another. We are deeply diverse in internal characteristics such as inherited fortunes, age, gender, general disabilities, particular talents, and proneness to illness and so on, as well as in external circumstances such as ownership of assets, social background, and environmental predicaments and so on. It is precisely because of such diversity that insistence on egalitarianism in one field requires rejection of egalitarianism in another. .

Women are the bridge builders over the dividing lines of conflict. In the legal profession, women advocates can play an important role by providing a deeper insight into conflict resolution from a human perspective. The legal profession in India has been 'gendered' but women are slowly but surely becoming prominent in the Indian legal community, striving to work towards fostering a legal community that represents the best and brightest that society has to offer.. It was difficult for women to break through rigid traditions. But, some women through their talent, their legal skills, their intellect and their capacity for hard work, have achieved permanence in the legal landscape today.

What, at times, forms a genuine impediment, is the reluctance that is felt among women that they are under closer scrutiny while balancing future family needs when contemplating their career. Overcoming this impediment is a complex task. It requires a wider systemic change within the legal fraternity that offers more support and diversity to women, and an enhanced sense of confidence. Overcoming the complex task, younger generation have responded and has made their career in lower judiciary. The study suggests that women must rise not only to speak before the Court but also to deliver judgement. That equal opportunity in legal practice is a daily reality. That law has moved to bring to practice the same virtues of fairness and non-discrimination that the law itself in India is supposed to preach.

7.6. A SUM UP

The chapter gives the following findings:

(i) The analysis addresses whether the legal profession can be classified as experiencing successful feminization.

(ii) The study suggests that relatively successful feminization occurs where (a) occupational growth is rapid, (b) graduate and specialized degrees are important, and (c) wages are increasing.

(iii) The study develops an argument for the legal profession as a case of successful feminization with data taken from Bar Council of India, National Commission for Women and Bar Council of West Bengal. The results suggest that there have been overall improvements in the economic standing of female lawyers.

(iv) With more women lawyers entering into the legal performance and performing lawyering task different from men has oriented the legal profession and has brought the increased presence of women on broad institutional effects.

(v) Women lawyers and judges are most likely to make an impact on legal matters affecting women's interests.

(vi) There is also evidence of a persistent 'glass ceiling' in the earnings distribution for women.

(vii) Analyses of change in evaluations of legal work settings suggest that changes in earnings that favour women's successful entry into law are occurring in a context of growing dissatisfaction with legal work settings

(viii) The constraints that women face in and outside the home also affect in their professional career.

(ix) Some scholars expect that increasing the number of female judges will make courts more receptive to the arguments of claimants in gender-coded cases

(x) One form of this argument goes so far as to expect female judges to 'seize decision-making opportunities to liberate other women' in deciding cases. Thus far, the validity of arguments that gender affects case outcomes.

(xi) Women would inhabit the role of lawyer differently than men if they could overcome men's domination of the profession;

(xii) Some feminist feel that women will reconstruct the profession and the legal system to be more comprehensive, more contextualized, less rule-bound, more responsible to others, as well as clients and more conscious of socially just ends; and

(xiii) Women's role as lawyers, judges and partners of law firms will refuse to capitulate to a 'macho' ethic of law and will try to incorporate their own integration of psycho-social health and family balance into their roles.

CHAPTER – VIII

A CRITICAL APPRAISAL

"Where the mind is without fear and the head
Is held high, where knowledge is free,
Where the world has not been broken up into
Fragments by narrow domestic walls,
Where words come out from the depth of
Truth, where tireless striving stretches its arms
Towards perfection,
Where the clear stream of reason has not lost
Its way into the dreary desert sand of
Dead habit.
Where the mind is led forward by thee
Into ever widening thought and action
Into that heaven of freedom, my father
Let my country awake."

GITANJALI - Rabindranath Tagore
(Nobel Prize Winner from India for Literature)

8.1. AN OVERVIEW

This research examines the conceptual framework of study of women and legal profession – a feminist approach. Through the historical developments and from judicial decisions based on past legislations, the study analyses women were prevented from entering the legal profession until the early twentieth century. Women were therefore required to bring lawsuits against the legal establishments while in others they mobilized the influence of fathers and husbands. These suits gradually brought reforms in the past legislations through which women were entitled to enter into the practice of law. Women were notably absent from legal education in most of the countries until the1960s. The study explores the existing admission pattern, the situation of women in legal education and found a small proportion of women studying law.

In many countries, women had great difficulties in accessing legal education and throughout their careers they seem to face greater obstacles. This study analyses the causative factors, varieties of forms of discrimination, legislative development, implementation pattern and inadequate representation of women in the various wings of the legal profession. While the enrollment of women in University education expanded, the actual participation of women in legal practice was increasing in a slower pace. The issues surrounding women in law have received some attention in recent years. From the available data, case studies and anecdotes it is possible to ascertain that women face serious obstacles succeeding in law.

Women were consistently rated negatively. The intensity of feeling against women varied with the size of the firm. However, discrimination showed varying faces to women job seekers, and each form had its consequences. Sometimes women were victims of discrimination and sometimes by statutes. The study investigates some of the judicial decisions of the Supreme Court of India, which reveals the discriminative and oppressive working conditions of women in general including women in legal profession.

In recent years, the legal profession has undergone significant change, with rapidly rising numbers of women among its membership. Though formal barriers have been have been removed in legal education, informal and structural barriers that impede women's full participation within the legal profession still exists even today. Although law schools have made advances toward achieving gender equality, there continues to be an inadequate representation of women. Despite their advances in gaining admittance to law school and law colleges, women continue to face gender-based barriers once they enter the profession, and partly as a result, they leave the profession at significantly higher rates than their male colleagues as we have seen in earlier chapters.

The study analyses the problems women face in the workplace regarding advancement opportunities. Women in many countries now constitute half or more of the workforce and they can be found in all professions. Yet, more analyses show that women's participation tends to be highly concentrated in only quite a narrow range of legal profession. Women are clustered in the lower echelons of professional hierarchies while elite positions are by and large the reserve of men which is apparent from the available datas shown in chapter two, three and six. This horizontal and vertical segregation means that female dominated occupations tend to be those with lower standing in terms of career opportunities, income and prestige. Over and over, the picture remains the same in most of the underdeveloped countries. Social awareness is necessary to attain goals envisaged in the Constitution to transform 'de jure' equality to 'de facto' equality as equality of women is a basic condition of social, economic and political development of the nation.

In many countries women now constitute close to half of all law students, although it will be the turn of the century before this representation is fully mirrored among practitioners. This study explores the meaning of these changes for the profession and women, through various theoretical frameworks. The influx of women into the legal profession has prompted speculations among both academics, political and social activists that women would bring about change in the nature of substantive law and how law is practiced. The study analyses the concept of feminization of legal profession and the impact. Feminist scholars wonder if the presence of women and a female voice would alter the way the law made decisions about women, and whether the profession would change to incorporate and accommodate women's life cycles, or simply force women to assimilate and adopt the typical male work pattern. One form of this argument goes so far as to expect female judges to 'seize decision-making opportunities to liberate other women' in deciding cases. The study reveals concludes the following findings.

8.2. FINDINGS:

A. *RELATED TO LEGAL PRACTICE AND LAW FIRMS*

1. On an average, female lawyers earn less than male lawyers. Even in between those having equivalent positions, experience, and qualifications there is disparity of income. Studies show that qualified women are only half as

likely as men to obtain partnership. This polarity of viewpoint across gender gives greater cause for concern given that employers within private practice remain predominately male.

2. Certain findings in the research suggest that there may be issues surrounding the position of the proportion of female lawyers. The study finds that women are paid less than others, are limited in terms of the quality and variety of work they are offered and do not achieve career progression. The position of women in the profession is a product of the interaction of all of these factors.

3. Women continue to face gender-based barriers once they enter the profession, and partly as a result, they are leaving the profession at significantly higher rates than males.

4. Increasing number of women is unable to cope in the first phase of profession. As a result they leave the practice in greater numbers than their male counterparts.

5. This deeper look into the hearts of these women provides important insight into why career patterns of women in the field of law are different than career patterns of men which concluded that the advancement of women in the legal profession continues to be undermined by insufficient accommodation for parental responsibilities.

6. Marriage and motherhood should not become a disability preventing women from fulfilling their full and proper role for which society including women themselves must accept their due responsibilities.

7. Some Bar reports in India have identified difficulties faced by women advocates. Reports of harassment have come from time to time mainly from the young female advocates who are shocked but most often accept such behaviour due to social and other reasons.

8. It can have a devastating effect upon the health, confidence, morale and performance of those affected by it. The anxiety and stress produced by such

harassment commonly leads to stress, being less efficient at work, or leaving the profession to seek work elsewhere.

9. Such acts have led to degradation in the legal profession as they set forth wrong behaviors and affect the career of a woman.

10. There is still long way to go in order to change the values and thinking of tradition bound people of countries like India.

11. The studies indicate the attitudes, environmental problem and difficulties in securing work. There is a feeling of resentment towards the competence of lawyers.

12. The departure of women professionals from the Bar is a great loss to the legal profession and an economic loss to the family and to the country.

13. India has witnessed many social changes post independence. Today, women have come out of homes and established an identity of their own in different areas of work. Though most women lawyers make an economic contribution in one form or another (including housework, working in family, working in the Bench and Bar etc.), much of their work has not been documented.

14. The problems women face is in the workplace, regarding equal salary and advancement opportunities that will not change over night. This study suggests that certain things that can be done that may at least partially aid this situation.

15. Society owes a special responsibility to women as mothers.

16. Safe bearing and rearing of children is an obligation that must be shared by the mother, the father and the society. The contribution made by an active house maker to the management of a family should be accepted as economically and socially productive and as essential for national development.

17. Marriage and motherhood should not become a disability preventing women from fulfilling their full and proper role in becoming successful professionals.

18. Through questionnaire and personal interviews, the study reveals that women belonging to upper class families experienced greater dissatisfaction with their career opportunities than do women who are from lower middle class.

19. It is essential for future studies to consider the interplay of gender, and other forms of identity in the context of a professional training program.

20. The legal profession, at the bar and the legal education possesses both the resources and the talent to provide manpower and skills to fulfill its professional educational obligations.

21. In our society the freedom of women to seek employment outside the family is a major issue. This freedom is denied in many cultures and this attitude in itself is a serious violation of women's liberty and gender equality.

22. The absence of this freedom militates against the economic empowerment of women, with many other deleterious consequences. The employment of women in the bench or in judicial service in post of law officers in the government departments reflected the barriers in their representation.

23. The denial of the right to work outside the home is rather a monstrous violation of women's liberty. There are so many women law graduates simply turned as housewives for want of proper support and encouragement to work outside the matrimonial home.

24. Ordinarily the prohibition may work more implicitly through the power of convention and in the guise of culture. Quite often there may not even be a clear ban on women seeking practice in the court, and yet women reared in the traditional values may be quite afraid to break with the traditions.

25. The prevailing perceptions of normality and appropriateness are quite central to this question. As this is applicable to women who would like to choose practice legal as their first choice but is afraid in doing so.

26. The responsibility to run the home and take care of the children is that of women. The idea still exists. Even where they join the Bar or Bench, not only have they to work in offices — both before going to and after returning from the office — but will have to carry out the household chores apart from attending to children and taking care of visitors.

27. As long as there is no understanding and sharing of household work between men and women and the family is solely dependent on the women of the house, it is a kind of deprivation to the women, of leisure or time for pursuit of other interests in addition to reducing the burden of the family cares.

28. In this area particularly where both the parents of the child are employed, the fact remains that the responsibility of the children is on both the parents and necessarily calls for sharing the burden but that may not be in many cases.

29. Statistics demonstrate that women in law are still the primary careers of children. They nevertheless spend three times as much time as men on caring for children. This pattern and the stereotype of women for bringing up the child , have put most of the career women in an disadvantage positions

30. As has been mentioned above, women are to look after the child and often resume work after childbirth on reduced hours. In many cases this is associated with a drop in income much greater than that on average in compared to male advocates.

31. The approach of the society is that the child instinctively looks to the mother rather than to the father forgetting the fact that it was the mother who was available to the child rather than the father.

32. In terms of employment as well as promotion in work and occupation, women often face greater handicap than men. A country like Japan may be quite egalitarian in matters of demography or basic facilities, and even, to a

great extent, in higher education, and yet progress to elevated levels of employment and occupation seems to be much more problematic for women than for men.

33. The findings of the report examined several aspects of gender equity affecting career and professional development and quality of life for lawyers.

34. Women are paid less than men in terms of fees have less opportunity than men and advance at slower rates than men. This disparity remains prevalent even when years in practice are factored into the equation.

35. There is a disparity among the kinds of activities in which women are involved and the connection of activities might have to advancement and income increase. Women are more often involved in committees that address diversity and issues affecting the organization. They are less likely to be involved in compensation, management, partnership and business development committees. Gender disparagement undermines women's authority in law practice

36. There are disparate perceptions of women's roles in the profession. For example, women lawyers are often mistaken as assistant of senior lawyers instead of independent practitioners. The range of unfair treatment experienced included: unfounded criticism, downgraded appraisals, not being declared as designated seniors or elevation to the bench.

37. There are significant differences between what men and women perceive as issues of gender equity. The majority of women reported that child care-related issues impact their participation in their careers and affect their choice of field of concentration, hours worked and the ability to participate in networking opportunities.

38. Some women lawyers who were interviewed experienced significant disadvantage by reason of pregnancy. Women's legal status has been linked to marriage, making them dependent on their husband's.

39. Many pregnant women lawyers who leave the work often struggle to return to their pre-maternity professional status. But those women who had husbands as lawyers are in a much more comfortable position than other women lawyers whose spouses belong to some other profession.

40. Women are more likely to go into public service areas of the law than men, because such jobs are more available. Often they prefer jobs which may give them economic stability.

41. Some women lawyers interviewed suggested satisfaction of work. They tend to be younger than the average age of male lawyers. Very few women lawyers stated that there was harassment in matters of getting brief. Many of them confessed and opined that networking is an important factor in the practice of law.

42. Many women lawyers believed that they faced various forms of discrimination and gender bias within the legal profession, which placed them at a disadvantage to their male peers. In addition, harassment continues to undermine professional relations in the practice of law

43. The demanding nature of legal practice, particularly in private practice makes difficult for women lawyers in reconciling with family responsibilities.

44. Gender barriers in private law firms were said to reflect a law firm culture that emphasized loyalty, dedication and a degree of commitment to the firm often to the exclusion of family responsibilities and differential treatment of men and women in terms of work allocation, access to clients, mentoring and remuneration.

45. There are often enough, basic inequalities in gender relations within the family or the household, which can take many different forms. Even in cases in which there are no overt signs of anti-female bias, survival or son-preference or education, or even in promotion to higher executive positions, the family arrangements can be quite unequal in terms of sharing the burden of housework and child care.

46. The reach of this inequality includes not only unequal relations within the family, but also derivative inequalities in employment and recognition in the outside world. Also, the established fixity of this type of 'division' or 'accumulation' of labour can also have far-reaching effects on the knowledge and understanding of different types of work in professional circles.

47. The one exception was in Matrimonial law which was seen as having a female dimension in the area where there were more women legal practioners. However there was a disparity of perception here according to gender. In respect of Civil, Corporate and Criminal Law, a majority of female lawyers believed that there was a perception that men were better suited to these areas. In two of these (Civil and Corporate Law) male lawyers did form a majority who actually undertook such work.

48. It should be noted that the general impression is that in areas where men dominate tend to be those which are regarded within the profession as being well paid whereas women form the majority in those areas are regarded as being poorly paid.

49. At the Bar, the male dominated character of work posed special problems for women lawyers. Obtaining a brief was said to be difficult for women advocates with some clients being resistant to briefing female advocates even to the extent of refusing to do so.

50. Indian women have been suffering from male domination, subjugation and oppression. In the midst of the prevalence of such male domination in almost every area, it becomes quite impossible for women to have access to power-sharing and decision making unless exceptional provisions are made and implemented.

51. Women make up between 24-30 percent of a nation's lawyers.

B. *RELATED TO LEGAL EDUCATION*

53. Many students have seldom considered legal Profession as the first choice. Very often, the value of the study of law is not really understood till quite late. Many drift into law either because they are related to some one who is doing well in the legal profession or because they have nothing else to do. They feel that a law degree can help them to get a good job in a commercial organization; or if nothing else, they can enroll themselves as advocates and start practicing. While doing so, many still look for an alternative career because of the initial frustration for not being able to make a significant headway at the Bar.

54. Nevertheless, like medicine, engineering, and management, law is also a highly rewarding profession. But the tendency of a good student is to sit in joint examinations of medicine and engineering rather than in law entrance examinations. There are also instances of students getting admitted at the law course to enable them to continue to stay in the hostels, which provide highly subsided board and lodging.

55. What is necessary is to take a decision to choose law as a career instead of drifting into it as the last resort, and vigorously pursue the course. In fact, the crowd of drifters who could not make a mark in the profession has diluted the quality of legal profession.

56. There are very few women who opt as a career in legal profession. In the state of West Bengal, there are disparities in matter of enrollments of men and women.The tendency is to go for teaching, nursing, medical profession and management.

57. The foremost problem is that of resource constraints faced by educational institutions. Due to financial constraints many law colleges are working with few faculties mostly on part time basis. The picture is grim in the state of West Bengal and Bihar.

58. Even when there is relatively little difference in basic facilities including schooling, the opportunities of higher education may be far fewer for young

women than for young men. Indeed, gender bias in higher education and professional training can be observed even in some of the richest countries in the world, in Europe and North America.

59. There are few women teachers in law schools and colleges and very few in the rank of Deans and Professors. Even the new law schools have few law faculties as women. In law schools, women faculties may find themselves in 'female' areas of the law: family law, contract, and criminal law.

60. That legal education stands in need of substantial modification. The process of change is predicated upon careful evaluation of diverse educational needs, successful marshalling of faculty and administrative skills, provision of viable channels of communication between faculty and students, provision of requisite research and consultative facilities, and co-operation between the three important constituent units of a law school : administration, faculty and students.

61. Importantly, change must bear a sophisticated relationship to the localized requirements of individual law schools and the clientele they serve.

62. Due to ignorance of the property rights and in matters of succession, in many societies the ownership of property is also unequal. Even basic assets such as homes and land have been asymmetrically shared. The absence of claims to property can not only reduce the voice of women, but also make it harder for women to enter and flourish in commercial, economic and even some social activities. This type of inequality has existed in most parts of the world, though there are also local variations. For example, traditional property rights have favoured men in the bulk of India. Thus, lack of legal education and awareness has prevented many women to assert their rights.

C. *RELATED TO JUDICIARY*

63. Women are disproportionately represented in lower positions within the different wings of judiciary despite increasing number of women graduating in law. On the bench, they are predominately at the lower rungs of the

courts. Only in last five years women have made their careers in lower judiciary in quite a few states in India.

64. Many of the women judicial officers are not posted in family courts, or as members in Juvenile boards or committees. Most often the family courts have men as judges who consider such postings as less prestigious.

65. Women should be encouraged to join into the judiciary and promoting them as judges was necessary. While young female members of the Bar may be encouraged in the profession by way giving assignments as Court Commissioners, for inspections and recording statements of witnesses, cross examinations, etc. Preference may be given to female lawyers in the matter of assigning legal aid work or amicus curiae briefs so that they have more and more effective appearances in courts.

66. Poor court facilities in the district level reflect the country's broken infrastructure so far judiciary is concerned. For example, most courts are not located in separate buildings and share space with other agencies. Any gender bias had to be carefully guarded against in the court room and this protection should be extended to any women present or appearing in the court either as a member of the staff, party, witness of member of legal profession.

67. The Family Courts generally suffer from unsatisfactory conditions. There is no proper place for the judges to be seated and working conditions, by and large, are unhygienic and poor. There is no proper space allotted for the children to meet their separated parents.

68. Family Courts lack essential public conveniences like drinking water, waiting room, etc and facilities like photocopying paid public telephone, availability of stamps, stationery etc. In the absence of basic infrastructure like a stamp office, typist and stationery, services of a notary or even adequate sitting arrangements, canteen and drinking water, the litigants are subjected to endless hardships.

69. The research found that many advocates and litigants expressed their dissatisfaction regarding their experience with Family Courts and stated that their expectations have not been met. The reasons for dissatisfaction found were: procrastination and dilatory decisions, overworked counsellors, and undue pressure exercised on women litigants for reconciliation, etc.

70. On average, a litigant had to visit the Family Court as many as 21 times before the case was decided. Only 14 percent of the cases were decided within the statutorily laid down time-frame of six months, while the remaining large number of cases were decided within a time frame ranging between more than six months and as long as nine years.

71. There are other deficiencies in basic facilities available to women, varying from encouragement to cultivate one's natural talents to fair participation in rewarding social functions of the community. The Family Courts should be located in easily accessible residential colonies where aggrieved women, for whose benefit the courts have been created, may go without hesitation. Women and children of rural area are deprived of its benefits because of the financial constraints and their inability to reach the courts, which are situated at the district levels.

72. The intimidating atmosphere of normal law courts generally overawes women in social distress seeking judicial relief. Efforts should be made to provide prompt and easily accessible justice to women in social distress and should not be nullified by the insistence of lawyers.

73. Gender justice should be a component for recruitment and it should be made essential for a judge to have undergone a gender sensitization course/training before taking the position as a judge. Courts dealing with sensitive issues needs to be empowered in the true sense.

74. There are just a handful of women who have been elevated as judges to High Courts and Supreme Court of India. Those women who were elevated to bench came from the legal background were their family consisted either of judges or of lawyers.

75. When reforms were introduced in various segments of personal law, it was thought that if women would be empowered they would perform certain functions that would create an atmosphere where women can progress resulting in betterment of the society but it hardly happened in the betterment of legal profession and in other associated wings.

76. Though the Constitution of India recognizes equality of the sexes and provides certain provisions under the chapter on Fundamental Rights which are more favorable to women, but in actual practice there has been breach in compliance.

77. Women would inhabit the role of lawyer differently than men if they could overcome men's domination of the profession.

78. Women will reconstruct the profession and the legal system to be more comprehensive, more contextualized, less rule-bound, more responsible to others, as well as clients and more conscious of socially just ends.

79. The legal profession in India has been 'gendered' but women are slowly but surely becoming prominent in the Indian legal community, striving to work towards fostering a legal community that represents the best and brightest that society has to offer though initially it was difficult for women to break through rigid traditions.

80. Women will refuse to capitulate to a 'macho' ethic of law and will try to incorporate their own integration of psycho-social health, and family balance, into their roles as lawyers.

81. The equal involvement of women in all walks of life, particularly in the legal profession, is therefore essential, to promote the wider interests and possibilities of the law.

8.3. RECOMMENDATIONS:

From the foregoing findings, following recommendations have been made for better and qualitative improvement of women in legal profession.

A. LEGISLATIONS

1. With the enactment of the *Consumer Protection Act 1986* (CP Act) for settlement of consumer disputes and for matters connected therewith. The aim of the CP Act is to provide for an effective, inexpensive, simple and speedy redressal of consumer grievances, which civil courts are not able to provide. Women consumers are to be made aware of the courts and the Alternative Dispute Resolution methods.

2. *The Family Courts Act* 1984 (FC Act) was enacted to provide for the establishment of Family Courts with a view to promote conciliation in, and secure speedy settlement of, disputes relating to marriage and family affairs and for matters connected therewith. The Law Commission of India in its 59th Report (1974) had also stressed that in dealing with disputes concerning the family, the court ought to adopt a humane approach different from that adopted in ordinary civil proceedings, and that it should make reasonable efforts at settlement before commencement of the trial. More initiative must be taken for proper implementing and executing that has been mention in the Family Courts Act 1984.

3. Section 16 of *The Advocates Act* classifies Advocates as Senior Advocates and other Advocates. Senior is "by virtue of his ability, standing at the Bar or special knowledge or experience in law". It may be worthwhile to examine if the classification of advocates needs to be re-defined and expanded to keep in line with the modern times giving preference to women. Advocates Act to be amended to give effect to the above proposals and to create new categories of specialized advocates. The Bar Council that has to look after ethics of lawyers, but it has rarely taken action against tainted lawyers. Everything becomes customary and loses meaning.

4. The Gram Nyayalayas Bill has been enacted to set up more trial courts at the intermediate Panchayat level. The welcome feature is that the procedures have been kept simple and flexible so that cases can be heard and disposed of within six months. It is also envisaged that these courts will be mobile, to achieve the goal of bringing justice to people's doorsteps. Training and

orientation of the judiciary, especially in frontier areas of knowledge, like bio-genetics, IPR and cyber laws, need attention.

B. EDUCATION

5. All India Examination in judicial services to be introduced for all those who apply for membership of Bar Council. In other words, a Bachelor of Law will get the right to practice only if he/she clears the proposed examination. Reservation for women in the entry level may be introduced.

6. Specialized Post-Graduate Certificate Courses and Exams (Conducted by Bar Council) for specialized branches of law. These may be open to advocates as well as to Chartered Accountants, Company Secretaries, Cost Accountants, and Engineers etc. and may give the right to practice in that field of law. This will help to bring women from other fields and improve the quality in legal profession.

7. Law colleges and Law schools to carry out awareness-raising campaigns among both men and women on the importance of women's full and equal participation in political and public life and in decision-making, as a necessary component of a democratic society, and create enabling, encouraging and supportive conditions for such participation. Accordingly a comprehensive strategy is called for which tackles equality issues on all fronts rather than in a piecemeal fashion.

8. Law Colleges all over the country are finding it increasingly difficult to attract motivated young teachers especially women to teach law. After all any law college needs highly qualified and motivated faculty members to train students for careers in the bar and the judiciary. The knowledge that is imparted through rigorous and engaging classroom discussions often proves to be an important influence in the future careers of students. If the processes of learning and evaluation are conducted in a professional and innovative manner, the seeds are planted for meaningful contributions in the future.

9. Another set of factors that deserve attention are the overall expectations from legal education. Students should not view the obtaining of a law degree as merely a means to the end of professional success.

10. There are several underlying reasons for the same, one of them being that talented law graduates are increasingly driven to more lucrative career options rather choosing litigation. While there is no doubt that today's law graduates have many career options to choose from, methods should be devised to attract some of the best among them to the teaching line. In order to prepare for such complexities, legal education must promote a strong inter-disciplinary agenda.

11. The insights gained through disciplines such as political science, sociology, economics, history and philosophy enrich our understanding of the evolution of laws and help us to engineer reforms for the future. Inter disciplinary studies should be encouraged in the university level courses. Computer facilities are to be brought in all institutions imparting legal education.

12. With the growth of specialized practice areas such as those related to natural resources, international trade, intellectual property and technology among others, such interdisciplinary inputs must also come from the natural sciences as well as commerce-related subjects.

13. In the present day and age, law students have unprecedented access to research materials since the decisions of Indian as well as foreign courts, legislations, treaties and academic writings are easily accessible through the internet.

14. University heads must urge teachers and students to make the best use of these resources and produce scholarship that will actively engage with the problems faced by our legal system.

15. A consensus on guidelines for incorporating the goal of gender equality into national level which can be benefited to all must be executed by the administration.

16. Young law students are always competing against each other to do well in academics and eventually secure good job opportunities. However, this spirit of competition should also be channeled into activities which give them better preparation for their careers.

17. Meaningful practical experience through participation in legal literacy programmes, involvement with NGO's and regular visits to institutions such as courts, police stations and prisons among others will give students a chance to observe the 'law-in-action' as opposed to the 'law-in-the-books'.

18. Lastly, higher education is not only a means of personal empowerment, but it also serves an instrument of social integration and transformation. Hence efforts should be taken so that students belonging to different backgrounds learn together in a conducive environment. This may eventually lead them to learn and to look beyond the traditional barriers of caste, regionalism, gender, class and religion.

19. While a law degree does enable a person to enroll as an advocate, the curriculum must also take on the broader mandate of sensitizing students to social, economic and political realities.

20. Law school curricula must encourage students to take courses in other departments of the university—courses related to their subject interests. Absent of this elastic provision, legal education is subject to the indictment of parochialism, and an unwillingness to fulfill the information needs of its students.

21. A faculty-student forum discussing, evaluating and formulating proposals for legislative action, would be both an educational and professional benefit. There are vast areas of the law that stand to benefit from such systematic evaluation. This will help the future lawyers to be well equipped.

22. One of the key challenges for our educational system is to ensure that the future generations dissolve the old social barriers. Needless to say, law colleges should be at the forefront of these efforts to remove old social barriers.

23. It is the duty of the law schools and colleges to provide the future lawyer with exposure to related disciplines in order to enable him/her to discharge his functions effectively as laws cannot be applied and interpreted in a mechanical and insulated manner.

C. *IN DIFFERENT WINGS OF LEGAL PROFESSION*

24. Women have made significant strides in the legal profession; gender inequity remains prevalent to a degree that is unacceptable. So, initiate must be taken for cultural and attitudinal change within the Profession.

25. Parliamentary and State legislative committee deliberations should be monitored. Opening the gates of academe to the practicing lawyer. The rigid distinction between the practicing and the academic is untenable and mischievous.

26. Legal journalism is an integral part of the law school program. It develops the disciplined skills that play an essential part in a lawyer's professional effectiveness: the ability to present a brief within the inexorable limits of time and space. A system of enabling women/men as trainee lawyers to work.

27. The present free apprenticeship system must be discouraged. While relevant details must obviously be worked out between law schools and professional institutions. Members of the Bar associations must assume the initial lead in developing a liaison system.

28. It is easy to see why the law and the justice process might seem an unfriendly and alien place for women Care should always be taken to recognize the difficulties faced by a person appearing before a tribunal that does not appear on its face to reflect their concerns or interests, and to take appropriate steps to ensure they are reassured.

29. Infrastructural facilities to improve in the Bar and the Bench for women. The directive principles of State policy provide for maternity relief as part of just and humane conditions of work as also assure "equal pay for equal work"

vis-à-vis men. Therefore it is suggested that all the courts in India must have proper crèche, toilets and medical rooms for women lawyers.

30. Setting objectives to ensure that each chambers has an adequate gender balance and has made appropriate provision for members of disadvantaged groups coming to the Bar

31. Sensitization of Lawyers both male and female through the active development of law journals that will stimulate interest in legal writing, and create avenues for publication of legal research findings to benefit the women.

32. To seek assistance from the Women Lawyers' Association's Group in developing the Bar's own structures for creating equality of opportunity for women at the Bar.

33. To promote measures to eliminate double standards and other discriminatory practices in briefing processes.

34. To take sustained legal and other measures to increase the representation of women in elected and appointed bodies and at the highest levels of the judiciary, and in diplomacy.

35. To introduce appropriate legal and other measures, including amending or replacing ineffective laws and adopting temporary special measures in accordance with article 4, paragraph 1, CEDAW and the Committee's general recommendation 25 to increase the number of women in judicial positions within a concrete time frame in line with the Committee's general recommendation 23

36. While interpreting the language of statutes and regulations, judges must be advised to take into account for the policy-concerns and legislative intent behind them.

37. Very often, judges are confronted with fact-situations that have neither been contemplated by the legislature nor discussed in past decisions. In deciding such difficult cases, judges need to draw insights from a wide variety of

sources, often going beyond the plain reading of statutes and the submissions made by the counsels.

38. A system of enabling women/men as trainee lawyers to work.

39. Strengthen efforts to promote the participation of women in all walks of public life as well as in the private sector especially law and corporate firms.

40. Awareness-raising campaigns be addressed to both women and men and media be encouraged to project positive images of women and of equal status and responsibilities of women and men in private and public spheres.

41. Law on Gender Equality provides for equal representation in decision-making processes. To harmonize the law on gender equality and strengthen and implement measures to increase representation of women in elected and appointed bodies and in decision-making positions as office bearers in State Bar Councils and the Bar Councils of India, and judiciary. Women lawyers are to be encouraged to reach in high positions in State-owned companies through, inter alia, implementation of special measures, in accordance in the lights and directions given in CEDAW .

42. More and more women lawyers to be involved in spreading legal awareness. Women judges to be involved in dealing with domestic violence and other allied issues.

43. In almost every High Court, there is huge pendency of cases and the present strength of the judges can hardly be said to be sufficient to cope with the alarming situation. The institution of cases is much more than the disposal and it adds to arrears of cases. The litigating citizens have a fundamental right of life i.e. a tension-free life through speedy justice-delivery system. Now it has become essential that the present strength of the judges should be increased manifold according to the pendency of cases. The government must think in terms of appointment more women to have a balanced ratio.

44. Women as judges to be recruited in Lok Adalats and Nyaya Panchayats.

45. Legal Services Authorities are also part of the campaign to take justice to the people and ensure that all people have equal access to justice in spite of various barriers like social and economic backwardness. Large population, more litigation and lack of adequate infrastructure are the major factors that hamper our justice system. Regular adjudication procedures through the constant efforts of Legal Services Authorities will act as catalysts in curing these maladies of our system.

46. Disposal of legal disputes at pre-litigative stage by permanent and continuous Lok Adalats would provide expense-free justice to the citizens of this country. It also saves the courts from additional and avoidable burden of petty cases enabling them to divert their court-time to more contentious and old matters.

47. Legal literacy and legal awareness are the principal means to achieve the objective for ensuring equality before law for the citizens of our country. Legal profession of the country, as we know it today, is more than two centuries old. We can legitimately expect that the future of this profession ought to be very bright, particularly in the context of the enormous strides our country is making in various fields and human rights awareness. Public interest has to be its motto and service in the cause of justice its creed. Provisions have been made in the Legal Services Authorities Act for settling cases through Lok Adalats; a Lok Adalat generally comprises a judicial officer, serving or retired, a lawyer, and a person of a social welfare association, preferably, a woman. Power has been given to Lok Adalats to dispose of disputes referred to them by arriving at a compromise or settlement between the parties; awards of Lok Adalats are deemed to be decrees of civil courts or orders of other courts or tribunals; every award made by a Lok Adalat is treated as final and binding on all the parties to the dispute, and no appeal lies to any court against the award.

48. All reforms need to take place in an integrated manner. The police, prosecution, lawyers and courts, must be thought of as being cohesive. The topic of judicial reforms has of late become very important because the

public has lost faith in the system. Judicial accountability is connected with the larger area of judicial reforms..

49. Currently there are backlog of cases, hence more women judges to be posted in fast track courts in different states in India.

50. In many districts, the family court did not have any separate building. One separate building should be constructed with all the facilities of family courts, for example., counselling centre, child centre (with recreation facilities), and so on for providing an informal atmosphere for the women litigants and their children, and this should not be within the premises of the District or High Courts.

51. Reservation issue for women, if actualized could be one of the important means for their empowerment and emancipation. This is a very necessary way of doing for women's liberation from the oppressive structure of our society. India is well known for having systematically instituted and constructed patriarchal and hierarchical structure of society. Hence, reservation for women is crucial and important. Administrative measures can be taken regarding it.

52. Article 15 asserts the full equality of women in civil and business matters, demanding that all instruments directed at restricting women's legal capacity 'shall be deemed null and void'.

53. Finally, in Article 16, the Convention returns to the issue of marriage and family relations, asserting the equal rights and obligations of women and men with regard to choice of spouse, parenthood, personal rights and command over proper. Therefore, the laws must also provide for appropriate measures to make the life of women easy, particularly when they are employed, by making provisions such as paternity leave and a culture must develop in our society whereby the burden is shared by both parents equally.

54. To comply with obligations under CEDAW to eliminate discrimination against women without delay, to include women in economic and social transformation processes in judicial service and also in higher echelon of

judiciary on a basis of equality with men and to make gender analyses an integral part of these processes on the lines of European Commission.

8.4 A CONCLUDING REMARK:

> *"Women must be in a position to solve their positions in their own way.No one can or ought to do this for them.Our Indian women are capable of doing it as any in the world."* Swami Vivekananda.

Closing the gap between the laws on the books and their implementation in the legal profession is one of the most pressing concerns. An established profession with a longer tradition of male exclusivity and a closer relationship to the exercise of citizenship were based on gender differences which were less significant in the push for women's access. The study will contribute in knowing about women's entering in the mainstream of professional culture and organizational structure from the Indian context. Many issues have cropped up which requires solution and hence the study recommends the need for amendment in the *Advocates Act* of 1961 with a ray of hope to create an environment that will make students aware of their role play in the legal profession.

The study draws an analysis from the angle of feminist jurisprudence to the sociology of the legal profession and sheds light on the processes which support women's continued subordination in employment as lawyers, corporate professionals and as judges. It continuously argues the status of woman solicitors and that the profession must not shirk from recognising how difficult the task is and how radical reforms are needed to bring a change. The study give an insight about the 'feminist' influence on the legal profession in India which includes changes in both the practice of law (e.g., adaptations of work of family) and substantive rules (like in areas of employment, discrimination in family law and criminal law). Much more research is therefore necessary. Thus, the study would contribute in women's empowerment, representation in policy formation for women in the stream of legal profession in India. With this optimistic note, the study emphasises on equality of occupational access between men and women that would be useful in the eventual creation of opportunities for women in the traditional 'liberal profession' of law.

Mahatma Gandhi practiced law without compromising truth. Abraham Lincoln said: "*Discourage litigation, persuade your neighbours to compromise whenever you can. Point out to them how the nominal winner is often a real loser in fees, expenses and time*".With more women passing in the All India Bar Examination shows the trend that in recent years the legal profession has experienced the influx of women. In many countries women now constitute close to half of all law students, although it will be the turn of the century before this representation is fully mirrored among practitioners. The influx of women into the legal profession has prompted speculations among both academics, political and social activists that women would bring about change in the nature of substantive law and how law is practiced. The legal profession getting 'feminized' therefore suggests further research

To sum up, we would like to share of wisdom of Swami Vivekananda which stand as true today even before. "It is our own mental attitude which makes the world what it is for us. Our thoughts make things beautiful, our thoughts make things ugly. The whole world is in our own minds. Learn to see things in the proper light. We are responsible for what we are; and whatever we wish ourselves to be, we have the power to make ourselves. If what we are now has been the result of our own past actions, it certainly follows that whatever we wish to be in future can be produced by our present actions; so we have to know to act. There is no chance for the welfare of the world unless the condition of the women improves. It is not possible for a bird to fly only on one wing."

CPSIA information can be obtained
at www.ICGtesting.com
Printed in the USA
BVHW051237060123
655725BV00016B/483